Decadent Catholicism and the Making of Modernism

Decadent Catholicism and the Making of Modernism

Martin Lockerd

BLOOMSBURY ACADEMIC
LONDON • NEW YORK • OXFORD • NEW DELHI • SYDNEY

BLOOMSBURY ACADEMIC
Bloomsbury Publishing Plc
50 Bedford Square, London, WC1B 3DP, UK
1385 Broadway, New York, NY 10018, USA

BLOOMSBURY, BLOOMSBURY ACADEMIC and the Diana logo
are trademarks of Bloomsbury Publishing Plc

First published in Great Britain 2020

Cover design: Eleanor Rose
Cover image: Religion, 1913–14, William Roberts. Estate of John David Roberts.
By permission of the Treasury Solicitor.

A catalogue record for this book is available from the British Library.

Library of Congress Cataloging-in-Publication Data
Names: Lockerd, Martin, author.
Title: Decadent Catholicism and the making of modernism / Martin Lockerd.
Description: London; New York: Bloomsbury Academic, 2020. | Includes
bibliographical references and index. Identifiers: LCCN 2020010905 (print) | LCCN 2020010906
(ebook) | ISBN 9781350137653 (hardback) | ISBN 9781350137660 (ebook) |
ISBN 9781350137677 (epub)
Subjects: LCSH: Decadence (Literary movement)–Great Britain. | English
literature–19th century–History and criticism. | English
literature–20th century–History and criticism. | Modernism
(Literature)–Great Britain. | Catholic Church–Influence. | English
literature–Irish authors–History and criticism. | Christianity and
literature–Great Britain–History–19th century. | Christianity and
literature–Great Britain–History–20th century.
Classification: LCC PR468.D43 L63 2020 (print) | LCC PR468.D43 (ebook) |
DDC 820.9/921282–dc23
LC record available at https://lccn.loc.gov/2020010905
LC ebook record available at https://lccn.loc.gov/2020010906

ISBN: HB: 978-1-3501-3765-3
          ePDF: 978-1-3501-3766-0
          eBook: 978-1-3501-3767-7

Typeset by Integra Software Services Pvt. Ltd.

To find out more about our authors and books visit www.bloomsbury.com
and sign up for our newsletters.

Contents

List of Figures

Preface

I would like to preface this study of literature and religion, faith and aesthetics with a note on its cover design. The image I chose for this purpose came as a surprise. All along, I had assumed that Aubrey Beardsley would receive pride of place on the cover. After all, he plays a significant role in two of its chapters and captures in much of his art the central concerns of my book. His pen-and-ink drawings were revolutionary in their time and have not lost their effect with the passing of the years; some still come as a shock to my students today. But, I am no Beardsley scholar, and this is not a book about decadence, per se. It is a book about the troubled relationship between decadence, Catholicism, and literary modernism.

So, in search of a fitting face for this Janus of a book—this story of art and faith that looks backward to decadence and forward to modernism simultaneously—I returned to a foundational text of literary modernity. *Blast*, the flagship magazine of "Vorticism" (one of the many -isms contained in the omnibus term "modernism"), was begun by Wyndham Lewis and Ezra Pound in 1914 and ran for only two issues. In that short time, however, it gave a face to the nascent literary movement that would define the early twentieth century. The first issue of *Blast* contains poetry, short stories, illustrations, and a series of manifestos that "BLAST" and "CURSE" everything from "THE BRITTANIC AESTHETE" to "HUMOUR" to the "years 1837 to 1900." That issue also contains two abstract illustrations by William Roberts: *Dancers* and *Religion*. Roberts was obscured, and continues to be obscured, by the shadow of Wyndham Lewis. Few among today's modernist scholars are likely to even recognize the name; nevertheless, Roberts's *Religion*, appearing where and how it does in *Blast*, speaks to a central concern of this book. Intentionally or not, Lewis and Pound chose to print *Religion* in the middle of Ford Madox Hueffer's "The Saddest Story," an early excerpt from what would become one of the defining examples of the modernist novel, *The Good Soldier*. The placement struck me as significant because, like most of the decadents, Hueffer (who later changed his name to Ford) was a convert. He joined the Catholic Church at the age of 18. Though his relationship with the faith was hardly orthodox or consistent, and his personal conduct treated Catholic morality as something better honored in the breach than the observance, Ford's life and art were always shot through with Catholicism. His children were educated in the faith. One of his daughters even became a nun. More importantly, for our purposes, his fiction took religion as a primary motif. *The Good Soldier* is a novel about adultery and the uncertainties of perception, but, more fundamentally, it concerns itself with the relationship between faith and action, whether it be the Tory Anglicanism of the serial adulterer Edward Ashburnham or the intractable Irish Catholicism of his long-suffering wife, Leonora. Ford's world was never secular, and neither was his art.

The fact that Ford receives no attention in the body of my book speaks to the surprising ubiquity of its subject and the surprising appropriateness of Roberts's illustration in the first issue of *Blast*. *Religion* presents the viewer with a vision whose subject would, at first glance, be nearly unrecognizable were it not for the title. Amid what the prophetic consciousness of T. S. Eliot's *The Waste Land* might call a "heap of broken images," we can discern a body bent with hands folded in a distinctly Christian form of prayer. Its fractured head portrays the painful psychic fracturing of the religious mind in the modern world. At the focal center of the image hovers the glowering half-face of a deconstructed deity whose countenance evinces the anger of a jealous God. The illustration expresses, through the ineluctable modality of the visible, what many modernist writers sought to express through their art: visions of a fractured world and a fractured humanity.

Many of the artists, both decadent and modernist, represented in this book, sought to make sense of this fractured world by returning to religion in new and surprising ways. Though few were conventional in their appropriation of the symbols, rituals, and beliefs of Catholicism, neither were many flatly antipathetic. Most sought, through irony, vice, epiphany, prayer, poetry, and prose, to come into contact with the transcendent reality to which art, often unbeknownst to itself, points. They picked up the pieces of a blasted religion.

Acknowledgments

This book began when I first read J. K. Huysmans's *À Rebours* as an MA student at St. Louis University. I credit Ellen Crowell and Vincent Sherry with introducing me to literary decadence and encouraging me to think about its many afterlives. Later, Elizabeth Cullingford and Alan Friedman generously helped me develop my fledgling interest into a respectable dissertation. Thank you both. Lee Oser, who has served as my Virgil in academia since my earliest days, went above and beyond to help me craft that respectable dissertation into this humble book. I owe all of these people a great debt and must apologize for the imperfections and infelicities that persist in spite of their best efforts. Any remaining errors are purely mine.

I would also like to thank the generous readers who provided formative feedback on bits and pieces of this book. They include Elizabeth Richmond-Garza (whose help to me at time of crisis will never be forgotten), Neville Hoad, James Campbell of UCF (scholar and gentleman), Steve Pinkerton, and Reid Echols. Ellis Hanson deserves special notice for encouraging me in this project at an early phase. I have not written a worthy companion to his *Decadence and Catholicism*, but who could have?

There are many people at the University of Texas who made this book possible by helping me to thrive in graduate school, keep food on my family's table, and get a job in an impossible market. They include the leaders of the incomparable British Studies Program—W. Roger Louis, Philippa Levine, and Holly Ghail; my wonderful colleagues at the University Writing Center—Alice Batt, Vince Lozano, Michele Solberg, and Trish Roberts-Miller; my excessively generous placement mentors—Jim Cox and Cole Hutchison; and the helpful folks at the Harry Ransom Center, which is just like home, but with better books. I have also received substantial support from my colleagues at Schreiner University, especially my department chair, Sally Hannay. At Bloomsbury, Lucy Brown advocated for this book and worked hard to get it into print. Thanks are also due to my anonymous readers for their invaluable feedback.

Earlier versions of portions of Chapters 3 and 4 have appeared as "'A Satirist of Vices and Follies': Beardsley, Eliot, and Images of Decadent Catholicism" in the *Journal of Modern Literature* (37, no. 4, 2014) and "Decadent Arcadias, Wild(e)

Conversions, and Queer Celibacies in *Brideshead Revisited*" in *Modern Fiction Studies* (64, no. 2, 2018). Grateful acknowledgment is given to the publishers for permission to use this material in the present work.

My siblings, Erika, Anna, Michael, and Marie, have cheered me on in all of my endeavors. My parents, Benjamin and Micheline Lockerd, have been staunch supporters since before I can remember, quite literally, and have done so with grace and love. Dad, you've read more of my bad first drafts than anyone should ever have to … thanks. My children, Madeleine, Mary Thérèse, Cecilia, Aibhin, and Bridget, were and are my most constant source of inspiration and motivation. Lastly, I wish to thank my wife, Jacqui, to say that this book would be nothing without you is silly. I would be nothing without you.

The author and publisher gratefully acknowledge the permission granted to reproduce the copyrighted material in this book. The following kindly granted permission to reproduce images:

The Victoria and Albert Museum:

Aubrey Beardsley, *Enter Herodias*. Plate IX from a portfolio of seventeen plates illustrating Oscar Wilde's *Salome*. John Lane, 1907.

Aubrey Beardsley, *The Dancer's Reward*. Plate XIV from a portfolio of seventeen plates illustrating Oscar Wilde's *Salome*. John Lane, 1907.

Aubrey Beardsley, *The Climax*. Plate XV from a portfolio of seventeen plates illustrating Oscar Wilde's *Salome*. John Lane, 1907.

Aubrey Beardsley, *The Wagnerites*. Pen and India ink, heightened with white, on paper. Reproduced as no. III in 'Four Drawings by Aubrey Beardsley' in *The Yellow Book*, vol. III, October 1894.

ART Resource, NY:

Édouard Manet, *George Moore*. The Metropolitan Museum of Art, New York. Photo Credit: © The Metropolitan Museum of Art. Image source: Art Resource, NY.

Gustave Moreau, *The Apparition*. Musée Gustave Moreau, Paris, France. Photo Credit: Erich Lessing/Art Resource, NY.

Nicolas Poussin, *Les Bergers d'Arcadie*. Musée du Louvre. Photo Credit: Erich Lessing/Art Resource, NY.

The Harry Ransom Center, The University of Texas at Austin, Image Credit for:

Aubrey Beardsley, *The Coiffing*. In *The Savoy* no. 3, 1896.

Aubrey Beardsley, *Et in Arcadia Ego*. In *The Best of Beardsley*. Edited by R. A. Walker. Spring Books. The Evelyn Waugh Collection, 1949.

Aubrey Beardsley, *Frontispiece*. In *A Full and True Account of the Wonderful Mission of Earl Lavender*. Ward and Dowdy, 1895.

Cover design for *Flowers of Passion* by George Moore. Provost & Co, 1878.

Evelyn Waugh. "[Crouching satyr holding flute, next to broken column]." Undated. Drawing from Evelyn Waugh Art Collection by Evelyn Waugh. Copyright © 2019 by Evelyn Waugh, used by permission of The Wylie Agency LLC.

"Frontispiece." In *The Poetical Works of Lionel Johnson*. Elkin Matthews, 1915.

The following publishers kindly granted permission to quote from the following texts:

From *Brideshead Revisited* by Evelyn Waugh, copyright © 1979, 1981, 1982, 2012. Reprinted by permission of Little, Brown & Company, a division of Hachette Book Group, Inc. Also reprinted with permission from Penguin, Random House UK.

From *The Complete Poems and Plays of T. S. Eliot* and *Inventions of the March Hare* by T. S. Eliot. Select T. S. Eliot excerpts from "Ash-Wednesday—Part IV" and "The Love Song of J. Alfred Prufrock" from *Collected Poems 1909-1962* © renewed 1964 by Thomas Stearns Eliot. Excerpts from "Opera" and "The Love Song of St. Sebastian" from *Inventions of the March Hare* © 1996 by Valerie Eliot. Reprinted by permission of Houghton Mifflin Harcourt and Faber & Faber. All rights reserved.

Abbreviations

AN	J. K. Huysmans, *Against Nature*
BR	Evelyn Waugh, *Brideshead Revisited*
CP	*The Collected Poems of Lionel Johnson*
CPP	*The Complete Poems and Plays of T. S. Eliot*
CYM	George Moore, *Confessions of a Young Man*
DG	Oscar Wilde, *The Picture of Dorian Gray*
ED	*The Poems of Ernest Dowson*
EP	Ezra Pound, *Selected Poems*
FP	George Moore, *Flowers of Passion*
MF	George Moore, *Mike Fletcher*
P	Oscar Wilde, *Poems*
PA	James Joyce, *A Portrait of the Artist as a Young Man*
SP	*Selected Prose of T. S. Eliot*
U	James Joyce, *Ulysses*
WBY	W. B. Yeats, *The Collected Poems of W. B. Yeats*

Anamnesis

As part of his decades-long effort to define the poetic landscape of the early twentieth century, W. B. Yeats accepted the task of editing the *Oxford Book of Modern Verse* in 1936, just three years before his death. The table of contents includes several poets associated with the decadent movement of the 1890s. Oscar Wilde (1854–1900), Ernest Dowson (1867–1900), Lionel Johnson (1867–1902), Francis Thompson (1859–1907), Arthur Symons (1865–1945), and other artists of the British *fin de siècle* are well represented. Glancing at this list, a casual reader might assume that Yeats (b. 1865) viewed his old peers as essential to "modern verse," but his preface tells another story. In it Yeats depicts most decadent poets as historically aberrant. Neither Victorian nor properly modern, these "Hamlets of our age" developed their own idiosyncratic tradition:

> Some of these Hamlets went mad, some drank, drinking not as happy men drink but in solitude…. Good manners in written and spoken word were an essential part of their tradition—"Life," said Lionel Johnson, "must be a ritual" … all had gaiety, some had wit:
>> Unto us they belong,
>> To us the bitter and the gay,
>> Wine and woman and song.
> Some turned Catholic—that too was a tradition.[1]

Johnson clung to ritual and "good manners." Dowson played wittily with the old hedonist's refrain, "Wine and woman and song." All lived lives of tragic gaiety. "Some" of this generation "turned Catholic." Mannered language, ritual, drunkenness, hedonistic wit, conversion—these are the hallmarks of the decadent movement. Immediately after characterizing decadence, Yeats assures his readers that the movement and its eccentricities passed into the haze of history along with the nineteenth century:

> In 1900 everybody got down off his stilts; henceforth nobody drank absinthe with his black coffee; nobody went mad; nobody joined the Catholic church; or if they did I have forgotten.[2]

The twentieth century is a saner time, a more serious time, a time when poets no longer indulge themselves in absinthe, madness, or, perhaps most importantly, Catholicism.[3] For it was the last item in the list that made the decadents un-modern. Rather than embracing the spiritual freedom afforded by a modernity that had cast off organized religion, these strange souls turned to an institution that repeatedly and forcefully denounced the errors of modernity and defended the supreme power of centralized religious authority. This artistic aberration, Yeats assures his readers, died with the nineteenth century.

The only problem with Yeats's characterization of the literary world after 1900 is its patent falsehood. Hemingway kept absinthe in vogue, though he substituted champagne for black coffee, and sent his broken characters to the occasional Mass in order to highlight their brokenness. European sanitariums were well stocked with mad poets, including T. S. Eliot, who put the finishing touches on *The Waste Land* (1922) while convalescing in just such an institution. Conversion never ceased among the literary set, claiming artists as aesthetically diverse as the experimental queer novelist Ronald Firbank in 1907, the Great War poet David Jones in 1921, and the "prince of paradox" G. K. Chesterton in 1922. By 1936 Yeats had indeed "forgotten" a great deal. My goal in this book is recollection. Perhaps *anamnesis* is the better term. Socrates uses the word in Plato's *Meno* to express the unforgetting of knowledge lost by the soul in the trauma of rebirth. Later, *anamnesis* denoted the moment in Catholic liturgy, immediately after the consecration, when the priest exhorts the congregation to remember the death and resurrection of Christ. David Jones provides this definition in a footnote to his masterwork, *The Anathemata* (1952):

> Anamnesis. I take leave to remind the reader that this is a key-word in our deposits. The dictionary defines its general meaning as "the recalling of things past." But what is the nature of this particular recalling? I append the following quotation as being clear and to the point: "It (anamnesis) is not quite easy to represent accurately in English, words like 'remembrance' or 'memorial' having for us a connotation of something absent which is only mentally recollected. But in the scriptures of both the Old and the New Testament *anamnesis* and the cognate verb have a sense of 'recalling' or 're-presenting' before God an event in the past so that it becomes *here and now operative by its effects.*" (Gregory Dix, *The Shape of the Liturgy*, p. 161)[4]

This book aims at *anamnesis* of a literary movement, the religion that animated it, and the lasting legacy of decadent Catholicism in the age of high modernism and beyond—a legacy that has affected not only modern converts but apostates, pagans, high church Anglicans, and postmodern atheists.

For almost a century, the literary-historical narrative contrived by Yeats and a cohort of other artists and critics—a subject I address in Chapter 2—was widely accepted. It presents decadence as an anomaly rather than a constituent element in the genealogy of modernism. With new ideas fit for a new age, the story goes, the modernist artists of the early twentieth century turned their backs on the forms and institutions of the immediate past in order to achieve an artistic movement unfettered by allegiances or debts to the decadent art of the *fin de siècle* and the Church that inspired it.[5] In the last twenty years, the histories established by these early critics have undergone significant dismantling, and decadence now receives considerable attention in discussions of modernist genealogies. David Weir's *Decadence and the Making of Modernism* (1995) began this work of revision by arguing that several modernist texts borrow elements from the earlier movement. Because of his focus on recovering decadence, however, Weir limited his discussion of modernism to just two representative exemplars: Joyce and Gide. Since then, numerous scholars have added evidence to Weir's general proposition. In *Literature and the Politics of Post-Victorian Decadence* (2015), Kristin Mahoney focuses primarily, but not exclusively, on artists who survived the *fin de siècle* and continued to employ decadent strategies in the early twentieth century. While Mahoney's project emphasizes literal survivors of the *fin de siècle*, Vincent Sherry's book, *Modernism and the Reinvention of Decadence* (2015), traces elements of a decadent aesthetic and temporality that helped define both central texts of "high modernism," such as Pound's *Hugh Selwyn Mauberley* (1920) and Eliot's *The Waste Land* (1922), and more peripheral works, such as Conrad's *The Secret Agent* (1907) and Chesterton's *The Man Who Was Thursday* (1908). The most recent attempt to trace this lingering decadent "influence," Kate Hext and Alex Murray's groundbreaking collection of essays titled *Decadence in the Age of Modernism* (2019), demonstrates that its two key terms are "not diametrically opposed, but mutually constitutive and thoroughly implicated in each other's aesthetic development and textual politics."[6]

In attempting to understand better the stakes of the current interplay of decadent and modernist scholarship, we might turn to Robert Volpicelli's review "The New Decadence" (2019), in which he examines three recent books on the subject—Sherry's *Modernism and the Reinvention of Decadence*, Murray's *Landscapes of Decadence*, and Stilling's *Beginning at the End: Decadence,*

Modernism, and Postcolonial History. Volpicelli notes that these books call to mind the "sort of expansion that the field of modernism underwent during the turn to a 'new modernist studies,' through which modernism was pluralized and proliferated in the name of multiple modernisms."[7] "The New Decadence," as Volpicelli christens this scholarly turn, traces "the broader context of decadence as a diverse set of aesthetic and cultural practices."[8] It also, especially in the case of Stilling, follows the "globalizing tendencies of the new modernist studies."[9] Together, my colleagues in "The New Decadence" have done a great deal to open up the critical discourse concerning the relationship between decadence and modernism; in the process, however, they almost completely elided an essential component of the modernist engagement with decadence: Catholicism.

If we are experiencing the birth of what might be called "new decadent studies" that mirrors and participates in the expansion of new modernist studies, then we are also still waiting for the "religious turn" that has played such a key role in modernist scholarship of the past decade and more to inform and inflect the discourse of new decadent studies. Stanley Fish's "One University under God?"—the 2005 *Chronicle of Higher Education* op-ed that many credit with announcing this religious turn—insisted that future scholars and educators would have to contend and engage with religion as both an historical reality and a "candidate for truth."[10] "When Jacques Derrida died," Fish tells us, "I was called by a reporter who wanted to know what would succeed high theory and the triumvirate of race, gender, and class as the center of intellectual energy in the academy. I answered like a shot: religion." New decadent studies, for all its success in broadening the scope of critical inquiry, has mostly stuck to Fish's familiar triumvirate and ignored religion. The scholars in this field have remained nearly as forgetful as Yeats concerning the legacy of decadent Catholicism after 1900. In 1998, Ellis Hanson's *Decadence and Catholicism* convincingly demonstrated the interdependence of decadent art, queer identity, and the theology, rituals, and symbolism of the Catholic Church. Furthermore, his conclusion called for greater consideration of decadent Catholicism in the work of such writers as Eliot and Waugh. Two decades later, religion receives only glancing attention in discussions of the relationship between decadence and modernism.[11] The otherwise excellent contributions to Hext and Murray's *Decadence in the Age of Modernism* make this oversight glaringly obvious. Neither the introduction nor a single one of the eleven essays grants sustained attention to religion. Joseph Bristow acknowledges religion briefly in a chapter on the Catholic poet Margaret Sackville, but only when the subject becomes absolutely unavoidable, for example, when discussing her poem "Nostra Culpa."[12]

No adequate understanding of the relationship between decadence and modernism is possible without Catholicism. Had the Catholic Church not existed—with its extra-rational economy of sin and grace, its storehouse of images for suppressed and sublimated desire, its reverence for celibacy (perhaps the most profoundly contra-normative mode of sexuality), and its eschatological worldview—then the decadent artists of the 1890s would surely have had to invent it. The tendency to ignore Catholicism in discussions of decadence after Hanson's groundbreaking 1998 study mirrors a similar tendency that persisted among scholars of modernism until relatively recently. Michael Levenson's *Modernism* (2011), for example, cites decadence as one of the avant-garde movements essential to the development of modernism but never once refers to Catholicism and only mentions Christianity in relation to Nietzsche's famous denunciation of the religion. Thanks to the recent work of scholars more attuned to the religious and spiritual dimensions of the era, we have started to move beyond the simple view that modernism's only concern regarding faith is with its irreparable loss.[13] We have yet, nevertheless, to fully appreciate the extent to which "high" and "peripheral" modernists like Eliot and Waugh looked to decadent artists like Wilde and Beardsley for models of what religious art might do in an age trending toward secularization.

As modernist scholars reevaluate and reject narratives that exclude the influence of organized religions, it is important to acknowledge the extent to which decadent Catholicism animated modernist texts. Only then can we fully appreciate how, for example, Stephen Dedalus's strange interweaving of sexual transgression and Marian devotion echoes the spiritual/sensual experimentation of that most decadent of antiheroes, Dorian Gray:

> If ever he was impelled to cast sin from him and to repent, the impulse that moved him was the wish to be her [Mary's] knight. If ever his soul, reentering her dwelling shyly after the frenzy of his body's lust had spent itself, was turned toward her whose emblem is the morning star, bright and musical, telling of heaven and infusing peace, it was when her names were murmured softly by lips whereon there still lingered foul and shameful words, the savor itself of a lewd kiss. (James Joyce, *A Portrait of the Artist as a Young Man*, 1916)

> He loved to kneel down on the cold marble pavement and watch the priest, in his stiff flowered dalmatic, slowly and with white hands moving aside the veil of the tabernacle, or raising aloft the jewelled, lantern-shaped monstrance.... The fuming censers that the grave boys, in their lace and scarlet, tossed into the air like great gilt flowers had their subtle fascination for him. As he passed out, he used to look with wonder at the black confessionals and long to sit in the dim

shadow of one of them and listen to men and women whispering through the worn grating the true story of their lives. (Oscar Wilde, *The Picture of Dorian Gray*, 1890)[14]

Only then can we understand the young T. S. Eliot's "The Love Song of Saint Sebastian" as a poem operating within a very recent Catholic literary tradition. The poem's sadomasochistic spiritual angst has unmistakable roots in the work of John Gray, who provided the inspiration for Wilde's Dorian Gray little more than a decade prior to his becoming a Catholic priest:

> I would come in a shirt of hair
> I would come with a lamp in the night
> And sit at the foot of your stair;
> I would flog myself until I bled,
> And after hour on hour of prayer
> And torture and delight
> Until my blood should ring the lamp
> And glisten in the light;
> I should arise your neophyte. (T. S. Eliot, "The Love Song of Saint
>   Sebastian," 1914)

> Last, that indeed a Mary thou may'st be,
> And that my love be mixed with cruelty—
>
> O foul voluptuousness! when I have made
> Of every deadly sin a deadlier blade,
>
> Torturer filled with pain will I draw near
> The target of thy breast, and, sick with fear,
>
> Deliberately plant them all where throbs
> Thy bleeding heart, and stifling with its sobs. (John Gray, "À une
>   Madone," 1893)[15]

If we believe that decadent Catholicism departed with the nineteenth century, then we lose an important point of reference for such texts as Eliot's "Love Song of Saint Sebastian," Joyce's *A Portrait of the Artist as a Young Man*, and Waugh's *Brideshead Revisited*—all of which engage with Catholicism using the language, symbols, and logic of decadence and with the crisis of modernity using the language of decadent Catholicism. Only by grasping the importance of Catholicism in discussions of decadent afterlives and modernist roots can we truly rewrite Yeats's nearly century-old narrative.

"Decadence"/"Modernism"/"British"

Scholars who have probed the relationship between decadence and modernism often obsess over terminology.[16] My insistence on reiterating and relying upon the very terms of strict periodization I plan to interrogate may seem counterintuitive, but the distinguishing labels are still useful if not too narrowly defined. We may say, for example, that "modernism" as a literary-historical period climaxed in 1922 with the publication of *Ulysses* and *The Waste Land* while still acknowledging a fairly broad historical range for the age of modernism. The same is true of decadence. Academic definition wrangling aside, Pound, Yeats, Eliot, Joyce, and other modernists referred to the artists of "the 'nineties" as participants in what clearly amounted in their minds to a school of art sufficiently coherent to be imitated, disavowed, or both.

Decadent Catholicism and the Making of Modernism focuses primarily on the artistic legacy of the relationship between Catholicism and "British decadence," by which I mean a particular literary movement of the last two decades of the nineteenth century comprising artists under the dominion of the UK and native to the British Isles, who, for the most part, lived and worked primarily in England. Thus I include Anglo-Irish artists such as George Moore and Oscar Wilde. Analogously, I refer to T. S. Eliot (an American until middle age), David Jones (a Welshman), and James Joyce (an Irishman) as participants in "British modernism." Decadence had a profound influence on modern and modernist writers beyond the UK, of course—notably the Southern American authors Flannery O'Connor, Allen Tate, Caroline Gordon, and Walker Percy. All were converts (excepting O'Connor); all were influenced to a greater or lesser extent by Charles Baudelaire and Edgar Allan Poe, whom Baudelaire famously declared the father of the decadent imagination; all dealt with "perversion," drunkenness, and sin. But their explicit engagement with what I have singled out as decadent Catholicism is less profound than that of the "British modernists" I discuss in this book. Such restrictive national terminology, of course, runs the risk of eliding the diversity of cultural landscapes in Great Britain both before and after the turn of the century. My fourth chapter, for example, pays particular attention to the specifically Irish expression of decadent *anti*-Catholicism in the novels of George Moore and James Joyce because the cultural experience of Catholicism in Ireland was significantly different than in England. Still, I find the term "British decadence" especially useful when discussing decadent Catholicism. Wilde, an Oxford-educated Anglo-Irish Protestant writing primarily for an English audience, had a personal experience of Catholicism that was significantly closer to those of English decadents such as Aubrey Beardsley and Ernest Dowson than to those of Irish Catholic apostates like Moore.

For the British decadents who came into contact with the Church in post-Tractarian Oxford, Catholicism was less a latent cultural force in need of revival or rejection than an exotic foreign entity to which one might defect. Since the Reformation, Catholics were regularly caricatured in popular theater and literature as evil foreigners. The Jacobean dramatists took particular delight in depicting Italian and Spanish Catholics as wanton, perverted villains set on corrupting the innocent. By the end of the nineteenth century, such public vitriol had become less widespread, but could still be found in the cartoons of *Punch*, where Catholic men were repeatedly portrayed as effete, un-English degenerates. The British decadents had to contend with long-standing national prejudice against Catholicism as the superstitious religion of continental Europeans. Unlike their French counterparts, they typically approached Catholicism as an alternative to a state-supported religion that, until recently, had legally excluded all dissenters from public life.[17] The Roman Catholic Relief Act of 1829 allowed a level of political, social, and economic inclusion, and this shift toward religious tolerance entered the educational system in 1866 when Oxford ceased requiring its students to be members of the Church of England. The nineteenth century witnessed a profound shift away from harsh, exclusionary policies. Despite these gains in legal equality, Catholics remained firmly in the minority at the turn of the century. The Catholic Church in England primarily comprised a motley crew of Irish immigrants, Old Catholics—landed gentry who formed rural enclaves— and the intellectual elite who congregated around centers of learning such as Oxford. All three subgroups of this minority religion were typically viewed with suspicion by their Anglican neighbors. Edward Norman, author of *Anti-Catholicism in Victorian England* (1968), points out that anti-Catholic sentiment remained prevalent beyond 1900. The history of religious conflict in Victorian England is well documented and too dense a topic to rehearse satisfactorily here,[18] but one literary example may help to illustrate the day-to-day reality of that conflict near the turn of the century.

In his autobiographical novel *Of Human Bondage* (1915), W. Somerset Maugham provides a humorous anecdotal expression of the anti-Catholic sentiment that gripped the citizenry of late Victorian England. The narrator relates a telling dispute between the Anglican vicar, Mr. Carey, and his churchwarden, Josiah Graves, over the inclusion of candlesticks on the church altar.

> [Mr. Carey] had bought them second-hand in Tercanbury, and he thought they looked very well. But Josiah Graves said they were popish. This was a taunt that

always aroused the Vicar. He had been at Oxford during the movement which ended in the secession from the Established Church of Edward Manning, and he felt a certain sympathy for the Church of Rome. He would willingly have made the service more ornate than had been usual in the low-church parish of Blackstable, and in his secret soul he yearned for processions and lighted candles. He drew the line at incense. He hated the word protestant. He called himself a Catholic. He was accustomed to say that Papists required an epithet, they were Roman Catholic; but the Church of England was Catholic in the best, the fullest, and the noblest sense of the term. He was pleased to think that his shaven face gave him the look of a priest, and in his youth he had possessed an ascetic air which added to the impression. He often related that on one of his holidays in Boulogne, one of those holidays upon which his wife for economy's sake did not accompany him, when he was sitting in a church, the *curé* had come up to him and invited him to preach a sermon. He dismissed his curates when they married, having decided views on the celibacy of the unbeneficed clergy. But when at an election the Liberals had written on his garden fence in large blue letters: This way to Rome, he had been very angry, and threatened to prosecute the leaders of the Liberal party in Blackstable.[19]

In this amusing reflection on papist panic, the vicar himself expresses suspect and unwholesome sympathies. Mr. Carey, a staunch "Catholic in the best, the fullest, and the noblest sense of the term"—a man who believes that papists should be referred to with the "epithet" Roman Catholic—has still fallen prey to some of the ritualism of the Oxford Movement. Manning's famous secession from the Church of England engendered some sympathy in the young Mr. Carey, which manifested itself as a secret yearning for ritual and, perhaps most damning of all, candles. Though incense remains a bridge too far for the vicar, his Anglo-Catholic sympathy for Rome informs a scandalous belief in the benefits of temporary celibacy that gets him into trouble with his congregation. Maugham's fictional anecdote seems merely funny and charming on the surface, but it conveys the depth of insecurity caused by the defection to Rome of Manning and other eminent Victorians. It also highlights the day-to-day reality of a uniquely British tension between the state-sponsored church and the Church of Rome.

My use of the term "British decadence" speaks to the unique cultural status of "Papists" in England. The phrase is part of an attempt to solidify our understanding of one manifestation of decadent Catholicism, a term that, by itself, can be applied much more broadly. Isolating a particular group of artists allows for greater sensitivity to the implications of Catholic allegiance in turn-of-the-century England. These British decadents—most notably Oscar Wilde, Aubrey Beardsley, Ernest Dowson, Lionel Johnson, Lord Alfred Douglas, John

Gray, Frederick Rolfe (a.k.a. Baron Corvo), and "Michael Field" (Katharine Bradley and Edith Cooper)—have been largely written out of literary historical narratives describing the trajectory from Victorian doubt to modernist disbelief. Because they represented Oxford education, ivory-tower poetics, ennui, and entropy, they have also been excluded from the commonly accepted time line leading from the sublime reveries of the Romantics to the superb disruptions of the futurists, imagists, vorticists, and other diverse artists delineated by the protean term "modernism." My project presents a counter-narrative, a counter-history, that challenges the truism of modernist newness and proposes a different genealogy, one in which decadent Catholicism becomes an essential constituent element in the development of British modernism.

Decadence and Catholicism

The ranks of British decadence include more converts to Catholicism than any other comparable artistic movement in post-Reformation British literature. Along with those already named, more peripheral converts might be included: for example, Robert "Robbie" Ross (1869–1918), Canadian journalist, art critic, and intimate friend of Wilde; and Henry Harland (1861–1905), editor of the infamous decadent journal *The Yellow Book*. Nonetheless, I focus here on Wilde, Beardsley, Dowson, Johnson, Douglas, Gray, Rolfe, Bradley, and Cooper because their art helps to define the phenomenon of decadent Catholicism most directly. All, to a greater or lesser degree, found in the Church of Rome new material and color for their art: a trove of evocative symbols, a source of exotic rituals, and a font of narrative inspiration. In this respect, they followed in the footsteps of both the Pre-Raphaelites, especially Dante Gabriel Rossetti, and the artist-critic Walter Pater. As Claire Masurel-Murray has pointed out, both Rossetti and Pater tended to treat Catholicism less like a living faith than a source of aesthetic experience.[20] They made extensive use of Catholic iconography and ritual in, for example, "The Blessed Damozel" (1850) and *Marius the Epicurean* (1885), respectively, but personal convictions seemingly never entered into what Masurel-Murray calls their "art Catholicism."[21]

The decadents have routinely been accused of following this tradition by pursuing artistic interests that were never ratified by sincere spiritual experience. Were the British decadents obsessed with the aesthetic trappings of Catholicism? Without a doubt. Bloody martyrs, dark confessionals, beautiful vestments, the smells and bells of the Roman liturgy—the decadents were enchanted by it all. Some of the figures I have named spent more of their lives fetishizing the rituals and flaunting the moral teachings of the institutional Church than they did in sober prayer and meditation. Wilde comes first to mind. But John Gray, transgressive poet turned priest, follows close behind. What links the two, aside from a love affair, is that both eventually participated in the ritual of conversion—the formal gesture of assent by which the Church measures sincerity of faith. Christ himself proclaimed a radically inclusive measure of salvific faith when he crafted the parable of the workers in the vineyard.[22] In the allegorical meditation on salvation, he praises a landowner who pays the same wage to workers who began their labor at the beginning and at the end of the day. Such equivalence of reward finds its corollary in the sacramental economy of the Catholic Church, where eleventh-hour converts like Wilde and Beardsley are as eligible for the reward of everlasting life as their more spiritually industrious peers. I feel no compulsion to outdo the pope in measuring efficacious spiritual sincerity. The British decadents examined in this study had complicated relationships with the Catholic Church that invariably went beyond their art and into their personal spiritual lives. In this respect, they conform more closely to the example of French novelist Joris-Karl Huysmans (1848–1907) than to the "art Catholicism" of Rossetti and Pater.

Those looking for a paradigmatic expression of the decadent aesthetic often turn to Huysmans's *À Rebours* (*Against the Grain* or *Against Nature*, 1884). Arthur Symons dubbed the novel the "breviary of the Decadence" in his influential 1899 study *The Symbolist Movement in Literature*, a lengthier reincarnation of an 1893 article for *Harper's Magazine* titled "The Decadent Movement in Literature."[23] The novel contains all the elements we most readily associate with decadence: preference for artifice over nature, Schopenhauerian pessimism, sensual experimentation, perverse pleasures, and Catholicism. *À Rebours* implicitly undermines much of the utopian aestheticism of William Morris and highlights the spiritual and physical toll of the continual pursuit of ecstasy and new sensations called for in Walter Pater's landmark conclusion to *Studies in the History of the Renaissance* (1873). The novel follows Duc Jean Floressas des Esseintes in his failed attempt to construct an aesthetic paradise. When we first meet Des Esseintes he already resembles Poe's degenerate aristocrat Roderick Usher: "A frail man of thirty … anemic and highly strung, with hollow cheeks, cold eyes of steely blue … [and] papery hands."[24] He is the last of a once-noble bloodline and the broken product of generations of excess and inbreeding. He is an embodiment of nineteenth-century Austrian social critic Max Nordau's degenerate, whose "*fin-de-siècle* disposition" and neurasthenia make him a sterile creature of "malformations and infirmities."[25] He is infected with the *mal du siècle*, and his sensual exploits have already left him impotent, neurotic, and incapable of enjoying even the mildest gastronomic delights. In order to escape the frenetic Parisian lifestyle, Des Esseintes flees to the isolation of the suburbs, where he creates a perverse monastery in which to "steep himself in peace and quiet for the rest of his days" (*AN* 10). Once established there, he surrounds himself with all the opulent artificial beauty and rare quartos and folios prescribed by the aesthetic movement. There he remains, in Huysmans's words, "brutishly determined to wallow in the mud of his own carnality" (*AN* 211). Instead of a conventional plot, Huysmans provides a lengthy catalog of this wallowing. Des Esseintes's various extravagances—the garden of artificial flowers, the jeweled tortoise that dies under the weight of its gold carapace, the collection of Catholic vestments, the finely bound editions of Baudelaire—have become the stuff of legend and inspired writers from Oscar Wilde to Ernest Hemingway to recent Man Booker Prize winners Alan Hollinghurst and DBC Pierre.

More important than a litany of Des Esseintes's excesses is an understanding that they all stem from his desire to separate himself from banal modernity by creating a sensual monastery in which his decadent desires and Catholic aesthetic sensibilities can feed off one another. One lavish creation provides an explicit example of his intentional commingling of decadent literature and Catholic sacred objects:

> As a finishing touch, in the center of the chimney-piece, which was likewise dressed in sumptuous silk from a Florentine dalmatica, and flanked by two Byzantine monstrances of gilded copper which had originally come from the old Abbaye-au-Bois de Bièvre, there stood a magnificent triptych whose separate panels had been fashioned to resemble lace-work. This now contained, under its glass frame, three works of Baudelaire copied on real vellum, with wonderful missal letters and splendid coloring: to the right and left, the sonnets bearing the titles of *La Mort des Amants* and *L'Ennemi*, and in the middle, the prose poem entitled *Anywhere Out of the World*. (*AN* 17)

For Des Esseintes, liturgical objects provide a natural setting for ornately rendered copies of the poetry of Baudelaire, whose verse likewise blends the sacred and profane into a decadent whole. Take, for example, the speaker of "Harmonie du soir" from *Les Fleurs du Mal*, who punctuates his contemplation of evening noises and a bloody sunset with a religious simile:

> The violin is trembling like a grieving heart,
> A tender heart, that hates non-being, vast and black!

The sad and lonely sky spreads like an altar-cloth;
The sun is drowning in its dark congealing blood …[26]

Baudelaire's evening spreads out, not like a patient etherized upon a table but like the cloth that covers the sacrificial altar of the Catholic Eucharist, which is itself perversely mirrored in the disk of the sun slowly "drowning in its dark congealing blood." These selections from *À Rebours* and *Les Fleurs du Mal* serve as succinct examples of the decadent Catholic aesthetic at work in literature, but they fall short of holistic representation of decadent Catholicism.

Following the publication of *À Rebours*, Huysmans began a gradual conversion process that played out in both his life and his art. Between 1891 and 1903 he published four novels that follow the semiautobiographical spiritual development of a writer named Durtal, who begins by investigating a Satanic cult in Paris and ends by becoming a Catholic oblate. Examining this dramatic shift from the decadent phantasmagoria of Des Esseintes to the long conversion narrative of Durtal, it is tempting to try to divide Huysmans's work into the two phases: pre- and post-conversion, decadent and Catholic. Critics often make this mistake with other converts. T. S. Eliot's work is routinely, and mistakenly, segregated along these lines. Looking back at his artistic career in a 1903 preface to *À Rebours*, Huysmans explicitly traces his development as a Catholic author to his most decadent artistic creation: "All the novels I have written since *Against Nature* are there in embryo" (*AN* 209). What began, he tells us, as an exercise in unrestrained fantasy drew his attention toward the mysteries and consolations of the Church into which he had been born and to which he would return in time:

> The strange thing was that, without my realizing it at first, I was drawn by the nature of my work itself to study the Church from a number of angles…. Not being a believer, I looked at her, a little defiant, taken aback by her greatness and her glory, wondering why a religion which seemed to me to have been created for children could have inspired such marvelous works of art…. Today, after surer and more extensive investigations, as I look over the pages of *Against Nature* which deal with Catholicism and religious art, I am aware that this miniature panorama, painted on the pages of notepads, is accurate. What I was painting then was succinct; it lacked development, but it was truthful. Since then I have simply expanded and elaborated my sketches. (*AN* 208)

Huysmans articulates the narrative of his own artistic development in relation to his spiritual development and vice versa. *À Rebours* induced belief in the faith it defiantly admired. Subsequent writings grew out of the stunted but essentially truthful examination of Catholicism contained in that novel.

Perhaps the greatest lesson the British decadents learned from Huysmans was that fascination with the aesthetic trappings of Catholicism can contain the germ of a sincere faith. That all the decadent artists examined in this study chose at some point to publicly profess their faith, however late or imperfectly, suggests that their interest in Catholicism has something in common with that of their artistic and spiritual godfather, Huysmans. For most, this interest begins in the aesthetic realm, but it never ends there. Still, the degree to which the individual members of even this fairly intimate decadent coterie can be defined by an interest in Catholicism (artistically, theologically, spiritually, or otherwise) varies too greatly to allow for any totalizing definition of decadent Catholicism. In Chapter 1, I attempt to capture the variety of decadent Catholic literature by reading several representative works from the artists mentioned above. For now, I would like to focus more generally on the historically rooted rhetoric of decadent Catholicism as an artistic phenomenon—a rhetoric at work in the literature of an ideologically diverse group of modernist writers.

Decadent Catholicism

The term "Catholicism" itself contains multitudes. If we define it in relation to discourse, it embraces not only all discursive acts associated with the institutional Church (the seven sacraments, the liturgy, the various prayers and feast days) but also, to a lesser extent, the cultural products of Catholics (Dante's *Commedia*, Guido Reni's *Saint Sebastian*, Graham Greene's *The Power and the Glory*). In its most expansive sense, then, decadent Catholicism delineates an imaginative space in which the discursive acts of decadence and Catholicism engage, interact, overlap, or simply breathe the same air. In this space, we may find an exhausted hedonist desiring the peace of Carthusian monks at prayer, a murderous coiffeur contemplating a Virgin and Child, a suicidal dandy attempting to seduce a nun, or a tortured gay alcoholic enumerating his sins in poetic imitations of Thomas Aquinas's august hymn, "Pange Lingua."[27] Whatever the particulars, this imaginative space is invariably concerned with sin as a real transgression of a divine order. Sin, with all of its consequences and consolations, is perhaps the obsession that most unites the decadents and their modernist inheritors. In 1930 Eliot would credit Baudelaire with perceiving "that what really matters is Sin and Redemption" (*SP* 236). Almost a decade earlier, Joyce, a practiced blasphemer, demonstrated his continued respect for the God he so fiercely sought to disavow by refusing Robert McAlmon's drunken toast "Here's to sin!" with the curt response "I'll not drink to that."[28] The social ills that enraged Dickens and the interpersonal betrayals that haunt the novels of Hardy held less interest for the artists explored in this book than the literal reality of sin. Evil, vice, perversity— in decadence, these words find meaning primarily in relation to a Catholic conception of spiritual corruption. Excess, no matter how exotic, risks banality if it poses no threat to an immortal soul.

This is not to say that the decadents simply adopted the Catholic notion of sin as a means of adding spice to their debauches. Quite the opposite. Sin was more than a source of titillation; it was a spiritual reality that spurred each of these artists in turn along diverse paths all leading eventually to the foot of the Cross. In *De Profundis*, Wilde's 1897 prison epistle to his once and future lover, Lord Alfred Douglas, the broken artist credits Christ with realizing the true artistic and spiritual value of pain and transgression:

> Christ, through some divine instinct in him, seems to have always loved the sinner as being the nearest possible approach to the perfection of man.... in a manner not yet understood of the world he regarded sin and suffering as being in themselves beautiful, holy things, and modes of perfection. It *sounds* a very dangerous idea. It is so. All great ideas *are* dangerous. That it was Christ's creed admits of no doubt. That it is the true creed I don't doubt myself.
>
> Of course the sinner must repent.[29]

It should come as no surprise that Wilde and his contemporaries found in the pleasure of sin and the struggle for repentance a fitting subject for their art. For all of its subtle ambiguities, *Dorian Gray* is essentially a parable about the wages of sin and the necessity of contrition. Denial of this fact is usually a form of elaborate sophistry. For all of its praise of wine, women, and song, the poetry of Ernest Dowson routinely decries excess as a hallmark of a corrupt and fallen world. For all its bawdy naughtiness, the art of Aubrey Beardsley presents a biting satire of banal modern licentiousness. All of these artists turned to Christianity, in part, as a source of moral authority against which to measure both their own sins and those of their creations.

This fixation on sin hints at one possible reason for the noticeable scarcity of decadent-feeling literature in our time. Ellis Hanson is very nearly correct in the conclusion to *Decadence and Catholicism* when he asserts (laments?) that he would "speak of Catholic postmodernism, but, as far as literature is concerned, it can scarcely be said to exist."[30] Modern secularization and Moralistic Therapeutic Deism,[31] greater threats by far to the survival of orthodox Catholicism than Nero's lions or Saladin's armies ever were, have not done away with morals but have nearly eliminated the notion of wrong action as sin from much of contemporary Anglophone literature. Excess abounds in the work of novelists such as Martin Amis and Edward St Aubyn, but that excess is never conceptualized in relation to a coherent hermeneutic of sin. Conversely, the decadent obsession with sin is one of the most readily apparent legacies of the British *fin de siècle* in the literature of the early twentieth century. Joyce spends most of *A Portrait of the Artist as a Young Man* exploring Stephen's conflicted relationship with Catholic morality. Eliot made diagnosis of modern sinfulness the work of a lifetime. And Waugh made the sweet and bitter consequences of sin the central focus of his grand conversion narrative, *Brideshead Revisited*. This abiding concern is part of their decadent Catholic inheritance.

Like the Church itself, the decadents did not give equal attention to all transgressions. Non-normative sexual desire and alcoholism are the staple sins of decadent literature. Alcoholism is the less problematic issue. From the perspective of the Church, drunkenness endangers the soul, but drink can elevate it. The decadents never managed to follow Chesterton's maxim that we "should thank God for beer and Burgundy by not drinking too much of them."[32] In principle, however, they tended to agree with Chesterton, and those who struggled with dipsomania treated it as a sin worthy of healthy disdain, repentance, and failed renunciation. Lionel Johnson was especially conspicuous in this respect. Like Waugh's broken dandy Sebastian Flyte, he sought escape from guilt in a bottle and found only more guilt. Issues of sexual identity and expression are more complicated.

Homosexuality in particular plays such an integral role in decadent literature that Hanson's book-length study of decadence and Catholicism approaches the phenomenon almost exclusively from the perspective of queer theory. Drawing on interpretive models developed by founding queer theorists, such as Eve Sedgwick, Hanson questions why the almost exclusively homosexual members of the decadent school—straight authors such as Ernest Dowson and George Moore get short shrift—were drawn inexorably to a religion that condemns homosexuality. His conclusion: "They regarded the Church as, among other things, a theatre for the articulation of homosexual desire and identity through faith and through ritual."[33] Hanson identifies the decadent attraction to Catholicism as essentially performative. Huysmans, Wilde, Johnson, and others found a religion whose suitability to the performance of aesthetic and sexual discursive acts suggests that the Church was always already decadent. Hanson's work calls into question the common treatment of Catholicism and homosexuality as inherently antithetical even as it occasionally insists on the inherent homophobia of the institutional Church. In the recent ideological fallout from the legalization of gay marriage in Ireland and the United States, the Church has taken center stage as the most prominent institution to openly decry the altered and expanded legal definition of marriage. Because of this modern opposition between Catholicism and mainstream queer culture in the developed world we might be tempted to simplify the spiritual-sexual politics of decadent Catholicism by writing off the phenomenon as inexplicably paradoxical. To be sure, paradox, as Chesterton repeatedly demonstrated, plays an important role in the sacred mysteries of orthodoxy; yet the seemingly strange sexual aspect of decadent Catholicism is far from mysterious.

For a poet to feel pangs of devotional fervor mingled with more fleshly desires is hardly surprising in a Catholic context. As we saw above in Gray's "À une Madone," an imitation of Baudelaire's poem of the same name in which he compares his lover to the Virgin Mary, sadomasochistic yearning can easily express itself in a Catholic register. Blurring the line between spiritual devotion and erotic desire may strike some as unwholesome or titillating but should surprise no one. The writings of two of the Church's greatest early modern mystics, St. John of the Cross and St. Teresa of Avila, regularly combine erotic and spiritual rapture. Bernini's masterpiece *The Ecstasy of Saint Teresa* was inspired by the account of Teresa's ecstatic experience of repeated penetration by the fiery arrow of an angel. As a religion founded on the literal incarnation of God, the most radical example of spiritual and physical unity in any major religion, Catholicism is actually suited to, if not always vocally in favor of, the poetic-mystic conflation of spiritual and sexual desires. Such theological suitability for the artistic expression of decadent sexuality suggests the extent to which the *fin-de-siècle* aesthetic can subvert stereotypes of Catholicism as a religion especially opposed to the body in general and to sexuality in particular. At the same time, the rare heterosexual decadents (e.g., Dowson) demonstrate the degree to which Catholic doctrine operates beyond the bounds of traditional normative-queer sexual binaries. Because it conceptualizes sexual fulfillment and transgression in terms of morality as opposed to cultural normativity, the Church presents serious obstacles to all "improperly ordered" acts, whether they be hetero- or homosexual. Furthermore, the decadent obsession with celibacy as an almost exotic form of sexual expression draws attention to a queer*ish* aspect of priestly and monastic life—something even queer theorists such as Benjamin Kahan, author of *Celibacies: American Modernism & Sexual Life* (2013), have managed by-and-large to ignore.[34] While exploring the aesthetic afterlife of decadent Catholicism in the age of modernism, this book builds on the work of Hanson and more recent queer theorists by highlighting the complex ways in which many of the artists associated with decadence and modernism (queer and otherwise) undermine commonplace distinctions between queer sexuality and Catholic doctrine.

Whether dealing with non-normative sexual desire, alcohol, or opium, the decadent subscription to Catholic notions of sin was made possible by the complementary sacramental economy of the Church. Sin realized its positive potential by leading to the grace offered most directly through the sacrament of confession. For this reason, much of decadent Catholic poetry is confessional in nature. Its preoccupation with sin stems largely from the need to name transgressions—a need learned from the discourse of the confessional. What separates the poetry from the sacrament is the distinct sense of efficacious action. Because the confessing poet engages in a one-sided dialogue, his reflections nearly always end on a note of failure. This aesthetic of failure typically voices itself as world-weariness, ennui, or melancholy. With rare exceptions, joy, happiness, and even hope remain muted possibilities at best. As we will see, the experience of happiness or fulfillment in decadent literature tends to arise when sins are sublimated into the rituals and sacramental economy of the Church rather than simply brooded on. More often than not, decadent authors emphasize their separateness from salvation and holiness. Earthly manifestations of the Church's moral authority, such as individual churches, monasteries, or cloisters, act as reminders of sinfulness and of the gulf between the desire for and the realization of salvation. There—as Eliot relates in homage to Ernest Dowson's "*Cynara*"—"falls the shadow." Part of this sense of separation may be ascribed to the fact that the British decadents were all converts. Consequently, much of decadent prose and poetry deals with the attraction of conversion. Perhaps this is why the Church always seems to feel like a rare thing discovered rather than a natural inheritance. Drawn to those elements of Catholicism that were always already alien, the British artists of the *fin de siècle* found those parts of their own souls and their own art that were always already Catholic.

Decadent Catholicism and the Making of Modernism

These generalizations do not present a satisfactory definition of decadent Catholicism. They are merely a way to begin conceptualizing the diversity of artistic expression covered under the umbrella term. Nor do the decadent artists I have mentioned provide anything like a complete survey of artists who might be included in this book. Several women authors of the *fin de siècle* have received increased attention for their contributions to decadent literature and even their engagement with Catholicism. Vernon Lee (1856–1935) spent most of her life on the continent, where she experienced both an aesthete's attraction to and puritan's repulsion from the art and cultural practices of the Catholic Church.[35] The Spanish novelist and feminist Emilia Pardo Bazán (1851–1921) wrote much about French decadence from a Catholic perspective. Unlike their more canonical decadent contemporaries, Lee and Pardo Bazán do not manifest as prominently in the network of modernist texts explored in this book. Neither scholars of decadence nor modernism will find here an exhaustive account of decadent Catholicism before or after 1900. It is my sincere hope that this book might help define a space for wider-ranging investigations by other scholars. There is much work still to be done in this line of inquiry.

A decadent Catholic text does not necessitate expression of untroubled belief or chastity or piety any more than it does unorthodoxy or perversity or blasphemy. As a category, it represents variety, not uniformity. We might theorize generally about why British decadents were drawn to the Church and chose to weave its symbols, rituals, and theology into their art. Speaking in broad terms about something as intimate as religious attraction and its role in aesthetic praxis, however, provides at best a pastiche of unsatisfying oversimplifications that are as often misleading as enlightening, especially since what the Catholic Church meant to artists like Wilde or Beardsley or Dowson changed significantly over the course of their lifetimes. I find it better to simplify the discourse of definition and focus on providing concrete evidence for the central argument of this study: that the modernist absorption of decadence involved, and could not help involving, the religious aspect of the movement. By partially eschewing the task of definition, we can move away from universalizing statements and focus on the complexities of particular manifestations of continuity. We can listen closely for resonances of decadent Catholicism in modernist works and trace those resonances back to their *fin-de-siècle* sources. The following chapters seek to enact this process of retracing and uncovering.

Since some of the names most familiar to scholars of decadence are still obscure to those interested in other literary periods, Chapter 1, "The Decadents: Profligates, Priests, Pornographers, and Pontiffs," returns to the 1890s in order to rediscover the phenomenon of decadent Catholicism and expand the current critical conversation concerning this strange cultural development. It provides a sense of the variety encompassed in the convenient term and surveys the artists who gave it life.

Chapter 2, "Yeats and Pound: Disavowing Decadence, Forgetting Catholicism," focuses on the efforts of W. B. Yeats and Ezra Pound to write decadence and Catholicism out of their own artistic legacies and the history of early twentieth-century literature. Yeats, who began his poetic career alongside the decadents as a member of the Rhymer's Club, repeatedly implicated Catholicism in the early deaths of Beardsley, Johnson, and Dowson. Though several poems from *The Rose* (1893) and *The Wind Among the Reeds* (1899) demonstrate that Yeats was inspired by some of the Catholic symbolism and iconography found in the work of his decadent peers, he never made what he saw as the fatal mistake of subscribing to a religion that repeatedly set itself against artistic and intellectual freedom. In his grand historic vision, the priests and acolytes of Christianity would soon give way to a new age of unfettered imagination in which symbolist poets would replace their clerical forebears as the arbiters of religious experience. To hasten this day, Yeats actively distanced himself from the more decadent tone of his early verse and worked to modernize his art. Pound, whose early verse evinces the unmistakable influence of *fin-de-siècle* poetry, similarly expended a great deal of energy denouncing the decadents and their religion in both his prose and his long poem *Hugh Selwyn Mauberley*. New archival evidence shows that Pound unsuccessfully sought to pass his prejudice on to his protégé, T. S. Eliot. Together, Yeats and Pound managed to disavow decadence and forget about Catholicism, but the same cannot be said of their modernist contemporaries.

Chapter 3, "T. S. Eliot's Decadent (Anglo)-Catholicism," considers the dual role of decadent Catholic art in the dark satire of Eliot's early poetry, as well as the troubled expressions of religious feeling in his post-conversion work. In his early phase as satirist, Eliot produced poetry that evokes the spirit of the *enfant terrible* of the naughty nineties, Aubrey Beardsley. The young Eliot, faced with some of the same accusations of vulgarity and perversity that hounded Beardsley, composed poetry that, if not directly influenced by the illustrator of the decadents, clearly shared a similar artistic vision. Understanding Eliot's early poetry as part of a longer Catholic literary tradition helps us to grasp some of the continuity between pre-conversion poetry, such as the "Love Song of Saint Sebastian," and post-conversion poetry, such as *Ash-Wednesday*. Conversion to Anglo-Catholicism altered Eliot significantly. In the development of his "religious" poetry, however, we can still find traces of the decadent Catholic aesthetic developed in such poems as Johnson's "Ash Wednesday."

Chapter 4, "George Moore and James Joyce: Decadent *Anti*-Catholicism and Irish Modernism," follows a counter-current. In it, I explore the early poetry and fiction of the Irish novelist George Moore and the adoption and transformation of his decadent *anti*-Catholicism in the work of James Joyce. Moore associated with Wilde in his youth, but, unlike his Protestant friend, he saw nothing to love in the notoriously Jansenist Irish Catholic Church. Driven by a desire for cosmopolitan freedom, the young Moore fled to Paris to pursue painting and compose Baudelairean knockoffs, including his book of poetry *Flowers of Passion* (1878). Loosely based on his own youthful rebellion, Moore's early novels *Confessions of a Young Man* (1886) and *Mike Fletcher* (1889) established the heroic figure of the disillusioned young Irish artist who rejects the authority of the Catholic Church by fleeing to France and England to pursue a distinctly decadent artistic vocation and lifestyle. Joyce recapitulates Moore's narratives of anti-Catholic rebellion in *A Portrait of the Artist as a Young Man* (1916), where Stephen Dedalus rejects his country's religion, flees to Paris, and crafts distinctly decadent verse, but he undercuts and complicates Moore's heroes by satirizing them in the figure of Stephen, who returns to Dublin in *Ulysses* (1922) as a failed artist excluded from Moore's fashionable literary parties and still bound by the chains of his abandoned country and faith.

Chapter 5, "Evelyn Waugh: Decadent Catholicism Revisited," reaches past the 1920s and 1930s into the Catholic literary revival of the mid-twentieth century. Evelyn Waugh's corpus includes several works that engage with the legacy of British decadence, from the atmosphere of decline and excess that pervades *Vile Bodies* (1930) to the late-born dandy Ambrose Silk in *Put Out More Flags* (1942). In these novels, Waugh expresses his well-documented fascination with decadence while simultaneously lampooning the movement with his sometimes-indiscriminate satirical wit. *Brideshead Revisited* (1945) broke with all that. Hailed and berated by early critics as the first "serious" and "Catholic" novel of Waugh's career, *Brideshead* offers perhaps the last great expression of decadent Catholicism as an artistic phenomenon. In addition to highlighting Waugh's allusive use of Beardsley and Wilde in ways that scholars have largely overlooked, I argue that Waugh's fiction carries on an important legacy of British decadence by troubling what many today think of as an essential opposition between queer communities and the Catholic Church. Aside from actually depicting queer Catholics—a practice Waugh learned in part from the first truly decadent modernist, novelist Ronald Firbank (1886–1926)—*Brideshead* eschews any easy distinction between straight Catholicism and queer decadence. Instead, as I argue, it subverts convenient religious-sexual alignments by emphasizing the queer possibilities of Catholic sexuality.

Waugh may have crafted the last great example of decadent Catholic literature, but the relationship between decadence and Catholicism continues to fascinate contemporary writers. My conclusion, "Alan Hollinghurst and DBC Pierre: Decadent Catholicism after Modernism," follows lingering traces of this fascination in the work of two twenty-first-century novelists. Both Pierre and Hollinghurst, winners of the Man Booker Prize in 2003 and 2004, respectively, clearly feel the attraction of decadent Catholicism. This attraction manifests in their novels in many recognizable forms: a titillating Saint Sebastian, a pseudo-sacramental wine called Marius (after the protagonist of Walter Pater's *Marius the Epicurean*), and direct invocations of Dorian Gray and Des Esseintes, to name a few. Pierre and Hollinghurst are notable not only because they still make creative use of decadent Catholicism, but also because they do so in novels that assume and reflect an almost unconscious secularism alien to both decadent and modernist literature.

Together, these chapters call into question the literary-historical narrative established by Yeats in 1936 and readily adopted by critics for generations. Critical attempts, conscious and otherwise, to remove decadent Catholicism from the story of modernism failed to erase the telltale traces of the former in the defining texts of the latter. *Decadent Catholicism and the Making of Modernism* both records that failure and attempts to set the record straight.

1

The Decadents: Profligates, Priests, Pornographers, and Pontiffs

The decadent school of the 1890s was the most substantial Catholic literary movement in Protestant Britain until the Catholic revival of the mid-twentieth century. There were, of course, individual Catholic writers of genius between the early sixteenth and late nineteenth centuries: Crashaw stood out as the only Catholic among the metaphysical poets of the early seventeenth century. Dryden immortalized his allegiance to Rome in *The Hind and the Panther* (1687). Hopkins, whose merits as a poet arguably outweigh those of all of his contemporaries, stood alone in his genius—a master of poetic form ahead of but also isolated from his time. Newman, Pusey, and other luminaries of the mid-nineteenth-century Oxford Movement argued the merits of ritual and reunification and helped solidify the Catholic conversion narrative as an important part of the modern British intellectual tradition. Later, Newman's *Apologia* (1864) and *Dream of Gerontius* (1865) would attest to his substantial literary merit, but his legacy rested primarily on apologetics and theology. The decadent authors and artists of the British *fin de siècle* were not theologians producing literature but poets drawn to the literary possibilities of a foreign theology and its Church. On the cusp of what many have characterized as an age of disbelief, the age of modernism, they formed a literary movement that openly embraced religion as a source of artistic inspiration and spiritual fulfillment.

This assertion may strike some as controversial. What could be more irreligious than decadence, with its emphasis on the "perverse," on alcohol and opium, on homoerotic love and sensual experimentation, on artifice and synthetic pleasure? What could be further from religious art than Wilde's *Picture of Dorian Gray*, or Dowson's "Non sum qualis" ("I have been faithful to thee, Cynara! in my fashion"), or Beardsley's salacious illustrations of Wilde's *Salomé*? As I have already suggested, the decadent relationship with Catholicism was never entirely orthodox; at least it has never been entirely acceptable to champions of orthodoxy such as G. K. Chesterton, who began his literary career with the express design of combatting the school of Wilde. Yet Chesterton himself acknowledged that, at least in the case of Wilde, the aesthete's pursuit of beauty led inevitably to God:

> Like a many-coloured humming top, he was at once a bewilderment and a balance. He was so fond of being many-sided that among his sides he even admitted the right side. He loved so much to multiply his souls that he had among them one soul at least that was saved. He desired all beautiful things— even God.[1]

Chesterton combines disapproval of Wilde's many-sidedness with grudging fascination and an acknowledgment of the sincere religious element in the artist's soul. It is true that the number of decadent converts treated in this chapter who actually challenged or rejected the established doctrines of the Church remains a matter of debate. Nevertheless, heterodoxy or immorality in "Catholic" literature should hardly come as a surprise. The Goliardic poets of the twelfth and thirteenth centuries were nothing if not irreverent. Chaucer, the father of English literature, was a Catholic who told bawdy tales set in the context of a holy pilgrimage. Even the most intellectually serious and devout artists in the broader Catholic tradition have never been entirely conventional. Dante, that exemplar of Thomistic imagination, had comparatively little interest in bawdy tales or poems in praise of wine, women, and song. Yet he constructed an afterlife that regularly pushes the boundaries of orthodox theology. The author of Europe's greatest Catholic epic places a living pope in Hell, employs the pagan Cato as the greeter at the foot of Mount Purgatory, and makes a woman other than his wife or the Virgin Mary into an object of near-idolatrous adoration. These eccentricities came from the mind of a man born into a Catholic city-state centuries before the crises of faith that shook nineteenth-century Europe. At a time when doubt was outstripping faith, at least among the educated and elite, the profligates, priests, pornographers, and would-be pontiffs who made up the decadent movement distinguished themselves simply by treating religion as something other than an absurdity, or worse, a subject of indifference.

Scholars of *fin-de-siècle* literature are familiar with the decadent converts to Rome, but they remain largely unfamiliar to many modernist critics. Anyone looking for a wide-ranging study of the phenomenon should begin with Hanson's *Decadence and Catholicism* (1997). In the following pages, I seek to sharpen Hanson's insights by focusing more exclusively on British decadence, somewhat broadly defined. It was, after all, the British decadents of the nineties whose influence, as I will discuss in Chapter 2, Pound and Yeats so emphatically sought to exclude from the literature of the early twentieth century. Most of this chapter is concerned with revisiting the work of those little-known figures, especially those neglected by Hanson. For this reason, Lionel Johnson and Ernest Dowson receive particular attention. It seems only fitting, however, to begin our survey of distinctly British decadent Catholicism not with an Englishman but an Irish Protestant.

Wilde and His Circle

Amid the obscure names that populate the roster of British decadence Wilde's stands out as an exception. Looking back on decadence from the other side of 1900, prominent literary men like Chesterton and Eliot thought nothing of referring to the whole movement as the "school" or "circle" of Wilde.[2] Not surprisingly, given the elasticity of his mind and the often-paradoxical expressions of his many opinions and beliefs, the nature of Wilde's relationship with Catholicism continues to instigate controversy. Following in the footsteps of Richard Ellmann, some critics remain dubious about the seriousness of Wilde's engagement with Catholicism and go so far as to proclaim that he was an atheist. Others indulge in the opposite extreme. In 2000, Catholic apologist Joseph Pearce published *The Unmasking of Oscar Wilde* with the express intention of overturning Ellmann's characterization of the artist's lack of faith.[3] Needless to say, his rebuttal did not produce any consensus in critical opinion, but it did illustrate the polarizing nature of a debate that continues to tell us more about its participants' views on Catholicism than Wilde's. Yet among Catholic intellectuals, usually keen on claiming converts of all stripes, Wilde's approach to religion, as well as that of his fellow decadents, continues to cause as much discomfort as interest.

Nowhere is this aestheticized Catholicism more evident than in the infamously decadent eleventh chapter of Wilde's *The Picture of Dorian Gray* (1890/91). Under the influence of an unnamed "poisonous book," presumably Joris-Karl Huysmans's *À Rebours* (1884), the previously innocent Dorian throws himself with abandon into the cultivation of strange new sensations:

> In his search for sensations that would be at once new and delightful, and possess that element of strangeness that is so essential to romance, he would often adopt certain modes of thought that he knew to be really alien to his nature, abandon himself to their subtle influences, and then, having, as it were, caught their colour and satisfied his intellectual curiosity, leave them with that curious indifference that is not incompatible with a real ardour of temperament, and that, indeed, according to certain modern psychologists, is often a condition of it. (*DG* 102)

We soon learn that Catholicism has a part to play in Dorian's decadent education and pursuit of experiences "alien to his nature":

> It was rumoured of him once that he was about to join the Roman Catholic communion, and certainly the Roman ritual had always a great attraction for him. The daily sacrifice, more awful really than all the sacrifices of the antique world, stirred him as much by its superb rejection of the evidence of the senses as by the primitive simplicity of its elements and the eternal pathos of the human tragedy that it sought to symbolize. (*DG* 102–3)

The Mass is not a tame thing for Dorian. In his mind, the "Roman ritual" is, paradoxically, both a sacrifice more terrible than those of pagan antiquity and a purely symbolic gesture. Wilde, always capable of staring paradox in the eye without blinking, depicts the central sacrament of the Catholic Church as simultaneously vacant of literal significance and more awe-inspiring than the older blood sacrifices it displaced. Such speculation might lead some to a more theologically serious engagement with Catholicism. Not so for Wilde's pretty, vapid, corrupt, superficial protagonist. Dorian desires only a gilded gesture and a beautiful pose. He attends Mass as a voyeur, watching the solemn priest and pretty altar boys wrapped in beautiful gowns and performing ancient rituals amid incensed smoke. He looks longingly at dark confessionals, beside which he wishes to sit and overhear the stories of others' sins. This Romish fascination, we are quickly reassured, never became anything more substantial:

> But he never fell into the error of arresting his intellectual development by any formal acceptance of creed or system, or of mistaking, for a house in which to live, an inn that is but suitable for the sojourn of a night, or for a few hours of a night in which there are no stars and the moon is in travail. (*DG* 103)

The narrator's closing metaphor defines Dorian's fascination with Catholicism as an ephemeral dalliance draped in overt sexual innuendo. Playing at being Catholic is, for him, like an assignation with an anonymous partner in a disreputable inn on a moonless night. Though Wilde's own flirtation with Catholicism was far more serious than Dorian's, he understood all too well the importance of keeping the hearth and the hotel separate.

Almost always the standard by which critics initially assess Anglophone decadence, *Dorian Gray* presents a frivolous and superficial picture of the decadent protagonist's interest in Catholicism. Dorian receives the lion's share of attention from critics who either celebrate or deplore his almost solely "aesthetic" appreciation of Catholic ritual. Converts among the generation of the nineties were well aware that their religious interests had been caricatured in art and the popular press as little more than superficial gestures, and they enjoyed elaborating on the theme in an ironic key. The same year that Wilde published his expanded edition of *Dorian Gray* (1891), Lionel Johnson, who introduced Wilde to "Bosie" (Lord Alfred Douglas) and found a degree of immortality with his quintessentially decadent poem, "The Dark Angel" (1893), wrote a satirical anatomy of young aesthetes titled "The Cultured Faun." Johnson's young "faun," disabused of all conventional ideas, steeped in paradox and epigrams, and infused with the nervous tension of Gautier and Baudelaire, cultivates an appreciation for Catholic ritual as a complement to his aesthetic development:

> Here comes in a tender patronage of Catholicism: white tapers upon the high altar, an ascetic and beautiful young priest, the great gilt monstrance, the subtle-scented and mystical incense, the old world accents of the Vulgate, of the Holy Offices; the splendor of the sacred vestments. We kneel at some hour, not too early for our convenience, repeat the solemn Latin, drinking in those Gregorian tones, with plenty of modern French sonnets in memory, should the sermon be dull.[4]

In keeping with the Dorian mood, Johnson's narrator scoffs at the idea of his cultured fauns actually converting to their pet religion:

> But join the Church! Ah, no! better to dally with the enchanted mysteries, to pass from our dreams of delirium to our dreams of sanctity with no coarse facts to jar upon us. And so these fine persons cherish a double "passion," the sentiment of repentant yearning and the sentiment of rebellious sin.[5]

Johnson, perhaps the most pious and theologically minded of his contemporaries, clearly took delight in ridiculing the spiritual superficiality of those young aesthetes of the time—imaginary and real—who were too caught up in cultivating sensations to actually produce art or save their souls.

As "The Cultured Faun" demonstrates, Dorian's superficial interest in religion should not be taken as definitive of decadent Catholicism as an artistic movement. Far from extoling purely aesthetic flirtation with religion, Johnson depicts such dabbling as shallow and risible. Arguably, this was partly Wilde's point as well. He portrays Dorian's flirtation with Catholicism, along with all of his other pursuits, as a pretty bimbo's attempt to live out someone else's hedonistic philosophy (namely, that of Lord Henry) and imitate the exploits related in a Huysmanian "poisonous book." Those who miss Wilde's irony miss the novel's essentially moral, if not moralistic, force. Nevertheless, some Catholic intellectuals have gone so far as to disparage the majority of decadent Catholic artists who associated with Wilde as frivolous Dorians. In *The Pen and the Cross: Catholicism and English Literature 1850–2000* (2010), Richard Griffiths begins his discussion of the generation of the nineties with the telling heading "A False Start: Aesthetic Catholicism." Griffiths lays the blame for this "false start" squarely at the feet of Walter Pater. He laments that the purely aesthetic approach to religion in Pater's *Marius the Epicurean* (1885) became "common among those of the generation of the nineties who saw in Catholic liturgy something purely picturesque, exotic and aesthetically pleasing."[6] From this perspective, Dorian Gray's fictive encounter with Catholicism becomes truly representative of the spiritual shallowness of most of the members of a diverse literary movement. Griffiths refrains from writing off all British decadents but still insists on dividing them into two camps: the dilettantes and the sincere converts. Wilde, of course, ends up in the first category. Like T. S. Eliot, who once accused the arch dandy of getting "all the emotional kick out of Christianity one can, without the bother of believing it,"[7] Griffiths writes off Wilde's interest in Catholicism as superficial. Both are wrong. Though never orthodox in his life or art, and certainly an unfit saint for literary hagiographers, Wilde had few more consistent or compelling muses than the Church his Protestant peers still denigrated as the Whore of Babylon.

Among his earliest verses, we find an earnest attraction to Catholicism that differs greatly from the trifling fascination of Dorian Gray. Wilde composed "Rome Unvisited" in the summer of 1875, when money troubles cut short a tour of Italy. In the poem, he laments the deferral of a journey to the eternal city and imagines all the ritual pomp he might have glimpsed there:

> A pilgrim from the northern seas—
> What joy for me to seek alone
> The wondrous Temple, and the throne
> Of Him who holds the awful keys!
>
> When, bright with purple and with gold,
> Come priest and holy Cardinal,
> And borne above the heads of all
> The gentle Shepherd of the Fold.
>
> O joy to see before I die
> The only God-anointed King,
> And hear the silver trumpets ring
> A triumph as He passes by!
>
> Or at the altar of the shrine
> Holds high the mystic sacrifice,

And shows a God to human eyes
Beneath the veil of bread and wine. (*P* 46)

Wilde's speaker shares Dorian's attraction to the trappings of Catholicism, but his enthusiasm is more like that of a sincere seeker after faith than an epicurean. He sees in the bread and wine a "mystic sacrifice" that "shows a God to human eyes." The transubstantiated God reveals himself in Rome, filling Wilde's English pilgrim with the hope that he might one day travel to the eternal city and experience the conversion he can only imagine:

Before yon field of trembling gold
  Is garnered into dusty sheaves,
  Or ere the autumn's scarlet leaves
Flutter as birds adown the wold,

I may have run the glorious race,
  And caught the torch while yet aflame,
  And called upon the holy name
Of Him who now doth hide His face. (*P* 47)

After returning to the UK, Wilde sent the poem to a delighted Cardinal Newman, a move suggestive of an early desire for conversion that would not reach fruition until the eleventh hour.[8]

Not all of Wilde's early verse treats the Catholic Church with the same degree of breathless enthusiasm. In the sonnet "Easter Day," the speaker watches a regal pope carried in procession through adoring crowds at St. Peter's: "Priest-like, he wore a robe more white than foam, / And, king-like, swathed himself in royal red, / Three crowns of gold rose high upon his head" (*P* 50). The poem's volta contrasts the princely "Holy Lord of Rome" with the homeless and suffering Christ of the scriptures. The message is simple and speaks to a latent puritanism. Christ's supposed representative on Earth leads a rather decadent and worldly lifestyle. Wilde's occasional English puritanism emerges elsewhere in *Poems*, as in "Quantum Mutata," in which he fondly recalls the days when Cromwell's ambassadors stood up for continental Protestants and made the pope shake in his boots. The poem berates England for its current decadence and failure to live up to the legacy of its political and poetic heroes:

How comes it then that from such high estate
We have thus fallen, save that Luxury
With barren merchandise piles up the gate

Where nobler thoughts and deeds should enter by:
Else might we still be Milton's heritors. (*P* 14)

Such poems, though far fewer in number than those that celebrate Catholicism, remind us that, like Whitman, Wilde never feared contradiction. His infatuation with Rome was real, but so too were his critical mind and his restless wit.

After much vacillation in his Oxford years, Wilde decided against conversion, but the *Urbs Sacra* played an important role in his later life. Less than a year before his death, the itinerant poet found himself among a crowd at St. Peter's receiving the blessing of Pope Leo XIII. According to Wilde, his ticket for the audience came from an angel at a café. Wilde was clearly moved by the experience, and he claimed that the Papal blessing healed him of a pernicious physical aliment. It shouldn't surprise us that Wilde's story is almost as whimsical as one of his fairy tales. As G. K. Chesterton proved repeatedly, earnest Catholicism and fairy tales are rarely antithetical. In spite of such fantastic bouts of papist enthusiasm, Wilde neither rushed to convert nor abjured fleshly pleasure. His was never going to be an Augustinian conversion narrative, moving more or less predictably from sin to repentance to sanctity, but those who seek to distance Wilde from Catholicism run the risk of dismissing an essential element in the artist's work.

Almost more surprising than Wilde's conversion is that of his sometime lover Lord Alfred Douglas (1870–1945), affectionately known as Bosie. After actively distancing himself from Wilde and attempting to establish himself as a respectable married gentleman, Douglas converted in 1911 and adopted an attitude of self-righteous piety, disavowing his early decadent verses such as the notorious "Two Loves," best known for the inspired line "I am the love that dare not speak its name."[9] Douglas composed the poem in 1892 and first published it in the 1894 issue of the Oxford periodical *The Chameleon*, which also included Wilde's "Phrases and Philosophies for Use of the Young;" a short story about chaste but passionate love between a priest and an altar boy; and homoerotic verses such as "Les Decadents" and "Love in Oxford." The Catholic register of most of Douglas's early poetry is muted, but some later poems, such as "Before a Crucifix" (1919), demonstrate how the persecution complex evident in "Two Loves" carried over into his post-conversion verse. Based loosely on the traditional Catholic "Prayer Before a Crucifix," in which the suppliant reflects on his or her own sinfulness and Christ's five wounds, Douglas's poem foregoes reflection on personal iniquity and focuses instead on a self-pitying identification with the betrayal suffered by the crucified God:

What hurts Thee most? The rods? the thorns? the nails? …

Is it Thy Mother's anguish? *"Search thine heart.*
Didst thou not pray to taste the worst with Me,
O thou of little faith." Incarnate Word,
Lord of my soul, I know, it is the part
That Judas played; this I have shared with Thee
(By wife, child, friend betrayed). *"Thy prayer was heard."*[10]

Without any shade of irony or suggestion of self-conscious exaggeration, the speaker empathizes with Christ and claims that his life has been equally marked by personal betrayal. In some ways, Lord Alfred Douglas the respectable convert is less sympathetic than Bosie the melancholic, conflicted young decadent.

Another of Wilde's acolytes and the presumed model for Dorian Gray, John Gray (1866–1934) is best known for his early work. With poems about homicidal beauticians and *femmes damnées*, as well as imitations of Verlaine, Rimbaud, and Baudelaire, his volume *Silverpoints* (1893) captures the essence of 1890s decadence, including its preoccupation with Catholicism. In his imitation of Baudelaire's "À une Madone," quoted in the introduction, Gray's speaker offers to build his beloved lady a "grotto altar of my misery" far from the corrupting force of the "world's cupidity" (XXXIII). After his Marian shrine is complete, this twisted lover promises to pierce the heart of his beloved with all the cultivated sins that he carries with him, thereby transforming her into a true Mary, a sinless virgin whose heart is broken by the transgressions of the sinful:

Last, that indeed a Mary thou may'st be,
And that my love be mixed with cruelty—

O foul voluptuousness! when I have made
Of every deadly sin a deadlier blade,

Torturer filled with pain will I draw near
The target of thy breast, and, sick with fear,

Deliberately plant them all where throbs
Thy bleeding heart, and stifling with its sobs.[11]

This combined act of veneration and violation speaks to a tension at the heart of nearly all decadent texts between ideal purity and cultivated depravity—a tension that R. K. R. Thornton refers to as "the decadent dilemma."[12] Gray's conversion in 1890 was followed by several years of lapse, near scandal, and debauchery that led to a reconversion in 1895, publication of a volume titled *Spiritual Poems* the following year, and ordination in 1901. He was also instrumental in the conversion of one of the neglected female poets of the *fin de siècle*, "Michael Field," the aunt and niece duo Katherine Bradley and Edith Cooper, who found religion after the death of their beloved dog Whym Chow in 1906. "Whymmie" received credit for this conversion and was commemorated in the sentimental, bathetic, and shockingly touching collection of poems *Whym Chow: Flame of Love* (1914). Aside from functioning as a sort of requiem for the Skye terrier, *Whym Chow* provided a space where Bradley and Cooper could bring together their pagan and Catholic identities.[13]

Late in their career, Bradley and Cooper found in their conversion a source of poetic inspiration that naturally expressed itself through the style and forms of decadent Catholicism that were already present in their earlier work. As early as 1892, Bradley and Cooper were producing poetry that resonates with and, in some instances, anticipates the decadent Catholic verses of their male contemporaries. Their poem "Saint Sebastian" singles out the patron saint of homoerotic decadence in an ekphrastic reverie on a painting by Correggio, in which the arrow-pierced martyr gazes lovingly up at the Madonna and Child surrounded by cherubs in the clouds above:

> While cherubs straggle on the clouds of luminous, curled fire,
> The Babe looks through them, far below, on thee with soft desire.
>> Most clear of bond must they be reckoned—
>>> No Joy is second
> To theirs whose eyes by other eyes are beckoned.
>
> Though arrows rain on breast and throat they have no power to hurt,
> While thy tenacious face they fail an instant to avert.
>> Oh might my eyes, so without measure,
>>> Feed on their treasure,
> The world with thong and dart might do its pleasure![14]

The beckoning gaze of "soft desire" that passes between Sebastian and Christ is, as several critics have pointed out, suggestive of the well-established homoerotic cult surrounding the martyr.[15] This critical tendency to read elements of coded homoeroticism in "Saint Sebastian," though valid to an extent, often misses the point that Catholicism has long fostered a sense of quasi-erotic attraction between Christians and Christ. The Catholic Church routinely discussed its role in relation to Christ as one of conjugal feminine receptivity; the Church is the bride waiting to receive Christ the bridegroom as Mary received the seed of God.

Bradley and Cooper's quasi-erotic description of Sebastian's adoring relationship with Christ taps into this ingrained theology of feminine receptivity. In doing so it suggests that specifically Catholic conceptions of spiritual conjugality provide a closer analogue to non-normative decadent sexuality than anything in mainstream British culture or the Anglican Church. To a greater or lesser degree, all the British decadents associated with "the Wilde circle" found echoes of their own "aberrant" sexual attractions in the hagiography and theology of the Church.

Other important English Catholic poets of the time touched the edges of the decadent network. Perhaps the most prominent was Francis Thompson (1859–1907), whom Chesterton praised as one of the greatest poets of his age and defended against public insinuations about "moral weakness."[16] Such insinuations had substantial basis in fact. Before being discovered and taken in by Alice Meynell, herself a poet associated with decadence,[17] Thompson struggled with opium addiction and experienced first-hand the world of urban degradation imagined in the later chapters of Wilde's *Dorian Gray*. He knew the other poets examined in this book well enough to be invited to a meeting of the Rhymers' Club in its heyday. It was not a success. Thompson, paralyzed by shyness, failed to share any of his work and never returned to the Club.[18] Nevertheless, his poetry contains many of the hallmarks of decadent verse, most notably a tendency to fixate on personal sinfulness and grasp after a partially realized and specifically Catholic redemption. We can see this tendency at work in one of the most well known and influential Catholic poems in English literary history, "The Hound of Heaven" (1893). Confessing a life of spiritual, aesthetic, and moral waywardness, the poem's speaker recounts the myriad ways in which he has fled from God over the course of his life, just as the hare flees the pursuing hound:

> I fled Him, down the labyrinthine ways
> > Of my own mind; and in the mist of tears
> I hid from Him, and under running laughter.
> > Up vistaed hopes I sped;
> > And shot, precipitated,
> Adown Titanic glooms of chasmèd fears
> > From those strong Feet that followed, followed after.[19]

Stripped of earthly pleasures and the fleeting contentment offered by the beauty of the natural world, the speaker finds himself eventually reduced to naked trembling at the feet of his pursuing God, where he asks, like Donne, to be ravished ("Naked I wait Thy love's uplifted stroke!").[20] Only at rock bottom, at the nadir of life does the speaker come to realize that what felt like the shadow of a hunter was the "shade of his hand, outstretched caressingly."[21] Thompson wrote some of the most iconic Catholic poetry of the 1890s, and his connection to his decadent contemporaries merits lengthier discussion,[22] but no poets captured the spirit of decadent Catholicism in all its variety as perfectly as Ernest Dowson and Lionel Johnson.

Dowson and Johnson served as the chief source of inspiration for Yeats's myth of the "tragic generation"—the narrative largely responsible for writing decadent Catholicism out of the history of modernism. Biographically, the two men have much in common. They converted in the same year (1891), died soon after the turn of the century, and were plagued by alcoholism, dissipation, and self-torturing sexual desires. They also moved in the same artistic circles, including the famous Rhymer's Club. In spite of their close association and many shared thematic concerns, their work is not uniformly decadent. Though both men are placed today in the pantheon of British decadence, they produced markedly different work. Strangely, Johnson and Dowson receive only glancing attention in Hanson's *Decadence and Catholicism*. Dowson's near absence is understandable, since his heterosexuality makes him one of many outliers in Hanson's assessment of Catholicism as a site for the performance of explicitly homosexual decadent desires. The limited attention paid to Johnson is more surprising, given his well-documented suppressed homosexuality and the abundance of his devotional poetry. Whatever the reason for these oversights, the work of these two peers embodies many of the tensions at the heart of British decadence. The following readings will address common elements in the poetry of Johnson and Dowson that identify their work as representative of decadent Catholicism, but also call attention to differences that demonstrate the term's variety and density.

Johnson in the Confessional

As decadent artists go, Johnson is less paradigmatic than his friend and peer Ernest Dowson. He never seems to have thought of himself as a decadent poet. As we saw in "The Cultured Faun," he actively distanced himself from the decadent label by lampooning his contemporaries. In a similar send-up titled "A Decadent's Lyric" (1896), Johnson's patronizing disdain is equally evident:

> Sometimes, in very joy of shame,
> Our flesh becomes one living flame:

And she and I
Are no more separate, but the same.....

Her body music is: and ah,
The accords of lute and viola,
When she and I
Play on live limbs love's opera! (*CP* 212)

Were it not for the overdone alliteration of "live limbs love's" and the almost comic rhyming of "ah" with "viola" the poem might feel at home in one of Dowson's collections. The final line feels like a parody of Dowson's favorite alliterative line of poetry from Poe's "The City in the Sea": "The viol, the violet, and the vine." Among Dowson's few strong opinions about verse was the notion that the letter "V" should be employed as often as possible. "A Decadent's Lyric" testifies to Johnson's facility with the verse aesthetic of his circle while demonstrating his desire to move beyond what Sturgis calls the "pseudo-Parisian cult of sin" in pursuit of a more serious poetic—one often concerned with the interplay of decadence and Catholicism.[23]

Aside from the "conspicuous" bottle of whiskey that George Santayana once noticed nestled on Johnson's desk at Oxford between *Leaves of Grass* and *Les Fleurs du Mal*,[24] a bottle that would follow the young poet throughout his short life, Johnson lived quite scrupulously. His corpus contains several homoerotic poems inflected by Catholic imagery, as we will see, but much of his poetry belongs to a more devotional genre. Johnson's poetry demonstrates a pious, theologically complex, ascetic Catholicism, especially when juxtaposed with the more obviously decadent work of his peers. It is hard to imagine Dowson, Douglas, or Gray writing "At the Burial of Cardinal Manning" (1892), though a young Wilde might have:

Victor in Roman purple, saint and knight,
In peace he passes to eternal peace:
Triumph so proud, knew not Rome's ancient might;
She knew not to make poor men's sorrow cease:
For thousands, ere he won the holiest home,
Earth was made homelier by this prince of Rome. (*CP* 63)

Here is no evidence of the *mal du siècle*. Johnson saw himself as a Catholic artist in a Catholic nation that had lost its way during the Reformation—a view reinforced by the title of his posthumously published collection of essays, *Post Liminium* (1911). The title translates as "after captivity" or "after slavery." Some ancient masters, including Cicero, used the word *liminium* as a shortened form of the single word *postliminium*, a Roman law ensuring that the property of captured citizens would be preserved until their return to Rome. The word was employed after the Reconquista when formerly Catholic dioceses taken as part of the Moorish conquest of Spain came under Rome's authority once again.[25] Johnson's poem "To Leo XIII" (1892) confirms his belief that England should one day return, *postliminium*, to Rome. It praises the "Vicar of Christ" and "Father of all," and it concludes with the prayer that "some, so proud to be / Children of England" might "bring / Thine England back to thee!" (*CP* 63). Such zealous papist cheerleading, however, is not characteristic of all of Johnson's religious poetry. Most of his verse is overtly inflected by decadence and marked by a tendency to brood on the world's many temptations.

"Before the Cloister" (1896), for example, opens with a plea that a spirit of repentance or "Sorrow" will return and save the speaker from his fiery desires:

> Sorrow, O sister Sorrow, O mine own!
>   Whither away hast flown?
> Without thee, fiery is the flowery earth,
>   A flaming dance of mirth,
> A marvel of wild music: I grow frail
>   Amid the perfumed gale,
> The rushing of desires to meet delights. (*CP* 150)

Tempted by sensuous earthly delights, the speaker fears that his frailty may lead to sin. So, he calls on Sorrow, now identified with the sorrowful Virgin Mary, the *mater dolorosa*, to "cool" him with her "bitter song" and remind him of Christ's suffering:

> Come, vestal lady! In my vain heart light
>   Thy flame, divinely white!
> Come, lady of the lilies! blaunch to snow
>   My soul through sacred woe!
> Come thou, through whom I hold in memory
>   Moonlit Gethsemani. (*CP* 150–1)

Only by remembering Christ's agony in the garden of Gethsemane can the poet suppress his decadent desires and avoid "the fatal sleep" of damnation that Augustine calls "the second death":[26]

> O Sorrow! come, through whom alone I keep
>   Safe from the fatal sleep:

Through whom I count the world a barren loss,
 And beautiful the Cross:
Come, Sorrow! lest in surging joy I drown,
 To lose both Cross and Crown. (*CP* 151)

There is nothing particularly unusual about a Catholic praying for temperance and reflecting on the suffering of Christ, but Johnson places himself outside the cloister, the secluded place reserved for those dedicated to a life of prayer and contemplation. In the liminal space between the world of the flesh and the world of the spirit, he allows his thoughts to linger on earthly desires in a perverse self-torturing way. The poem ends not with triumph over temptation but with a premonition of loss: "Come, Sorrow! lest in surging joy I drown, / To lose both Cross and Crown." The falling note that concludes "Before the Cloister" resonates with the aesthetic of failure so prominent in earlier decadent Catholic texts, including the poetry of Wilde's Oxford days.

Wilde first learned of Johnson, a promising young poet in New College, Oxford, while visiting Walter Pater in February of 1890. After waking Johnson up by calling on him at the crack of noon, Wilde proceeded to smoke all of his host's cigarettes and leave him generally enchanted.[27] This enchantment reached its artistic climax in Johnson's homage to *Dorian Gray*, "In Honorem Doriani Creatorisque Eius" ("In Honor of Dorian and His Creator," 1891). After receiving an inscribed first edition of the novel from Wilde, Johnson responded with the following lines of grateful adulation:

Benedictus sis, Oscare!
Qui me libro hoc dignare
 Propter amicitias:
Modo modulans Romano
Laudes dignas Doriano,
 Ago tibi gratias. (*CP* 209)

(Blessed be you, Oscar!
Who deem me worthy of this book
For the sake of friendship:
Modulating in the Roman mode
Praises fitting for Dorian,
I give you thanks.)[28]

The poem goes on for three more stanzas reveling in the beauty of the novel's *avidus amores* (greedy loves) and *peccata dulcia* (sweet sins). What a casual reader (even a casual reader of Latin) might miss is that Johnson's poem is more than the pedantic exercise of a Winchester-educated classicist. Its very rhythm is expressive of a specifically Catholic poetic form, epitomized in Medieval hymns such as the "Stabat Mater," "Dies Irae," and "Hymn of St. Thomas Aquinas" (also known as the "Pange Lingua Gloriosi"):

> Pange lingua, gloriosi
>> Corporis mysterium,
> Sanguinisque pretiosi,
>> Quem in mundi pretium
> Fructus ventris generosi
>> Rex effudit Gentium.

> (Sing, my tongue, the Saviour's glory,
> Of His Flesh, the mystery sing;
> Of the Blood, all price exceeding,
> Shed by our Immortal King,
> For the world's redemption,
> Fruit of a noble Womb to spring.)[29]

The above translation was completed by Edward Caswall (1814–78), an Oxford-educated Anglican curate who converted to Catholicism in 1847 and, in 1851, published a translation of the complete hymns of the Roman Missal and Breviary titled *Lyra Catholica*. Written in praise of the Eucharist by the most influential theologian in the history of the Catholic Church, the "Pange lingua" was composed in trochaic tetrameter with alternating catalectic lines. The regular trochaic tetrameter of the first line ("Pange lingua, gloriosi") alters in the second, catalectic line of only seven syllables, which ends on an incomplete foot ("Corporis mysterium"). When chanted, the last syllable in mysterium is elongated (mys-ter-i-u-um), which resolves the metric variation that appears on paper. Johnson's poem follows this same accentual rhythm as St. Thomas's hymn and imitates its six-line stanzas. As if to avoid charges of blasphemy, he alters the form slightly by limiting himself to two catalectic lines per stanza. Perhaps he sensed that a poem written in praise of Oscar Wilde and *Dorian Gray* should differentiate itself slightly from a hymn written in praise of the transubstantiated flesh of God or the sorrows of the Virgin Mary at the foot of the cross. Even with this slight alteration, "In Honorem Doriani Creatorisque Eius" provides one example of the inventive ways in which the artists in Wilde's circle appropriate the forms of Catholicism to engage with decadence.

Not long after composing "In Honorem Doriani Creatorisque Eius," Johnson turned from adoration of Wilde to disdain. His enthusiastic song of praise died on his lips when he realized that the sweet sins of Wilde's novel were more than fiction, more than the invented immoralities necessary for a morality tale. After witnessing Wilde's exploits with his beloved friend Lord Alfred Douglas, Johnson condemned his onetime master in "The Destroyer of a Soul" (1892): "Mourning for that live soul, I used to see; / Soul of a saint, whose friend I used to be: / Till you came by! a cold, corrupting, fate" (*CP* 74). Johnson was perhaps the only person in England who saw in Douglas the "soul of a saint" or thought that soul worth defending and mourning in verse. Furthermore, his infatuation with *Dorian Gray* leaves one wondering, how could someone enamored of Wilde's decadent masterpiece be horrified by sex between men? Tortured by his own homosexual desires, Johnson seemingly found in the novel what many readers do, an essentially moral tale about the dire consequences of sin. Before taking up the ludicrous position of defender of Bosie's honor, Johnson looked to Wilde as a model of what an artist might do with the raw material of a sinful world and a troubled soul—one of the older artist's most consistent themes. Take, for example, Wilde's poem "San Miniato," first published in 1876 after a summer tour of Italy when Wilde's early fascination with Catholicism was at its peak. After climbing to the famous Florentine Basilica, the speaker stands at the threshold of "this holy house of God," looks out over the moonlit city, and falls into a Marian reverie that seems to anticipate Johnson's own in "Before the Cloister":

> O crowned by God with thorns and pain!
> Mother of Christ! O mystic wife!
> My heart is weary of this life,
> And over-sad to sing again.
>
> O crowned by God with love and flame!
> O crowned by Christ the Holy One!
> O listen, ere the searching sun
> Show to the world my sin and shame. (*P* 40)

Like Johnson's speaker, Wilde calls upon the *mater dolorosa*, "crowned by God with thorns and pain," in a series of apostrophic outbursts and sets her in opposition to his dark inner desires. Upon reading her son's poem, Lady Wilde objected to the last line. "*Sin*," she wrote her son, "is respectable and highly poetical, *Shame* is not."[30] Johnson seems to have shared this sentiment. The influence of Wilde's decadent Catholic poetry is evident in such poems as "Before the Cloister," but, as we will see, Johnson's work is more seriously concerned with the theological complexities of sin and repentance than with the simple experience of shame expressed in "San Miniato."

One of the most salient motifs in decadent Catholic literature is the struggle between Catholic mores and fleshly desires, a struggle in which religion plays the role of spiritual foil to physical longings. Nowhere is this motif more apparent than in "The Dark Angel" (1893), one of Johnson's few widely read and anthologized works:

> Dark Angel, with thine aching lust
> To rid the world of penitence:
> Malicious Angel, who still dost
> My soul such subtle violence!
>
> Because of thee, no thought, no thing,
> Abides for me undesecrate:
> Dark Angel, ever on the wing,
> Who never reachest me too late!
>
> When music sounds, then changest thou
> Its silvery to a sultry fire:
> Nor will thine envious heart allow
> Delight untortured by desire.
>
> Through thee, the gracious Muses turn,
> To Furies, O mine Enemy!
> And all the things of beauty burn
> With flames of evil ecstasy. (*CP* 52)

Ellis Hanson's reading of "The Dark Angel" as an expression of the "shame and paranoid violence of homosexual panic,"[31] though astute, is incomplete. In his exploration of Johnson's interest in recusancy as a dwindling mode of English Catholicism, Alex Murray warns of the dangers of reading decadent Catholicism as a primarily sexual literary phenomenon and neglecting its theological depths.[32] Reading "The Dark Angel" as an expression of internalized homophobia risks ignoring the poem's theological depth as well as its interrogation of the philosophical foundations of decadence. Driven by a sadistic "aching lust," the "Malicious Angel" surely embodies Johnson's well-documented homoerotic desires, but this demon also embodies the morally subversive aesthetic philosophy of the elder statesman of decadence, Walter Pater. Drawing out the speaker's suppressed lusts, this torturing devil makes "all things of beauty burn / With flames of evil ecstasy." Johnson's diction recalls a founding text of British decadence—Pater's "Conclusion" to *The Renaissance*:

> To *burn* always with this hard, gemlike *flame*, to maintain this *ecstasy*, is success in life.... While all melts under our feet, we may well grasp at any exquisite passion, or any contribution to knowledge that seems by a lifted horizon to set the spirit free for a moment, or any stirring of the senses, strange dyes, strange colours, and curious odours.[33]

It is misleading to present this brief excerpt as representative of Pater's ethical and aesthetic theory as a whole. By 1893, however, his seemingly amoral injunction to multiply sensual and spiritual experience had taken on a life of its own and represented for many the corrupt philosophy behind decadence. In Johnson's poem, the constant burning ecstasy that Pater calls for results not in liberation but in torment; embodied as the Dark Angel, it perverts and desecrates all simple pleasures and beauties. Because of this spirit, gentle music turns "sultry" and the happy "land of dreams / Becomes a gathering place of fears" (*CP* 53). Johnson's speaker burns with a gemlike flame that threatens to engulf his soul. In spite of this poetic repudiation of the consequences of decadent philosophy, however, Johnson was in many ways a Paterian devotee.

Unsurprisingly, Johnson was drawn more to Pater's notion of *ascesis*, that discipline of mind and body epitomized by Spartans and monks alike,[34] than to the idea of limitless experimentation and indulgence in novelty. In "Mr. Pater and His Public," Johnson contends that Pater "was never more characteristically inspired than in writing of the discipline of art, its immense demands, its imperative morality."[35] According to Johnson, Pater was inspired by asceticism and repelled by "dissolute and lawless art, flung upon the world in a tumultuous profusion and disorder."[36] In the old aesthete, he saw a man devoted to order, morality, and self-discipline in art. No doubt this view was partially informed by Pater's condemnation of Wilde's character Dorian Gray: "an unsuccessful experiment in Epicureanism."[37] The threat presented by Johnson's "Dark Angel," the spirit of a twisted Paterian philosophy of art, is not simply that it might breed riotous art. Rather, Johnson's speaker is tormented by the idea that the philosophy of decadence might rob him of the knowledge of good and evil and thereby "rid the world of penitence," excluding him from the salvation promised by the Catholic Church, with its strictly defined moral code and sacramental economy.

Within this economy, sins are clearly delineated as venial or mortal. A quick "Hail Mary" or "Our Father" can expunge the former, but the latter can only be forgiven through participation in the well-choreographed sacrament of confession. Hanson's conceptualization of the decadent Catholic tension between piety and debauchery as part of a "dialectic of shame and grace,"[38] with its equation of sin and shame, falls short of the mark here. Lady Wilde, as we have seen, distinguished between the two on the grounds of respectability and poetic quality. Saint Augustine (354–430), one of Johnson's spiritual masters,[39] takes a more theologically informed position. He treats shame as a consequence of sin that can be traced back to the original sin of Adam and Eve. Feelings of guilt and actual transgression, especially in the realm of sexuality, are not the same. In *The City of God*, for example, Augustine argues that shame "attends all sexual intercourse" whether "unlawful" or "legitimate and honorable."[40] The fact that all people are secretive about sex, to a degree, attests to this shame; but this universal experience of shame does not mean that all sex is sinful. Since all people, according to Augustine, bear the "shame-begetting penalty of sin," whether they have actually transgressed or not, even the sacraments of the Church cannot fully eradicate feelings of shame. The repentant sinner, granted forgiveness in confession by the priest's *te absolvo*, the efficacious utterance "I absolve you," receives purifying grace. That grace offers no immediate or guaranteed cure for the shame and remorse that accompany sin. Johnson's speaker in "The Dark Angel" is wracked by shame but ultimately more concerned with salvation, an end made possible, if not inevitable, by confession.

In the final stanza, the penitent speaker claims victory over the demon of decadence in language that is less incontrovertibly triumphant than it first appears:

> Do what thou wilt, thou shall not so,
> Dark Angel! triumph over me:
> *Lonely, unto the Lone I go;*
> *Divine, to the Divinity.* (CP 53)

The defiant cry, "thou shall not so, / Dark Angel! triumph over me," seems uncertain at best because the second line resonates as if with a separate imperative, "Dark Angel! triumph over me." By addressing his tormentor in bold, poetic apostrophe, Johnson ensures that the word "triumph" follows with all the force of a whimper. In doing so, he also demonstrates a key difference between poetry and prayer, which are both, to an extent, dependent on the apostrophic voice. In *Poetry and Its Others* (2013), Jahan Ramazani devotes an entire chapter to the permeable border space that separates poetry from prayer. Lyric poetry, rooted as it is in the author's "idiosyncratic individualism," demonstrates awareness of itself as fictive artifice and consciousness of its self-consciousness in a manner generally foreign to the genre of prayer.[41] A prayer that is too individual, too conscious of its own artifice, slips into the realm of lyric poetry. Johnson's sympathy with decadence, a school known for its devotion to artifice, makes this distinction all the more weighty. In spite of the inherent differences between poetry and prayer, and the fact that many poems intentionally "thumb their noses" at prayer, Ramazani points out several instances of modern poetry "drawing sustenance and inspiration" from its liturgical cousin (or parent).[42] Such "prayer-infused" poetry stands out more in the work of modern poets than it does in the devotional verses of Crashaw or Herbert because of the pronounced ambivalence or even hostility toward conventional prayer evident in much of the literature of the nineteenth and twentieth centuries. Hopkins and Eliot receive the bulk of Ramazani's attention, but his essential insights regarding the recontextualization and decontextualization of prayer in their poetry might be applied equally well to Johnson's "Dark Angel." Perhaps his most salient observation regarding Hopkins's intensely devotional work is that "the 'poetry' of the poetry and the 'prayer' of the poetry" often "turn in different directions."[43] The prayerful posture of the humble suppliant, the petition for divine aid, and the repeated insistence on God's goodness and justice can at times falter under the weight of the poet's individual suffering and doubt. An "Our Father" or "Hail Mary" leaves little room for the assertion of idiosyncratic angst that defines the concluding stanza of Johnson's prayer-poem "The Dark Angel." Rather than directly affirming the unending goodness of God, the poem evinces a desperate desire to believe this goodness can exist in a universe where ecstasy is so often evil and pleasure is so often dark.

At this point the importance of specifically Catholic ritual, beyond the individual or communal act of prayer, asserts itself. Imperfect and distressing as it may be as a prayer, Johnson's poem resists despair because its speaker takes some comfort in the larger economy of sacramental ritual. For the believer tortured by forbidden desires and hedonistic habits, the sacramental economy of the Catholic Church offers some hope of salvation from sin, if the sinner is capable of true penitence. In the *Catechism of the Council of Trent* (1566), a primary repository of Catholic teaching until the Second Vatican Council in the mid-twentieth century, the faithful are warned about the danger of insincere repentance:

> If … we read in the pages of inspiration, of some who earnestly implored the mercy of God, but implored it in vain, it is because they did not repent sincerely and from their hearts…. A disease may be said to be incurable, when the patient

loathes the medicine that would accomplish his cure; and, in the same sense, some sins may be said to be irremissible, when the sinner rejects the grace of God, the proper medicine of salvation.[44]

The fear of insincere repentance torments Johnson's speaker and makes the Dark Angel both insidious and essential to his salvation. Though Johnson's demon embodies an amoral pseudo- or semi-Paterian philosophy that threatens to "rid the world of penitence" and separate the speaker from a salvific confession, the speaker's struggle against it also functions as a potential source of true repentance: "I fight thee, in the Holy Name! / Yet, what thou dost, is what God saith: / Tempter! should I escape thy flame, / Thou wilt have helped my soul from Death" (*CP* 53). In this stanza, we learn that the Dark Angel does only "what God saith" and that his temptations may well save the speaker's soul from "Death." As Ian Fletcher points out, temptation here becomes more than just a form of spiritual torture. Rather, "Temptation is constructive: it can elicit Grace."[45] In this way, Johnson's reading of the seemingly amoral Paterian philosophy that undergirds decadence as well as his own struggles with non-normative sexuality and alcoholism are manifest in the guise of an evil spirit that paradoxically drives the speaker into the confessional by baiting him with sinful thoughts. To put it another way, decadence propels the speaker toward Catholicism, as opposed to Catholicism drawing him away from decadence.

Michel Foucault argues that the Catholic sacrament of confession—the site of this counterintuitive reconciliation between decadent desires and Catholic needs—involves substantially more than, or at least something other than, a redemptive unburdening of conscience. In *The History of Sexuality*, Foucault interprets confession as a site of discourse between the individual and the moral authority of the Church that always reinforces the latter's power. After the Council of Trent (1545–63), which solidified the Church's position in relation to emerging heresies and initiated the Counter-Reformation, confession became an act in which sexual transgressions were treated with a combination of extreme delicacy and intense scrutiny: "Under the authority of a language that had been carefully expurgated so that it was no longer directly named, sex was taken charge of, tracked down as it were, by a discourse that aimed to allow it no obscurity, no respite."[46] This discourse obliged the penitent to do more than "admit to violations of the laws of sex, as required by traditional penance;" now a Catholic took on "the nearly infinite task of telling—telling oneself and another, as often as possible, everything that might concern the interplay of innumerable pleasures, sensations, and thoughts which, through the body and the soul, had some affinity with sex."[47] In "The Dark Angel," Johnson's speaker mercifully avoids recounting all of his imagined and actual transgressions of "the laws of sex" laid down by the Church. He was a queer celibate who never—as far as we know—acted on his sexual desires. It is worth noting that his perception of his own sin does not rest on any specific "sinful" act. Johnson seemed to have taken to heart Christ's declaration that "whosoever looketh on a woman to lust after her hath committed adultery with her already" (obviously substituting man for woman and him for her).[48] Johnson's speaker participates in the confessional discourse described by Foucault by not only giving voice to his actual transgression of the moral laws governing sexuality but hinting at his unexpressed queer desires in the "aching lust" engendered by the demon's "flames of evil ecstasy."

We should exercise caution, nonetheless, that in accepting Foucault's description of confession we are not too quick to accept his conclusions uncritically. Foucault's description transforms what believers such as Johnson view as an efficacious sacrament into a brutal ritual of disclosure and conformity in which the Church exercises moral authority and power over the victimized believer. For Johnson, confession offered more than an outlet for ingrained cultural neurosis. It offered grace and a means of reconciling his passions and ideals. In other words, it served what he understood as a healthy purpose. The speaker of "The Dark Angel" fears that his suppressed desires may eventually rob him of the penitence necessary for remorse and forgiveness but also credits those desires with teaching him humility and penitence, which, even in a voluntaristic postmodern society, are considered virtues by most.

Catholic sacramentality is the key element in Johnson's attempts to resolve Thornton's "decadent dilemma," the tension between the ideal and the real. Just as the confessional mode provides him with a vocabulary for interpreting his decadent desires as the dangerous but necessary material for repentance and salvation, the Catholic Mass provides a stage on which the poet can aestheticize and spiritualize his sexual impulses. On this stage, he acts out chaste same-sex desire—a sort of queer celibacy—as a force that complements and enriches religious rites. In his poem "A Dream of Youth" (1890), the combination of homoerotic fantasy and Catholic ritual is only thinly veiled. Johnson dedicated the poem to Lord Alfred Douglas, and, as Ian Fletcher notes, it originally bore a suggestive Greek epigraph taken from Pindar that translates "the bloom of delightful golden-garlanded youth."[49] The poem begins with a dream procession of beautiful youths:

> With faces bright, as ruddy corn,
> Touched by the sunlight of the morn;

With rippling hair; and gleaming eyes,
Wherein a sea of passion lies;
Hair waving back, and eyes that gleam
With deep delight of dream on dream:
With full lips, curving into song;
With shapely limbs, upright and strong:
The youths on holy service throng. (CP 43)

These youths, with their "shapely limbs," "full lips," and passionate eyes, populate a dream that, at first, seems far more moist than pious. Johnson's detailed description of comely boys must have delighted Bosie. It idealizes the homoerotic worship of youth in a manner that anticipates Wilde's *Dorian Gray* and Housman's "To an Athlete Dying Young." In the second stanza, however, the erotic dream takes on a specifically Catholic tone and folds itself into a more complex fantasy about the unification of the sensual and the spiritual:

Vested in white, upon their brows
Are wreaths fresh twined from dewy boughs:
And flowers they strow along the way,
Still dewy from the birth of day.
So, to each reverend altar come,
They stand in adoration: some
Swing up gold censers; till the air
Is blue and sweet, with smoke of rare
Spices, that fetched from Egypt were. (CP 43)

While he eroticizes his beautiful youths by wreathing them in "dewy boughs" and surrounding them with an oriental aura, the speaker also turns them into flower-strewing altar boys. These lily-white boys are active rather than passive; they engage in ceremonies reminiscent of the Mass, complete with an altar ready for the Communion sacrifice. Their procession also calls to mind one of the most public acts of devotion in the Catholic Church, the Corpus Christi procession. Corpus Christi is a springtime feast in commemoration of the institution of the definitive sacrament of the Catholic Church, the Holy Eucharist. The feast is typically celebrated with a public procession that, historically, would have been led by groups of boys and priests wearing flowery wreaths. Johnson's dream vision highlights the potential erotic undertones of this practice, but his obsession with these flower-crowned boys does not simply betray his suppressed homosexuality. "A Dream of Youth" comingles homoerotic desire with Catholic ritual so that the author can bring his queer desires in line with the Church's own sacramental economy by sublimating them into the Mass and the mystical body of the Church. Like any good celibate, Johnson refuses to just suppress his sexuality in an act of frigid chastity; he directs his sexual energy toward God.

This positive conflation of religious ritual and same-sex desire may seem contradictory at first, but it participates in a long tradition of Catholic homosociality found, for example, in the life of Newman, who treated the pursuit of intimate but chaste male-male relationships as laudable. For several decades, Newman played an essential role for scholars studying same-sex desire in Victorian England. In *The Love That Dare Not Speak Its Name: A Candid History of Homosexuality in Britain* (1970), H. Montgomery Hyde argues that Newman sublimated his homosexual desires in his relationship with his fellow convert Ambrose St. John.[50] The two lived together for thirty-two years sharing all the intimacy possible to celibate men and maintaining a bond of affection closer than that of many married couples. When Ambrose died, Newman lay in mourning with the body all night. Newman later directed that he should share his friend's grave after his own death. Building on these observations, Frederick Roden suggests that Newman's "queer virginity" expressed itself both in intense homosocial relationships and, more perfectly, in the Eucharistic communion with the body of God.[51] Roden's notion of queer virginity strikes me as partially true, but it runs the risk of falling back on an expressivist model of sexuality that primarily conceptualizes intense male bonds as evidence of repressed or subconsciously sublimated homosexual desire. While it's true that priestly celibacy provided centuries of men with a vocation free from the restraints of compulsory heterosexuality and procreation and open to the formation of sometimes passionate same-sex friendships, it cannot be thought of as mere cover for the acting out of otherwise illicit desires in a sanctioned manner. The contra-normative nature of Catholic celibacy, a way of life that has long attracted hostility from anti-Catholic Anglicans and still baffles many today, lies in its intentional refusal to play by the standard rules of expressivist sexuality and its fusion of spiritual, sexual, and ethical ideals. This type of celibacy might be understood best as a positive mode of sexuality, not a negation. Johnson lacked a vocation, but he clearly shared some of Newman's ability to fuse his spiritual convictions with his sexual desires and aesthetic ideals. "A Dream of Youth" demonstrates how the aestheticized and sublimated homoeroticism associated with decadence formed a complementary relationship with the sacramental economy of the Catholic Church.

Dowson's Search for Peace

Unlike Johnson, for whom we still have no authoritative academic biography and little in the way of critical secondary work, given his relatively large corpus and sphere of influence, Ernest Dowson inspired numerous biographies, and the "Dowson legend" cultivated after his untimely death has come to define decadence.[52] As one recent biographer notes, "He was the purest representative of the legendary group of British artists of the 1890s called the decadents."[53] His life was plagued by unrequited love for the daughter of a Polish restaurateur, Adelaide "Missie" Foltinowicz. The two met in 1889 when she was only 11. Dowson never acted on his pedophiliac desires, choosing instead to exorcise his demons in the beds of prostitutes and in the pages of his poetry. He spent years pining for Adelaide in the hope that they might marry when she came of age. His bid for her affection was ultimately rejected. Crippling alcoholism, coupled with the privations of nearly constant penury, led him to an early death. When news of Dowson's passing reached Wilde, the exiled dandy produced a fitting homage in a letter to Leonard Smithers: "Poor wounded wonderful fellow that he was, a tragic reproduction of all tragic poetry, like a symbol, or a scene. I hope bay leaves will be laid on his tomb, and rue, and myrtle too, for he knew what love is."[54] Under Wilde's hyperbole lies an earnest appreciation of Dowson's poetic achievement. Today, the myth of Dowson has largely overshadowed his poetry.

More than anyone else, Arthur Symons can be credited with the construction of the Dowson legend. In August of 1896, he published a portrait of an anonymous young poet of note. Following closely upon Dowson's death in 1900, an expanded version of the piece appeared as the preface to *The Poems and Prose of Ernest Dowson*. In Dowson's "immaterial snatches of song," Symons finds "implied for the most part, hidden away like a secret, all the fever and turmoil and the unattained dreams of a life which had itself so much of the swift, disastrous, and suicidal impetus of genius."[55] Symons recalls his first impression of the young poet as a "demoralized Keats," a frail man of excessive passions who displayed a "comradeship with madness" and proved "too weak for ordinary existence."[56] By shrouding Dowson in purple prose and playing up the young poet's love of cabmen's shelters and brothels, Symons attempted to write his own version of British decadence, one devoid of Catholicism. The Dowson myth, which grew out of Symons's embellished reflections, came to define British decadence, but the self-destructive excesses of Symons's demoralized Keats were, in reality, counterbalanced by a deep-seated spiritual desire for peace, which led Dowson to the Church.

Victor Plarr, a survivor of the *fin de siècle* who delighted the young Ezra Pound with stories of the decadent nineties, viewed Dowson's conversion as disgracefully superficial: "Lionel Johnson, at least, could give chapter and verse for his conversion. Hardly so Dowson."[57] Plarr's skepticism about the sincerity of Dowson's conversion has become a scholarly truism, with some critics impugning almost all decadent conversions as spiritually deficient. Norman Alford, in his otherwise sound study of the Rhymers' Club, makes the absurd claim that "neither Johnson nor Dowson was a Christian in the true theological sense."[58] Whether or not Dowson's conversion immediately transformed him into a different person (an unrealistic expectation in any case) is a moot point, since his art reveals a mind that conceives of sin and virtue, salvation and damnation, beauty and truth, in Catholic terms. True, his poetry never took on the pervasively pious and devotional flavor of Johnson's. That would be setting the bar rather high. Moreover, the poems dedicated to Dowson by his contemporaries reveal that many of them viewed the Church as an essential part of his identity. In *Silverpoints*, for example, John Gray dedicates his translation of Verlaine's ekphrastic poem "A Crucifix" to Dowson. The homoerotic sadomasochism of the poem is mixed with a sincere spiritual devotion to the central icon of Catholicism—the crucified Christ. Gray worships the perfect and mostly naked male figure of the tortured Savior in a nearly idolatrous manner that would have scandalized his more historically iconoclastic countrymen:

Under the torture of the thorny crown,
The loving pallor of the brow looks down
On human blindness, on the toiler's woes;
The while, to overturn Despair's repose,
And urge to Hope and Love, as Faith demands,
Bleed, bleed the feet, the broken side, the hands.[59]

After this extended reverie on the sacrifice of Christ, we learn that the poem is about a copy of the crucifix in question, which was left to the speaker in a gesture of friendship:

A poet, painter, Christian,—it was a friend
Of mine—his attributes most fitly blend—
Who saw this marvel, made an exquisite
Copy; and, knowing how I worshipped it,
Forgot it, in my room, by accident.
I write these verses in acknowledgment.[60]

By dedicating the poem to Dowson, Gray cast his fellow decadent in the role of the speaker's friend—a friend whose three attributes "poet, painter, Christian" blend "most fitly."

Johnson presents a similar image of Dowson in another dedicatory poem, "Our Lady of France" (1891). The title paired with the dedication alludes to a specific London church, Notre Dame de France, which Dowson used to attend and which inspired his own poem "Benedictio Domini." Written in the year of their shared conversion, "Our Lady of France" depicts Johnson and Dowson as "children" far from home, longing for a mother whom the Reformation has banished from England:

> Our Lady of France! dost thou inhabit here? Behold,
> What sullen gloom invests this city strange to thee!
> In Seine, and pleasant Loire, thou gloriest from of old;
> Thou rulest rich Provence; lovest the Breton sea:
> What dost thou far from home? Nay! here my children fold
> Their exiled hands in orison, and long for me. (*CP* 14)

This depiction may seem somewhat dramatic considering the fact that Mary was not evicted from the post-Reformation Anglican Church, but rather demoted from her near-divine status. Yet, Pius IX's 1854 declaration of the dogma of the Immaculate Conception of Mary, which asserted the already common belief that the mother of Jesus was endowed with special grace upon conception and thereby spared the original sin of Adam and Eve, reinforced the adoration of Mary as one of the firmest points of differentiation between Catholics and Protestants. Johnson implies in his poem that he and Dowson remain strangers in their own homeland because the people of England have wrongly abandoned veneration of the Virgin and failed to accept the Mariology that partially defined the Catholic opposition to modernity. This sense of alienation from British culture creates an aesthetic distance that allows Johnson to challenge the Anglican beliefs of his own country. "Our Lady of France" depicts Catholic identity as necessarily cosmopolitan and spiritually international. The metrical imitation of the alexandrine also suggests that English poets should look to France for both spiritual and artistic inspiration.[61]

Though Johnson clearly saw Dowson as a fellow traveler—a fellow alien, Catholic poet—the two men lived very different lives. Incapable of or uninterested in Johnson's rigid self-control in sexual matters, Dowson routinely sought satisfaction of his fleshly desires. One of his most notorious and wonderfully wrought poems, "Non sum qualis eram bonae sub regno Cynarae"[62] (1894),

takes place in a brothel, where the speaker muses on his beloved Cynara while
making love to a prostitute:

Last night, ah, yesternight, betwixt her lips and mine
There fell thy shadow, Cynara! thy breath was shed
Upon my soul between the kisses and the wine;
And I was desolate and sick of an old passion,
    Yea, I was desolate and bowed my head:
I have been faithful to thee, Cynara! in my fashion. (58)

The poem contains no traces of the Catholicism that is so central to most other
paradigmatically decadent texts. Instead, Dowson sticks to the three topics
approved for artistic treatment in his "Villanelle of a Poet's Road," namely "wine
and woman and song." Taken by itself, "Non sum qualis" is purely pagan. In the
context of his other poetry, it establishes the hedonistic and dissolute existence
that Dowson contrasts with the peace offered by the Church.

In much of Dowson's work, the Church, especially in the guise of the
monastery or cloister, functions as a place of escape from the temptations of
the world—a place both infinitely attractive and inaccessible to his decadent
poetic persona. This tension between the boisterous city and monastic solitude
recalls the struggle of one of the archetypal characters of French decadence,
J. K. Huysmans's deranged Des Esseintes. Worn down by years of excess, the
protagonist of *À Rebours* decides to construct an aesthete's monastery far from
the madding crowd only to find that, like Milton's Satan, he brings Hell with him
into his beautifully appointed sanctuary. As we have already seen, Huysmans
saw in his character's perverse fascination with mysticism and monasticism the
beginnings of his own conversion and eventual vocation as a Benedictine oblate,
a layperson affiliated with a monastery who attempts to follow the Rule of that
Order. Wilde expressed admiration for Huysmans's vocation and once applied
unsuccessfully for a six-month retreat at a Jesuit monastery; the rejection
reportedly left him in tears.[63] Dowson felt this same attraction to and separation
from monasticism. As Joseph S. Salemi puts it, "Dowson's most overtly religious
poems are those that deal with monastic renunciation of the world, or that
contrast cloistered peace with worldly turmoil."[64]

In "Nuns of the Perpetual Adoration" (1892), originally published in the *Book
of the Rhymers' Club* under the title "Carmelite Nuns of the Perpetual Adoration,"
Dowson's speaker draws a familiar contrast between the holy cloister and the
depraved outside world and projects his own spiritual dilemma, the choice
between extreme alternatives, onto the nuns themselves:

They saw the glory of the world displayed;
They saw the bitter of it, and the sweet;
They knew the roses of the world should fade,
And be trod under by the hurrying feet.

Therefore they rather put away desire,
And crossed their hands and came to sanctuary;
And veiled their heads and put on coarse attire:
Because their comeliness was vanity. (42–3)

Like Dowson, the nuns know that "they are not long, the days of wine and roses." Unlike the poet, the sisters choose separation from the transient world of fleshly desire and devote themselves to the dream of eternity. Their decision fascinates the speaker, who cannot forget that their sanctuary would separate him from his own passions: "Calm, sad, secure; with faces worn and mild; / Surely their choice of vigil is the best? / Yea! for our roses fade, the world is wild; / But there, beside the altar, there, is rest" (*ED* 43). The scriptural resonances of the ecstatic "Yea!" and the word "Surely," which are meant to convince reader and speaker alike, are undercut by the lingering uncertainty of the question mark. Dowson's nuns are "calm" and "secure," unlike his speaker; they are also "sad." This sadness, however, may be joy in another form. As we will see, Dowson elsewhere defines sadness among self-sacrificing Catholics as the full realization of pleasure. Understood in this way, the pleasurable sadness of the nuns contrasts with the bitter pleasure of the speaker's world of frenetic desire. Worldly pleasure is bitter. Heavenly sadness is sweet, we are told. Yet the poet cannot cast a cold eye on the world of wine and roses in order to, like the nuns, fix his heart on the eternal reward of heaven. Like St. Augustine, the arch-confessor, Dowson would joyfully receive the gift of chastity and peace, just not today. In spite of this imperfect devotion, Dowson's desire for the peace promised by the altar, where the drama of salvation unfolds in the consecration of Holy Communion, is undeniably central to his aesthetic and that of decadence in general.

Dowson lacked Huysmans's calling to monastic discipline but found fuel for his poetry in the vocations of others. One visit to a Carthusian monastery inspired the poem "Carthusians" (1899), one of the truly fine poems in Dowson's corpus that rarely sees the light of day. He begins by contemplating the silence and solitude cultivated by the monks as well as the cost of obtaining such a beautiful and fearful discipline: "A cloistered company, they are companionless, / None knoweth here the secret of his brother's heart: / They are but come together for more loneliness, / Whose bond is solitude and silence all their part" (*ED* 107). Just as in "Nuns of the Perpetual Adoration," Dowson highlights the solitude and sadness of his subjects but goes on to praise their steadfast vocation and bemoan the myopia of his world of ephemeral pleasures:

> Ye shall prevail at last! Surely ye shall prevail!
> Your silence and austerity shall win at last:
> Desire and mirth, the world's ephemeral lights shall fail,
> The sweet star of your queen is never overcast.
>
> We fling up flowers and laugh, we laugh across the wine;
> With wine we dull our souls and careful strains of art;
> Our cups are polished skulls round which the roses twine:
> None dares to look at Death who leers and lurks apart.
>
> Move on, white company, whom that has not sufficed!
> Our viols cease, our wine is death, our roses fail:
> Pray for our heedlessness, O dwellers with the Christ!
> Though the world fall apart, surely ye shall prevail. (*ED* 108)

On one level, Dowson is denouncing the follies of his life and asking the monks to continue their work by praying for the lost souls of the world. But he cannot help reveling in the exquisite nature of his own pleasures even as he decries them as distractions from the reality of death and judgment. There are few more carefully crafted and decadent lines in all of British poetry than "our cups are polished skulls round which the roses twine." Dowson was a poet above all else. His soul yearned for new sensations that might inform his art. Along with that yearning, however, came a desire for release from sensation. Death was his constant companion. Catholic monasticism offered him a terrible and undeniably alluring vision of life fixated on death as the doorway to eternal peace.

If the Church stands as an inaccessible but necessary sanctuary and place of rest in the otherwise riotous, decadent poetry that gave substance to the Dowson legend, his prose reveals a much more devout and serious commitment to Catholicism. His short story "Apple Blossom in Brittany," which appeared in the notoriously decadent *Yellow Book* the same year that "Non sum qualis" was first published, follows a young Catholic poet and critic of modest fame who bears significant resemblance to Dowson. Conscious of his shortcomings, Dowson creates a more virtuous version of himself in the protagonist Benedict Campion, an exceptionally saintly name that reflects Dowson's preoccupation with monasticism as well as his alienation from mainstream English culture. Benedict was the fifth-century founder of monasticism, and Edmund Campion was an English Jesuit martyred during the reign of Queen Elizabeth. Unlike

Dowson, who came to the Church through conversion, Benedict Campion is the last in a long line of Catholics. He combines deep-seated faith with a typically decadent disdain for all things modern:

> He had come to view modern life with a curious detachment, a sense of remote hostility: Democracy, the Salvation Army, the novels of M. Zola—he disliked them all impartially. A Catholic by long inheritance, he held his religion for something more than an heirloom; he exhaled it, like an intimate quality; his mind being essentially of that kind to which a mystical view of things comes easiest.[65]

Living his religion is like breathing, rather than torture. Catholicism provides an escape from the banality of a modern world characterized by the rule of the masses, puritan charity, and the naturalist novel. This holy protagonist's faith nearly reaches a breaking point when his much younger French ward and unofficial fiancé, Marie-Ursule (yet another saintly name), realizes that, in spite of her love for him, she may have a calling to join the Ursuline sisters. When she places her decision between the convent and the world before her guardian and would-be lover, he finds that the only way to perfectly possess her is to give her over to the Church:

> And it rested with him; he had no doubt that he could mould her, even yet, to his purpose. The child! how he loved her.... But would it ever be quite the same with them after that morning? Or must there be hence-forth a shadow between them; the knowledge of something missed, of the lower end pursued, the higher slighted? ... He felt at once and finally, that he acquiesced in it; that any other ending to his love had been an impossible grossness, and that to lose her in just that fashion was the only way in which he could keep her always. And his acquiescence was without bitterness, and attended only by that indefinable sadness which to a man of his temper was but the last refinement of pleasure.[66]

Campion fears that some "shadow" will fall between himself and his beloved child if he does not give her over to the higher pursuit of sanctity. Wishing to avoid the baseness of earthly love and possess Marie-Ursule more perfectly, he embraces renunciation. By recasting his scandalous real-life attraction to the juvenile Adelaide in a fictive world where even the local priest encourages the romance, Dowson sanctions his desires before transcending them and embracing "that indefinable sadness which to a man of his temper was but the last refinement of pleasure." He enshrines his love object among the chaste nuns and denies his fictive counterpart the pleasure of consummating the relationship in favor of the more perfect, self-torturing pleasure of sacrifice. In this way, Dowson weds his alter ego to the same pious sadness that characterizes the nuns and monks celebrated in his poetry.

There is no evidence that Dowson would have followed Campion's self-sacrificial example if given the chance to wed Adelaide. He failed in his ambition. He then transmuted that failure into a fiction of self-sacrifice and chaste pedophilia that turned young girls into ideal objects to be lusted after but never had. By allowing Benedict Campion to make the righteous decision, Dowson imagines an alternate reality in which his love of the Church outweighs his desires and leaves his love object perpetually undefiled. In this other reality the Church can figuratively consume his beloved and thereby overcome the tension between faith and desire. "Apple Blossom in Brittany" provides an alternative to the endless cycle of excess that tortures the speaker of Dowson's most quintessentially decadent poem, "Non sum qualis," and invites us to enter a world in which decadent desires and Catholic ideals coalesce into a self-sacrificial, sad, and peaceful synthesis.

Dowson and Johnson found eternal peace early in life. Like Beardsley and Wilde they seemed destined not to outlast the turn of the century, at least not for long. They ended their lives painfully in relative destitution, tormented by the same demons that inspired much of their art. If Wilde was correct in his assertion that Catholicism is the only religion beautiful enough to die in, then perhaps these deaths were still, somehow, beautiful. With them died decadent Catholicism, and a new, vital literary movement sprang up to define the twentieth century. At least this was the narrative produced by Ezra Pound and W. B. Yeats, who worked hard and unsuccessfully to write the decadent nineties out of the narrative of modernism.

Yeats and Pound: Disavowing Decadence, Forgetting Catholicism

The first edition of *The Poetical Works of Lionel Johnson* (1915) is fairly unremarkable in appearance. Unlike many texts of the decadent era—George Moore's *Flowers of Passion* (1877); Oscar Wilde's *Salomé* (1894), illustrated by Aubrey Beardsley; Victor Plarr's *In the Dorian Mood* (1896); Ernest Dowson's *Decorations in Verse and Prose* (1899); and W. B. Yeats's *The Wind Among the Reeds* (1899), the latter two illuminated by Althea Gyles—Johnson's *Poetical Works* is no objet d'art. The pages are ungilded; the cover lacks skulls, bleeding thorns, vulvic orchids, and broken lyres; the print is conventional and unornamented. The book is remarkable, not for its beauty but because one particular copy, housed in the archives of the Harry Ransom Center, evinces the complicated relationship between decadence and modernism. The inside cover of this artifact reads, "to T. S. Eliot from E. P." Pound wrote the preface to the book in 1915 and gave a copy to Eliot in 1918 in what seems like an attempt to exercise influence over his contemporary. But what was Pound so keen to convey? Put simply, that decadence is dead.

Pound: Wrong from the Start

Pound's preface to *The Poetical Works of Lionel Johnson* is less concerned with exploring Johnson's poetry than asserting the passing of an old school and the ascendency of what he calls "our present doctrines."[1] There is some backhanded praise of Johnson, but only in so far as he breaks with the trends of decadence:

> The "nineties" have chiefly gone out because of their muzziness, because of a softness derived, I think, not from books but from impressionist painting. They riot with half decayed fruit.

> The impression of Johnson's verse is that of small slabs of ivory, firmly combined and contrived.[2]

Of course, being praised for "contrived" verse is little better than being accused of "muzziness." What offends Pound most about the "nineties" is that artists such as Johnson, Wilde, and Dowson embraced the "painted speech" of the Elizabethans and turned it into their own affected idiom: "Johnson cannot be shown to be in accord with our present doctrines and ambitions. His language is too bookish a dialect."[3] Johnson's poetry simply does not belong to the current age.

Eliot must have realized the importance to Pound of this declaration of difference, because, as editor for Faber and Faber, he included it in the collection *Literary Essays of Ezra Pound* (1935) and referenced the preface in his introduction to Pound's *Selected Poems* (1928). There he claims that the shadows of both Dowson and Johnson "flit about" Pound's earliest poetry and notes that Pound "has edited a volume of the poems of Lionel Johnson, some few copies of which contained an introduction by the editor, hastily withdrawn from circulation by the editor and now a bibliophile's rarity."[4] Eliot's comments seem almost subversive, given that four years prior, in a 1924 letter to Pound, he had sought to reassure the godfather of modernism that they held similar views on the essential unimportance of nineties' verse:

> Probably the fact that Swinburne and the poets of the nineties were entirely missed out of my personal history counts for a great deal. I never read any of these people until it was too late for me to get anything out of them.... I am as blind to the merits of these people as I am to Thomas Hardy.[5]

No doubt Pound found this disavowal comforting at the time. It was, of course, a lie. In spite of his claim that the "poets of the nineties" played no role in his early development, Eliot himself said that John Davidson, Ernest Dowson, and Lionel Johnson were among his earliest poetic models.[6] In what seems like a transparent attempt to appease *il miglior fabbro*, Eliot pays lip service to Pound's crusade against decadence.

One can hardly blame Eliot for his duplicity given the scorn Pound heaps on the "nineties." In Pound's preface to Johnson's poems, as if to show that his criticism is not idiosyncratic, he attributes his own distaste for the affected speech of the decadents to popular opinion:

> Some say the "nineties" spoke as they wrote. I have heard it said that "A generation of men came down from Oxford resolved to talk as prose had been written" ... They loved the speech of books and proposed to make daily speech copy it.[7]

It should come as no surprise that Pound overheard these clever quips about affected Oxonians considering the fact that he wrote and published them himself the previous year. Writing under the pseudonym Ferrex, Pound aimed nearly identical jibes at the decadents in the inaugural issue of *The Egoist* (1914), one of the flagship journals of what we now term "modernism." With the air of a manifesto, Pound's essay calls on young artists to embrace "petulance" in order to unsettle London's literary set. A key element of this petulance is the refusal to imitate the style of the decadents—a generation who came "down to London resolved to speak as they wrote."[8] Pound's generation, he insists, "tries to write as it speaks." It is worth noting that the futurists and imagists generally failed in this dubious endeavor.

Only a handful of years before his call to petulance, Pound had produced a wealth of verse heavily inflected by British decadence, especially by the poems of Dowson and Swinburne. None of Pound's early poems matches his description of the poetic language of the new generation that writes as it speaks. His early publications, *A Lume Spento* (1908), *A Quinzaine for This Yule* (1908), and *Personae* (1909), show clear traces of the decadence he would so vociferously disavow in his prose. "In Tempore Senectutis: An Anti-stave for Dowson" and "The Decadence" present the most overt evidence of influence; however, we can witness Pound aping the language and style of decadence in many other early poems. "Praise of Ysolt," for example (which was originally titled "Vana" in *A Lume Spento*):

> In vain have I striven
> > to teach my heart to bow;
> In vain have I said to him
> "There be many singers greater than thou."
>
> But his answer cometh, as winds and as lutany.
> As a vague crying upon the night
> That leaveth me no rest, saying ever,
> > "Song, a song."
>
> Their echoes play upon each other in the twilight
> Seeking ever a song.[9]

Compare this dialogue between the poet and his "heart" (in which the latter urges the former to cast off his fears and sing in the twilight) to that between the poet and his inner "voices" in Dowson's "Sapientia Lunae," in which the latter urges the former to cast off the vain strivings of the day and contemplate the beauty of the moonlit night:

> Then said my inner voices: "*Wherefore strive or run,*
> > *On dusty highways ever, a vain race?*
> *The long night cometh, starless, void of sun,*

> *What light shall serve thee like her golden face?"*
> For I had pondered on a rune of roses,
> And knew some secrets which the moon discloses. (*ED* 68–9)

Aside from the fact that both Pound and Dowson conceive of the poet's vocation as a twilight occupation, best suited to those given to talking to themselves, neither poet seems interested in writing in the manner of speech. The syntax and diction of lines such as "his answer cometh, as wind and as lutany" produce an effect closer to that of *"the long night cometh, starless, void of sun"* than to the sparse imagism of Pound's later work.

Another early poem, more Swinburnian than Dowsonian and originally published in *A Quinzaine for This Yule*, Pound's "Night Litany," reveals some fascination with a Catholic God, whom Pound would later consign to history in favor of a poetic paganism. Contemplating the beauty of Venice, the speaker repeatedly calls upon the "God of the night," the "God of silence," the "God of waters" to "Purifiez nos coeurs" (make clean our hearts) in a manner that recalls various liturgical rites as well as the lamentations and paeans so characteristic of Wilde, Johnson, Dowson, and other decadents at different times in their careers:

> Yea, the glory of the shadow
>   of thy Beauty hath walked
> Upon the shadow of the waters
> In this thy Venice.
>   And before the holiness
> Of the shadow of thy handmaid
>   Have I hidden mine eyes,
>   O God of waters.[10]

The shadow of Venice playing on the water is the shadow of God's "Beauty," the "holiness" of which forces the speaker to cover his eyes in reverence. It could be argued that Pound is simply speaking *in persona* here, as he often did; however, given Pound's later attempts to distance himself from "Night Litany," it appears that the poem was more a product of the poetic unconscious than a self-consciously crafted impersonation. Astounded by the poem at the time of its composition and calling it a product of impulse rather than technique, Pound almost refused to sign his name to it.[11] Clearly, the impulses that moved the young poet to adopt the language and fascinations of the poets of the nineties also caused him significant discomfort. Pound saw himself as part of, if not the leader of, a generational movement away from the languor of the 1890s and toward a vital new artistic future. Simply changing the aesthetic feel of his verse was not enough. As his prose repeatedly demonstrates, Pound felt the need to disavow decadence and exclude it from the history of modernism.

Central to Pound's overt disavowal of decadent style in his preface to Johnson's *Poetical Works* and the inaugural issue of *The Egoist* is a more covert attempt to forget one of its constituent elements, Catholicism. Johnson's corpus contains more explicitly devotional and confessional Catholic verse than that of any of his contemporaries, with the possible exception of John Gray, but Pound's preface never so much as hints at the spiritual dimension of Johnson's poetry. Pound once calls Johnson's "taste" "catholic,"[12] but nowhere is the term used with a capital C. The importance of Johnson's Catholicism could hardly have been lost on Pound. The frontispiece for nearly all of Johnson's collections of poetry, including the one containing Pound's preface, depicts a Catholic bishop complete with miter, crosier, and vestments patterned with the fleur-de-lis (Figure 2.1). The same frontispiece appears on both *Poems* (1895) and *The Religious Poems of Lionel Johnson* (1916). Its explicitly Catholic nature reflects a central concern in Johnson's poetry—a concern conspicuously ignored by Pound.

To be sure, Pound was a poet's poet, a man obsessed with the art of the line. Naturally, his primary concerns were formal and stylistic. As "In Praise of Ysolt" and "Night Litany" demonstrate, however, his own early poetry repeatedly engages with many of the defining concerns of decadence. Viewed in this light, his refusal to address the content of decadent verse in his criticism seems almost willful. With his dislike of Christianity and interest in a rejuvenated modern paganism, Pound had particular incentive to ignore the odd phenomenon of decadent Catholicism.

Though he avoided discussing Catholicism in his early attacks on the artists of the nineties, by 1920 Pound was prepared to enshrine his rejection of decadence and its religion in verse. *Hugh Selwyn Mauberley* (1920), one of the iconic long poems of modernism, begins with a version of Pound's own mistaken attempts to "resuscitate the dead art / Of poetry" by imitating the verse of a bygone era—attempts he dismisses as "wrong from the start" (*EP* 173). Following this recognition of a false start, Mauberley recounts his uneasy awakening to modernity. Far from celebrating the new age of speed in which he finds himself, Pound's poetic alter ego repeatedly voices his disgust with the demands of the new age. Section III elaborates on the ugly usurpations of modernity, which substitutes "tawdry cheapness" for the art and cultural relics of the distant past (*EP* 174). Perhaps his most damning critique of the modern age is that it represents a degradation of medieval ideals of beauty, which are

POETICAL WORKS OF
LIONEL JOHNSON

LONDON: ELKIN MATHEWS
CORK STREET   MCMXV

Figure 2.1 Frontispiece from *The Poetical Works of Lionel Johnson* (1915). London: Elkin Matthews. Used with the permission of the Harry Ransom Center, The University of Texas at Austin.

themselves, Pound implies, degraded forms of classical ideals. In one stanza, both decadence and Catholicism are included in a list of dead and supplanted things of the past: "Faun's flesh is not to us, / Nor the saint's vision. / We have the press for wafer; / Franchise for circumcision" (*EP* 174). Coming to consciousness of the new age in which he lives, Mauberley realizes that the modern world has no use for the pagan faun, the mystic saint, or the Communion "wafer." This list reflects an historical progression from the goat god Pan of ancient paganism to the mysticism and sacraments of the Catholic Church, that defining institution of medieval and early modern Europe. On this surface level, Pound comments on the ouster of religion and beauty by the modern gods of media and politics. On a subtler level, he reiterates an ongoing narrative about the incongruity of modernity and decadent Catholicism. The faun and satyr functioned interchangeably as recurring symbols of decadent art in the last decade of the nineteenth century. These lascivious and indulgent forest gods abound in the art of Aubrey Beardsley, and, as we saw in Chapter 1, Lionel Johnson once wrote a satirical assault on his decadent contemporaries titled "The Cultured Faun." Taken together, the three concepts (faun, saint's vision, wafer) coalesce into a complex allusion to the poets of the nineties, whose art often combined Attic or Roman hedonism with medieval spirituality and sacramentality. *Mauberley* casts such men as relics of a dead world. Both pagans and Christians are things of the past, so nothing could be more out of place in the modern world than a decadent Catholic. Pound is, of course, highly critical of this brave new post-romantic world run by "the press" and ruled by the political whims of the unwashed masses. He presents the passing of decadence and Catholicism not as a sign of progress but merely as incontrovertible historical fact, evidence of the radical newness of the now.

Section III of *Mauberley* makes only oblique reference to the death of decadent Catholicism, but Section VII, titled "SIENA MI FE; DISFECEMI MAREMMA," is explicitly devoted to writing decadence into history and out of the present. In it, Mauberley learns about the poets of the nineties from one of their surviving contemporaries, Monsieur Verog, a character based on Victor Plarr (1863–1929). Plarr was a member of the Rhymers' Club, which also included Yeats, Dowson, and Johnson. The Rhymers met regularly in a private room at Ye Old Cheshire Cheese pub on Fleet Street and published two books of verse. Though Pound's Verog fixates on the scandalous and ridiculous aspects of the nineties, Plarr had a profound respect for his contemporaries and wrote extensively about Dowson and Johnson. Mauberley distills Verog's reflections on these poets into two stanzas of derogatory caricature:

> For two hours he talked of Gallifet;
> Of Dowson; of the Rhymers' Club;
> Told me how Johnson (Lionel) died
> By falling from a high stool in a pub ...
>
> But showing no trace of alcohol
> At the autopsy, privately performed—
> Tissue preserved—the pure mind
> Arose toward Newman as the whisky warmed.
>
> Dowson found harlots cheaper than hotels. (*EP* 177)

Basing his literary history on the apocryphal story that Johnson died while drinking at the Green Dragon pub on Fleet Street, Pound adds some intrigue to the story by questioning the validity of his "privately performed" autopsy. Dowson gets one line, made unforgettable by the symmetry of "harlots" and "hotels"—hardly a fitting epitaph for a man who, in Wilde's words, "knew what love is."[13] The speaker in *Mauberley* is convinced that decadence is a thing of the past, a movement memorable only because of the eccentricities of its members and best remembered with a smirk. Only twenty years after the fact, Dowson is little more than a cheap john, and the only legacy of "Johnson (Lionel)" is an absurd death. The placement of Johnson's first name in parenthesis insinuates that less than twenty years after his death no one could recognize the poet solely by his surname, as if confused readers might conclude, say, that Dr. Johnson was resurrected by the members of the Rhymers' Club only to die soon after by falling from a stool. Only Verog, a man "out of step with the decade, / Detached from his contemporaries, / Neglected by the young" (*EP* 177) keeps the fading memory of this bygone time alive. The message is simple. Johnson and Dowson, forgotten names to all but a few survivors of the nineties, have gone to join Cardinal Newman in the dubious heaven of another age, the age of Dante and Pia de' Tolomei.

These stanzas may seem like mere "petulance": a brash author disparages his predecessors so that he and his generation can make their voices heard. But there is more at work in Pound's disavowal of decadence than a personal anxiety of influence. What we see in *Mauberley* is part of a larger effort to write both the *fin de siècle* and Christianity out of what is supposed to be a radically new age. In the early days of what we now term *modernism*, Virginia Woolf could say without joking that "human character changed on or about 1910." The date she gave was less precise than that offered by Pound. In the Spring

1922 issue of *The Little Review*, he produced an elaborate Julian calendar for a new age—a post-Christian age initiated on October 30, 1921, the day after he received word of the completion of *Ulysses*. Similarly, Yeats's grand *Vision* allowed him to predict with confidence the end of the Christian era and the advent of something both wholly new and eternally old. More than that, his poetry made him a part of that monumental transition. Pound and Yeats were especially given to historical fantasies and assertions of shifting paradigms, but none of their grand pronouncements was meant to erase all of the past. Ancient paganism received pride of place in the modernist project of historical revision. In Pound's "The Return," the old gods come back to Earth to preside over the new regime. In Yeats's "Second Coming," too, the rough god of a pre-Christian era returns to reassert its ancient claim on humanity. Yeats and Pound never attempted to divorce themselves from the ancient world. Antiquity had lessons to teach and terrors to reveal. Conversely, the recent past was too close for comfort. After all, what visionary school of literature could acknowledge its debt to its immediate predecessors (especially Catholic ones) and still retain its claims to newness?

The assertion of such newness necessitated an overt disavowal of the immediate past, of the most recent literary movement to break the mold of convention. This need for discontinuity prompted not only an attempt to move beyond the decadent art of the 1890s but also an attempt to exclude it from the present. For Pound, the exclusion of the recent past was especially vital to his assertion of the new present. Decadence, the late romantic school of the 1890s, was one of the many movements that he had to disavow in order to design the new calendar for what Hugh Kenner famously christened "the Pound era." But, in order to be successful, Pound would need a powerful ally.

Yeats's Strange Souls

> In the first decade of the century the situation was unusual.... It was the tail end of the Victorian era. Our sympathies, I think, went out to those who are known as the English poets of the 'nineties, who were all, with one exception, dead. The exception was W. B. Yeats.... And Yeats himself had not found his personal speech. (T. S. Eliot, "American Literature and the American Language", 1953)[14]

Writing these words in the middle of the twentieth century, Eliot reveals the extent to which Yeats's own myth of the "tragic generation" influenced the thinking of his modernist contemporaries. The very act of recollection taxes Eliot and invites uncertain and half-true sentiments. He "thinks" that the sympathies of the young artists of the first decade of the new century "went out" to the unindividuated mass of "nineties" poets. Whether those sympathies extended to the literature of the deceased or only to their corpses remains ambiguous. Eliot could be sure only of one thing: Yeats was the sole survivor still shrugging off the style of his dead peers and searching for his "personal speech." This story, untrue in nearly all its particulars (e.g., "nineties" poets such as John Gray, Victor Plarr, Lord Alfred Douglas, "Michael Field," and others lived well into the twentieth century), rehearses a myth established by Pound and elaborated by Yeats himself—a myth that begins with one of the more famous dual apprenticeships in literary history.

In 1908, having found Swinburne too senile to apprentice under, Pound turned to the next greatest living poet. Twenty years his senior, Yeats saw promise in the young man, who, at the time, dressed with a flamboyance to rival Wilde. During his time as Yeats's amanuensis at Stone Cottage in Sussex (1913–14), Pound sought to modernize his elder colleague. Before long, he observed with satisfaction that "Uncle William" was coming along quite nicely. His only lament was that the elder poet was "still dragging some of the reeds of the 'nineties in his hair."[15] Characteristically, Pound credits himself with too much. There can be no doubt that he assisted with Yeats's transition from decadent collaborator to modernist insurgent, but Yeats was engaged in distancing himself from the Rhymers' Club and establishing his own legacy well before the winter of 1913. To employ a chemical analogy, Pound's influence was an accelerant, a catalyst, not an initiating reagent in Yeats's transformation. As James Longenbach points out in *Stone Cottage: Pound, Yeats, and Modernism* (1988), Yeats began shaking off shadows of the past and mythologizing the deaths of his decadent peers in public lectures as early as 1910:

> To remake himself as a lyric poet, Yeats first needed to push the successes of the eighteen-nineties securely behind him. In order to show his public that he was more than one of the members of the Rhymers' Club who happened to live into the twentieth century, he began to lecture about his dead companions, fixing them at a point in history that only he himself had transcended.[16]

Yeats's desire to transcend the ghosts of Johnson and Dowson paralleled Pound's ambition to create a new poetic elite in the unassuming Stone Cottage. "By sequestering himself in the country with Yeats," Longenbach writes, "Pound was finally able to recreate the aspect of the Rhymers' Club that he admired most: the sense of a poetic aristocracy."[17] In what feels like a somewhat sardonic nod to the religious fixation of the decadents, Pound described this new Rhymers' Club of two in specifically Catholic terms. In a letter written just prior to his time at Stone Cottage, he fantasized with playful enthusiasm about founding an order of "Brothers Minor," an "order more human than the Benedictines who should preserve even the vestiges of our present light against that single force whereof the 'ha'penny' press and the present university and educational systems are but the symptoms."[18] There was something of the retreat of both the monk and the aristocrat in the move to Stone Cottage, something of an escape from the world sought by St. Benedict and Des Esseintes alike. Two of the greatest literary minds of a generation temporarily abjured the world in order to craft in relative isolation their own vision of art and beauty for a new century.

The process of Yeats's modernization took more time. Only after his editorial collaboration with Yeats on the collection *Responsibilities* (1916) could Pound publicly announce that the older poet was no longer tainted by decadent sentiments. Pound begins a review for *Poetry* magazine on an uncharacteristic note of humility and deference, calling Yeats's work "immortal" and claiming that there is "no need for him to recast his style to suit our winds of doctrine."[19] Then, with a distinct sense of self-satisfaction, Pound draws attention to the "manifestly new note" in *Responsibilities*,[20] a note he privately credited himself with introducing. The degree to which Pound can actually be recognized for bringing Yeats on board with the doctrines of the modernist moment remains a point of contention; nevertheless, Pound's disdain for the softness of the nineties seems to have played a role in Yeats's own movement from sympathetic contemporary of the British decadents to chronicler of their extinction.

It was only later, in his autobiographical writing, that Yeats invented the myth of the "Tragic Generation," wedded the British *fin de siècle* to an aesthetic of failure, and established himself in writing as both sole survivor of decadence and guiding light of modernism. In order to explain his miraculous survival, Yeats drew attention to the most significant difference between himself and his dead colleagues. Instead of rejecting decadence for the affectation of its verse and taking subtle jabs at its religious preoccupations, as Pound had done, Yeats, as we saw earlier, explicitly disavowed the religion that informed and helped define the major texts of decadence. Construing the history of early twentieth-century poetry in his 1936 preface to the *Oxford Book of Modern Verse*, Yeats excludes all the trappings of the naughty nineties from the new century and gives Catholicism special attention: "In 1900 everybody got down off his stilts ... nobody joined the Catholic church, or if they did I have forgotten."[21] Yeats's insistence on segregating decadent Catholicism from the twentieth century is hardly surprising. He articulated and enshrined his belief in the incompatibility of art and organized religion early on in his career, most notably in the verse play *Mosada* (1886) and the narrative poem *The Wanderings of Oisin* (1889).

The Moorish heroine of *Mosada* is a manifestation of Yeats's confused romantic conception of Eastern magic.[22] Her Nietzschean resignation to the machinations of fate is wedded to a fierce artistic nature and undefined magical powers. As a magician and a poet, she stands in heroic contradistinction to the petty arbiters of the Church and its Inquisition.[23] In the opening lines of the play, as Mosada mourns the loss of her Christian lover, Yeats establishes an explicit opposition between his poet heroine and the forces of the Church:

> Three times the roses have grown less and less,
> As slowly Autumn climbed the golden throne
> Where sat old Summer fading into song,
> And thrice the peaches flushed upon the walls,
> And thrice the corn around the sickles flamed,
> Since 'mong my people, tented on the hills,
> He stood a messenger....
> Along the velvet vale I saw him come:
> In Autumn, when far down the mountain slopes
> The heavy clusters of the grapes were full,
> I saw him sigh and turn and pass away;
> For I and all my people were accurst
> Of his sad God.[24]

Mosada borrows some of the autumnal twilight imagery of the *fin de siècle* to poeticize her sorrow over the lover she lost to the "sad God" of the Christians. Dying roses and over-ripe grapes mark the passage of time since he left her behind to join the Spanish Inquisition and torment her people. In a cruel twist of fate, this same lover returns as the leader of the inquisitors who are responsible for Mosada's suicide. The play is an overt and unalloyed indictment of Catholicism as an ideology that stifles art and destroys the artist.

Yeats continued his youthful war against the Church in *The Wanderings of Oisin*, an epic poem in the form of a dialogue between the pagan hero Oisin and the patron saint of Ireland, St. Patrick. After centuries of wandering in Fairyland with his lover Niamh, Oisin returns to Ireland only to find it under the authority of Patrick and his new religion: "O Patrick! for a hundred years / The gentle Niamh was my wife; / But now two things devour my life; / The things that most of all I hate: / Fasting and prayers" (*WBY* 360–1). As much of his corpus testifies, Yeats often shared his hero's distaste for Patrick's religion; however, Yeats's relationship with Catholicism in the 1890s was complicated by collaboration and interaction with his decadent contemporaries. Lionel Johnson stands out among Yeats's influential decadent Catholic peers. The decadent poet "comes first to mind" in "In Memory of Major Robert Gregory" (1919) when an older, more experienced Yeats summons the ghosts of long dead friends, including his uncle George Pollexfen and the playwright John Synge. Johnson self-identified as Irish and played an important role in the Celtic Twilight, partly by lending Yeats certain Catholic bona fides.[25] Yeats's position among his countrymen was always somewhat suspect, partly because of his family's Anglican background and partly because of his eccentric occult preoccupations. It is easy to forget that in the 1890s Johnson showed as much if not more poetic promise than Yeats. The latter was still an apprentice of sorts, and there was good reason to believe that his English, Oxford-educated contemporaries were more likely to become household names in time. Yeats, who was not the first among the writers of that generation, drew on his contemporaries for inspiration. While actively collaborating with the decadent Catholic poets of the Rhymers' Club, he seems to have taken a greater interest in Catholicism, if not as a religion to be believed in, then at least as a potentially fruitful storehouse of symbols for his art.

For evidence of Yeats's growing Catholic sympathies in the 1890s, we need only look to *The Countess Cathleen* (1892). The play details the Christ-like self-sacrifice of an explicitly Catholic heroine. Such a dramatic shift in attitude toward Catholicism from the unequivocally antagonistic *Mosada* can be largely attributed to Yeats's infatuation with the Irish nationalist and Catholic sympathizer (and eventual convert) Maude Gonne. In voicing his love for Gonne in verse, Yeats allowed Catholic symbols and the decadent style of his contemporaries in the Rhymers' Club to inform his poetry. Yeats's warming to Catholicism was met with either cool indifference or active censure by the Irish Catholic public, who rightly sensed the heterodox undercurrents of the poet's work. Vexed by conservative opposition to the play, Yeats nevertheless continued to incorporate Catholic imagery in his two most decadent collections of poetry—*The Rose* (1893) and *The Wind Among the Reeds* (1899).

In *The Rose*, a collection born from his obsession with Gonne and shot through with decadent language and imagery, Yeats repeatedly articulates an essentially occult poetic vision that nevertheless draws heavily on Catholic symbolism. The central symbol of the Rose is such an all-encompassing representation of terrestrial and spiritual beauty and desire that assigning it particular meaning often leads to oversimplification. Still, its Catholic resonance is undeniable, calling to mind the mystical rose at the heart of Dante's *Paradiso*—the visual manifestation of the Empyrean: the seat of God that exists outside of and gives animation to the physical universe. As if to signal his engagement with decadent Catholicism in particular, Yeats dedicated *The Rose* section of *Poems* (1895) to Lionel Johnson and attached a Latin epigraph from Augustine's *Confessions*: "*Sero te amavi, Pulchritudo tam antiqua et tam nova! Sero te amavi*" (Too late did I love Thee, O Beauty, so old and yet so new! Too late did I love Thee). For Augustine, this "Beauty" is the same God that Johnson so fervently sought in the mystical reveries of his verse. The passage of *Confessions* from which the epigraph is taken contains a meditation on life's many temptations that reads like a decadent Catholic prose poem:

> Too late did I love Thee, O Beauty, so old and yet so new! Too late did I love
> Thee. For behold, Thou wert within, and I without, and there did I seek Thee; I,
> unlovely, rushed heedlessly among the things of beauty Thou madest. Thou wert
> with me, but I was not with Thee. Those things kept me far from Thee.[26]

Recognizing God as the essence of Beauty, Augustine laments his misguided attempts to capture that perfection by wallowing in worldly pleasures. As we saw in the previous chapter, British poets of the *fin de siècle* were obsessed with their failure to reconcile the ideal with the "real"—a failure that Thornton conceptualizes as "the decadent dilemma."[27] No decadent poet gave voice to this failure more frequently or eloquently than the dedicatee of *The Rose*, Lionel Johnson. Yeats's appropriation of Augustine's confessional lament in *The Rose* demonstrates his ability to absorb the influences of his Catholic peers and synthesize them into his own self-consciously paradoxical poetic vision.

In one poem from *The Rose*, "The Ballad of Father Gilligan," Yeats creates a surprisingly positive portrayal of an Irish priest. The poem's eponymous cleric, whose constant ministrations to the dying tax him to the point of exhaustion, rails momentarily against his vocation: "I have no rest, nor joy, nor peace" (*WBY* 53). Quickly realizing the sinful nature of his complaint, Father Gilligan repents and, in the act of praying, falls asleep. Awaking to find that his rest has caused him to neglect a dying man, Father Gilligan rushes to the man's house only to find that an angel administered the last rites while he slept. The poem ends with the good priest's heartfelt praise of a benevolent and merciful God: "He who hath made the night of stars / For souls who tire and bleed, / Sent one of His great angels down / To help me in my need" (*WBY* 53). This surprisingly touching and simple ballad appeared in the first *Book of the Rhymers' Club* (1892) alongside patently decadent Catholic poems such as Dowson's "Carmelite Nuns of the Perpetual Adoration" and Johnson's "A Burden of Easter Vigil." In this context it represented a specifically Irish contribution to an emerging Catholic literary movement. Yet, beneath Yeats's willingness to incorporate Catholic imagery into his verse, lay a distinct wariness. Some of Yeats's early work demonstrates that he considered his contemporaries' attraction to Catholicism inherently dangerous and self-destructive.

One such work appears in the infamous *Savoy* magazine. Founded by Aubrey Beardsley, Arthur Symons, and the publisher/pornographer Leonard Smithers in 1896 after the *Yellow Book* had become too tame for some, *The Savoy* was an incubator for decadent art. Symons initially attempted to distance his new periodical from aesthetic labels in his editorial preface to the magazine's inaugural issue: "We have no formulas, and we desire no false unity of form or matter. We have not invented a new point of view. We are not Realists, or Romanticists, or Decadents."[28] In spite of these protestations, *The Savoy* became a metonym for British decadence and contained work by most of the leading figures now associated with that movement. It served as the original venue for what is perhaps Yeats's most profound early rejection of a specifically decadent brand of Catholicism. "The Tables of the Law" (1896) focuses on one of the recurring figures in Yeats's corpus, Owen Aherne. Based largely on Lionel Johnson,[29] Aherne possesses a "nature, which is half monk, half soldier of fortune, and must needs turn action into dreaming, and dreaming into action."[30] Born in Ireland and educated in Paris (that hotbed of decadence), Aherne comes from a family that has produced a substantial number of energetic priests. Initially tempted to follow this family tradition, Aherne turns away from the priesthood at the eleventh hour and becomes entangled in the millenarian visions of the twelfth-century abbot Joachim of Flora. He travels the world for a decade in the hope of using his occult knowledge to overthrow the Ten Commandments of the Old Testament and craft new laws for a new age. Aherne is convinced "that the beautiful arts were sent into the world to overthrow nations, and finally life herself, by sowing everywhere unlimited desires, like torches thrown into a burning city."[31] His avocation is to speed this Armageddon on its way and hasten the end of time. Predictably, Aherne's experiments end not in revelation or apocalypse but in madness. The narrator finds his priest/mystic wandering the streets of Dublin a sad and broken man with nothing more to show for his ambitions than ivory tablets covered with the Latin scrawling of a mad theologian. The story is ultimately a cautionary tale warning about the dangers of mixing art and religion.

Yeats warns us that Catholic artist-mystics like Aherne and his real-world model, Johnson, are inevitably doomed to a life in which "there is no order, no finality, no contentment."[32] At times, the poetry of Johnson and Dowson seems to confirm such an assessment. Dowson's sonnet "Epilogue," later renamed "A Last Word," which was first published alongside "Tables of the Law" in the *Savoy*, demonstrates all the mad, discontented passion and self-annihilating despair that Yeats epitomizes in Aherne and implicitly ascribes to decadent Catholicism:

> Let us go hence: the night is now at hand;
> The day is overworn, the birds all flown;
> And we have reaped the crops the gods have sown;
> Despair and death; deep darkness o'er the land,
> Broods like an owl; we cannot understand
> Laughter or tears, for we have only known
> Surpassing vanity: vain things alone
> Have driven our perverse and aimless band.
> Let us go hence, somewhither strange and cold,
> To Hollow Lands where just men and unjust
> Find end of labour, where's rest for the old,
> Freedom to all from love and fear and lust.
> Twine our torn hands! O pray the earth enfold
> Our life-sick hearts and turn them into dust. (*ED* 138)

Dowson's "perverse and aimless band," who have "only known / Surpassing vanity," suggests the whole decadent entourage of the 1890s. Far from falling back on comforting notions of a paradisal afterlife, Dowson's speaker insists that he and his companions can pray for nothing better than annihilation. As we saw in Chapter 1, Dowson and Johnson feared their final ends and often expressed anxieties about the corrupting influence of their artistic pursuits on their eternal souls. These anxieties were often fleeting or ameliorated by moments of hope and joy. Yeats, who viewed such sentiments as corrosive, perceived an internal conflict between art and religion pervading the work of his colleagues. Such conflict, he eventually concluded, was responsible in large part for the depression and despair that drove his contemporaries to self-destructive excess and led to the premature death of decadence.

After "The Tables of the Law," Yeats's poetry continued to wear some of the trappings of decadent Catholicism. "The Travail of Passion," published in his most noticeably decadent collection of poetry, *The Wind Among the Reeds*, eroticizes the passion of Christ in a manner that would have put his Catholic contemporaries to shame if most were not already halfway in their graves and focused on final things:

> When the flaming lute-thronged angelic door is wide;
> When an immortal passion breathes in mortal clay;
> Our hearts endure the scourge, the plaited thorns, the way
> Crowded with bitter faces, the wounds in palm and side,
> The hyssop-heavy sponge, the flowers by Kidron stream:
> We will bend down and loosen our hair over you,
> That it may drop faint perfume, and be heavy with dew,
> Lilies of death-pale hope, roses of passionate dream. (*WBY* 68)

The royal "we" employed in this poem ("We will bend down and loosen our hair over you") implies that the speaker is representative of a larger group of artists who associate themselves with Mary Magdalene. According to tradition, this reformed prostitute became a disciple of Christ. In the middle ages she came to be identified with nearly every unnamed woman in the gospels. Yeats reflects this tradition by compacting three separate incidents in which the composite Magdalene washed the feet of Christ with her tears and hair, anointed his head with costly perfume, and risked death to witness his crucifixion. Yeats associates the "we" of his poem with this composite faithful sinner. If he speaks for any group here, it can only be the decadents—those sin-besmirched poets who approached their God with tears of penitence and the perfume of poetry. For a time, Yeats seems to have taken a certain mimetic pleasure from imitating the verse of his more devout contemporaries. This period of artistic sympathy came largely to an end in the twentieth century.

Soon after the turn of the century, several of the most prominent Irish and English decadents were dead or dying, and Yeats emerged as one of the preeminent poets of his time. It fell to him to dictate the legacy of his decadent contemporaries. His most profound and totalizing rebuke of decadent Catholicism came in his autobiographical *The Trembling of the Veil* (1922). Immersed in the material that would later inform *A Vision* (1925), Yeats managed to explain the dissipation of his contemporaries by pointing out that they were born in the wrong phase of history.

> I think that (falling back upon my parable of the moon) I can explain some part
> of Dowson's and Johnson's dissipation:—
>
> > What portion in the world can the artist have
> > Who is awakened from the common dream
> > But dissipation and despair?[33]

According to Yeats, these anachronistic Christians, for whom religion "deepened despair and multiplied temptation," could not survive because they were born with "strange souls," which their moment in history could not satisfy.[34] Sickness and alcoholism did more than religion to ensure the early deaths of Beardsley, Johnson, and Dowson, but Yeats insists that Catholicism acted as a spiritual contaminant, a sort of decadent accelerant. Moreover, he implicitly connects his own survival as a poet to his participation in the modern shift away from what he saw as medieval spirituality.

Yeats embraced the Irish literary revival as an antidote to the poisonous influence of Christ-haunted decadence. In "The Autumn of the Body" (1898), published just two years after "The Tables of the Law," he envisions a new future for art following the death throes of the decadent artists of the *fin de siècle*. In anticipation of a new, fruitful springtime of imaginative creation in which the arts might "take upon their shoulders the burdens that have fallen from the shoulders of priests,"[35] he recasts decadence as a fleeting moment rather than a movement:

> I see, indeed, in the arts of every country those faint lights and faint colours and faint outlines and faint energies which many call "the decadence," and which I, because I believe that the arts lie dreaming of things to come, prefer to call the autumn of the body ... We are, it may be, at a crowning crisis of the world, at the moment when man is about to ascend, with the wealth, he has been so long gathering, upon his shoulders, the stairway he has been descending from the first days.[36]

Caught up in something like the millenarian fervor of Aherne, Yeats produces a thoroughly anti-decadent vision based on an historical sense of progress that is antithetical to the ethos of decay and that conforms to a very different narrative of cultural recrudescence.

In one of his more optimistic moods, Yeats entered the twentieth century believing that the "faint lights" of decadence would soon be washed out by the bright effulgence of a new springtime for humanity. Priest would give way to artist; man would begin his ascent into new realms of enlightenment. Less than twenty years later, a young poet from St. Louis, a man whose work would come to define modernist verse, a man scarred by the horrors of the first major war in a century defined by global conflict, a man forever skeptical of progress and aware of the demands of tradition, would produce art infused with the "faint energies" of decadent Catholicism.

T. S. Eliot's Decadent (Anglo)-Catholicism

In his "In Memory of W. B. Yeats," W. H. Auden, with a clear intimation of what would someday happen to his own art, laments that the dead poet's genius will inevitably face the ready and easy moralizing scrutiny of another age and place:

> Now he is scattered among a hundred cities
> And wholly given over to unfamiliar affections,
> To find his happiness in another kind of wood
> And be punished under a foreign code of conscience.
> The words of a dead man
> Are modified in the guts of the living.[1]

Like Yeats, Eliot has proven an easy target for such "punishment" as well as some simplistic modification. Part of this modification has involved turning Eliot into the stodgy, homophobic opponent of an iconoclastic, queer decadence. Note how the introduction to *Decadence in the Age of Modernism* dismisses Eliot's critique of the Paterian philosophy most readily associated with decadence with one word from the foreign code of postmodern conscience:

> Pater's dictum of "art for art's sake," Eliot continued, "impressed itself upon a number of writers in the 'nineties, and propagated some confusion between life and art which is not wholly irresponsible for some untidy lives." Eliot's moralizing denigration of Pater and the movement he spawned is clearly homophobic.[2]

Clearly. But what do we make of his critique of the decadent "confusion between art and life"? What seems clear to me is that Eliot, like some of the decadents themselves (Lionel Johnson in particular), understood that such a conflation between the created world and the artist's creation could engender a potentially dangerous moral vacuum.

Eliot turned his critical gaze on decadence more than once. At other times, he acknowledged a kinship with the artists of the *fin de siècle*. We need only look to his own words in "Tradition and the Practice of Poetry" (1936) to get a clear sense of Eliot's understanding of his debt to decadence:

I cannot help wondering how my own verse would have developed, or whether it would have been written at all, supposing that the poets of the 'nineties had survived to my own time and had gone on developing and increasing in power. Perhaps they were men who could not have developed further, but I am making that assumption. I certainly had much more in common with them than with the English poets who survived to my own day.... Had they survived, they might have spoken in an idiom sufficiently like my own to have made anything I had to say superfluous.[3]

The loosely affiliated group of British decadents, acolytes of French "Symbolism" who worshipped the classics, scandalized Victorian propriety, and disdained materialism and secularism, anticipated and found an inheritor in T. S. Eliot.

In 1936, Louis Untermeyer, one of Eliot's harshest early critics,[4] acknowledged the poet's decadent Catholic heritage in a review of *Collected Poems* for the "New Poetry" section of the *Yale Review*:

T. S. Eliot has become a symbol of all that is advanced in poetry, and yet he is an anachronism in the sense that he is both futurist and *fin de siècle*. No one, as far as I know, has compared him to the aesthetes of the Nineties; yet his course and theirs are curiously similar.... They—Lionel Johnson, Ernest Dowson, Oscar Wilde, Aubrey Beardsley—could no longer face their own distortions and turned to the Catholic church, which supplied them with new color as well as a new impetus; he, unable to dwell in the Waste Land, with its nightmares of vulgarity, has found an Anglo-Catholic haven, and in return, the church has given him another kind of subsistence as well as fresh subject matter.[5]

Untermeyer's insights are brief and impressionistic: Eliot and his decadent precursors, including Beardsley, turned away from art that fixated on the perverse and toward traditional religions that both revivified their work and offered them a means of personal salvation. Untermeyer insightfully anticipates the later work of critics who have identified many of Eliot's stylistic, formal, and thematic debts to Johnson, Dowson, Wilde, Swinburne, and others.[6]

Tellingly, Untermeyer undercuts his keen insight by segregating the aesthetic and the spiritual, in this case decadence and Catholicism. To claim that the work of either the British decadents of the 1890s or their most prominent and direct modernist inheritor can be cleanly divided into the dubious categories of pre- and post-conversion overlooks the fact that Eliot and his late Victorian precursors created what we might recognize as decadent Catholic art at diverse points in their careers and often independent of their formal conversions. Johnson and Dowson, it is true, converted before the publication of some of their most famously "decadent" verses. Wilde was a deathbed convert (we think), but his early sonnets, *Dorian Gray*, *De Profundis*, and especially *Salomé*, bear the dual marks of decadence and Catholicism despite having been written prior to this moment of formal communion with Rome. John Gray, upon whom Dorian was based, converted after the publication of his most notorious verses in *Silverpoints*, but, according to him, the next several years were the most prodigal of his life.[7] Aubrey Beardsley's deathbed conversion (this one more certain than Wilde's) was preceded by the production of drawings that, while they shocked and disturbed, also contained the germ of that conversion. Such, I will argue, is also the case with Eliot.

Eliot's conversion was indeed significant, but his early poetry does not fail to anticipate it. Beardsley, whose illustrations, in the words of a contemporary, distill "the very essence of the decadent *fin de siècle*,"[8] was also recognized by his contemporaries as an ironic critic of the sinful excesses and extravagances he depicted. Thus, his conversion becomes a logical extension of his decadent art rather than a sudden spiritual spasm. Likewise, Eliot's "religious" poetry grows into, not out of, his darkly satirical and overtly decadent early work. Grasping this continuity allows us to appreciate the essential link between Eliot the experimental late decadent and Eliot the orthodox religious poet.

"A Satirist of Vices and Follies"

In spite of renewed interest in Eliot's ties to decadence, the parallels between Aubrey Beardsley's art and that of Eliot, which were apparent to Untermeyer in 1936, remain largely unexplored. Nancy Hargrove has devoted considerable attention to Eliot's study of art history at Harvard and the profound influence on him of artists such as Mantegna. Also, the *Edinburgh Companion to T. S. Eliot and the Arts* (2016) contains four chapters on the influence of the visual arts; however, Beardsley's infamous illustrations have yet to receive any attention in Eliot studies. Such a critical lacuna is hardly surprising, considering that the archive of Beardsley's influence is nowhere near as vast as that of, for example, Laforgue, whose name crops up repeatedly in Eliot's prose and whose poetry overtly impacted the formation of his aesthetic. Beardsley's name appears on the syllabus for a course that Eliot taught in 1917 on modern English literature along with other "personalities" from "the group of the 'Yellow Book'" under the general category of "The 'Nineties,"[9] but he is absent from both the letters and the published prose, with one important exception.

In the sixth of his Clark Lectures (1926), which he devotes to Crashaw, Eliot portrays the British decadents of the 1890s not as absinthe-swilling degenerates but as religious artists with roots in a particular literary tradition. After establishing Crashaw as a "devotional" and "fervent" Roman Catholic who "had more in common with Cardinal Newman than with Thomas Aquinas,"[10] Eliot traces this religious impulse in art through Newman and along a rather unexpected trajectory. He claims that the "current of feeling" that links Crashaw and Newman "passes through Arnold, Ruskin, and Pater to Francis Thompson, Lionel Johnson, Aubrey Beardsley, and even in a degraded and popularized form to Oscar Wilde."[11] In this schema, the British decadents (Thompson, Johnson, Beardsley, Wilde) function as nineteenth-century Crashaws—fervent, devotional, and Roman Catholic. True to form, Eliot provides no justification for or explanation of Beardsley's inclusion in this genealogy of devotional fervor. One possible reason presents itself in the form of a letter that Eliot acquired for publication in the *Criterion* shortly before delivering his Clark Lectures.

Eliot wrote twice to Lionel Johnson's executrix in pursuit of a letter written by Johnson regarding Beardsley's death, and Eliot's correspondences with Frederic Manning and Geoffrey Faber reveal that this epistle was not a casual addition to the *Criterion*. Its acquisition inspired Eliot to ask Faber if he would consider publishing a book of Johnson's letters.[12] The book never made it to print, but Johnson's reflection on the relationship between Beardsley's notoriously obscene art and his deeply felt religious impulses did:

> He [Beardsley] became a Catholic with a true humility and exaltation of soul, prepared to sacrifice much.... he would have dismissed from it [his work] all suggestion of anything dangerously morbid: he would have made it plain that he was sometimes a satirist of vices and follies and extravagancies, but not, so to say, a sentimental student of them for their curiosity and fascination's sake. I believe that he had some thoughts of entering some order or congregation, in which he could have followed his art, and dedicated it directly to the service of the faith .... He was not the man to play with high things, still less with the highest of all: he would never have been a fantastical, dilettante trifler with Catholicism, making it an emotional foil to other and base emotions.[13]

The devout, humble, pious Aubrey Beardsley depicted in this eulogy hardly resembles the young artist whose outrageous illustrations of Wilde's *Salomé*, the infamous *Yellow Book*, and *Lysistrata* challenged and subverted Victorian propriety. Yet few could have guessed that the "dangerously morbid" poetry of young Tom Eliot, with its lusty Tinker, murderous Saint Sebastian, fleshly Sweeney, and impotent Prufrock, contained the seed of a complex but largely orthodox religious sensibility. The work of both artists represents what Eliot claims he would "like" to find in religious literature: art that is "*unconsciously*, rather than deliberately and defiantly, Christian" (*SP* 100).

Nine days prior to his death, Aubrey Beardsley, the man whom Roger Fry dubbed the Fra Angelico of Satanism, the man who once claimed to have "one aim—the grotesque,"[14] wrote a brief but poignant missive to his publisher.

Jesus is our Lord and Judge

Dear Friend

I implore you to destroy *all* copies of *Lysistrata* and bad drawings. Show this to Pollitt and conjure him to do the same.
By all that is holy *all* obscene drawings.

Aubrey Beardsley
In my death agony.[15]

Had his epistle been addressed to anyone other than Leonard Smithers, the daring publisher and arch pornographer, the author might have harbored some hope of success. Fortunately for posterity, Smithers's lack of scruples and his desire to squeeze as much money as possible out of Beardsley's work preserved the "bad drawings" and secured the legacy of the illustrator of the decadents.

A convert to Roman Catholicism who was facing death at the age of twenty-five and fearing the verdict of his accepted "Lord and Judge," Beardsley clearly viewed his work as a liability. His contemporaries did not share the artist's ultimate assessment of his work as obscene or sacrilegious. As we have already seen, Johnson viewed his friend and contemporary as "a satirist of vices and follies and extravagancies, but not, so to say, a sentimental student of them for their curiosity and fascination's sake." Yeats, who agreed with this sentiment, defended Beardsley's art as an expression of "rage against iniquity."[16] For Yeats, Beardsley's task was to "take upon himself ... the knowledge of sin" as the saint takes upon himself the "consequence" of sin when he heals the sick.[17] Similar contemporary readings of Beardsley's work abound. Even Roger Fry, who depicted Beardsley as "the archpriest of a Satanic cultus," also saw in his decadent contemporary "all the stigmata of the religious artist."[18] These reflections are by no means the last word on Beardsley, but, seen in their light, his drawings become more than "bad" and "obscene": they become expressions of decadence divided against itself. They become manifestations of an aesthetic both Catholic and obscene; they become perverse reflections of the fervent, devotional feelings of Crashaw and Newman; they become visual precursors of Eliot's own artistic dilemmas.

The aesthetic affinities shared by Beardsley and Eliot make themselves felt in their treatments of one of the most pronounced obsessions of decadent Catholic art: the opera of Wagner. Ellis Hanson identifies Wagner as "a touchstone for the peculiar dialectic of shame and grace that is the foundation of decadent Catholicism."[19] He sees in the German composer an artist celebrating "a highly sensual and ritualistic conception of the faith that was visionary in its temptations, exquisite in its repentance, medieval in its intensity, and mystical in its tone."[20] Inspired by the celebration of perverse beauty and abject piety in *Tannhäuser*, Beardsley composed his own version of the myth in the unfinished erotic novel *Under the Hill* (1896), parts of which originally appeared in *The Savoy*. He also produced illustrations of scenes from *Siegfried* and *Tristan und Isolde*, among others. Eliot's fascination with Wagner's music manifests itself most powerfully and transparently in the echoes of *Tristan und Isolde* that haunt *The Waste Land* (1922). Surprisingly, the two artists converge not in their reimagining and reconstituting of Wagner's art but in their satiric treatment of his followers. If, as Johnson suggests, Beardsley's Catholic sensibility manifests itself in his decadent art through the satire of "vices and follies," then what we see in his illustration *The Wagnerites* (1894) and Eliot's early, unpublished poem "Opera" (1909) is a shared artistic sensibility situated at the intersection of decadence and Catholicism.

The first stanza of Eliot's "Opera," with its emotive instruments, self-torturing love, and romantic paroxysms, describes the sound and fury at a performance of Wagner's *Tristan und Isolde*. Eliot's is the thundering Wagner Lady Henry praises in *Dorian Gray* for being "so loud that one can talk the whole time without other people hearing what one says" (*DG* 40). This display of tragic power, though certainly loud enough to enable good conversation, offers no lasting revelation to Eliot's speaker: "We have the tragic? oh no! / Life departs with a feeble smile ... And I feel like the ghost of youth / At the undertakers' ball."[21] The passion of the music only highlights the ennui of experiencing lofty emotions that have no place in the banal, indifferent modern world. This realization that debased modernity is devoid of true tragedy leaves the speaker feeling denuded and spectral. Just as Eliot's poem reveals the banality of life after the music stops, Beardsley's drawing, *The Wagnerites* (Figure 3.1), represents the backs of a ghostly audience and scarcely hints at the spectacle of the stage.

The only figure aware of the viewer's gaze is a frail creature craning over its shoulder with a look of spleen. The only clearly male character is a Prufrockian balding man in spectacles surrounded by what Chris Snodgrass calls "vicious women."[22] Linda Zatlin describes the effect: "The collection of thick-lipped and

Figure 3.1 Aubrey Beardsley, *The Wagnerites* (1894). © The Victoria and Albert Museum, London. Image used with permission.

hard-looking women in *The Wagnerites* is the artist's ironic comment on those affected women whose emotional involvement with the composer's *Tristan und Isolde* appears to be on the same limited plane as would be their involvement with their fellow human beings."[23] These women are the ideal attendants at the "undertakers' ball" that is Eliot's opera house. What Zatlin reads as their limited "emotional involvement" with Wagner's work resonates with Eliot's speaker's conclusion that modern audiences do not, in fact, "have the tragic." Wagner can bring them to the edge of the tragic abyss, but he cannot force them to confront it.

Whether Beardsley's illustration directly inspired or informed Eliot's poem is uncertain. As Emma Sutton insists in *Aubrey Beardsley and British Wagnerism of the 1890s* (2002), "In biographical terms, we can only speculate whether the image was conceived as a scathing critique of contemporary Wagnerites ... or as an approving delineation of the decadence, the sensuality, of Wagner's music and its admirers."[24] Sutton makes a good point but develops a troubling binary since Beardsley's tendency toward satire does not preclude some sympathy with his subject. Beardsley's 1892 self-portrait, for instance, manifests his facility with what we might call sympathetic satire. In *The Wagnerites*, however, the scales seem to tip toward satire in a manner that makes the picture a tenable model for the scathing critique of the audience in Eliot's "Opera." For Eliot and Beardsley, the Wagnerites who leer at performances of grand passions are little more than empty shells, pale shadows of the heroic humanity being dramatized on stage. Eliot's poem allows us a glimpse into the psyche of one member of Beardsley's crowd from the position of the self-ironizing poetic "I." Such an argument for the complementarity of the work of Eliot and Beardsley is speculative, but the convergence of sensibility evident in *The Wagnerites* and "Opera" is far from an isolated example.

"The Love Song of Saint Sebastian" is the most overtly decadent of the poems in Eliot's early, unpublished work. Riquelme, for one, insists that the poem is "obviously indebted to Wilde" and to *Salomé* in particular.[25] As we will see, *Salomé* does inform Eliot's work, but those seeking a possible antecedent for "Saint Sebastian" will find a richer model in Beardsley's poem "The Ballad of a Barber," which appeared in the July 1896 issue of *The Savoy*. The poem tells the tale of Carrousel, a barber who "cut, and coiffed, and shaved so well, / That all the world was at his feet."[26] His work exemplifies the decadent preference for artifice over nature. Renowned for his prowess as both a barber and a lover, Carrousel attracts "reigning belles" and "beaux" alike. Disastrously, his skills fail when he attempts to coif the hair of a thirteen-year-old princess. Infuriated by his failure as an artist, Carrousel snaps, and mangles his failed masterpiece:

The Princess gave a little scream,
Carrousel's cut was sharp and deep;
He left her softly as a dream
That leaves a sleeper to his sleep.

He left the room on pointed feet;
Smiling that things had gone so well.[27]

His assault ambiguously suggests both murder and rape. Several commentators link this horrendous act with the murderous aesthetician in John Gray's poem "The Barber."[28] Browning's "Porphyria's Lover" also seems a poetic model for both Beardsley's Carrousel and Eliot's Sebastian.[29] All three poems involve the murder of an objectified beloved inspired by a deranged desire for control and possession. Eliot's poem and Beardsley's illustration share a distinctly Catholic undertone beneath their decadent surfaces that is missing in "Porphyria's Lover."

The speaker of "Saint Sebastian," who approaches his beloved as a self-flagellating worshiper, enacts a grotesque parody of asceticism:

> I would come in a shirt of hair
> I would come with a lamp in the night
> And sit at the foot of your stair;
> I would flog myself until I bled,
> And after hour on hour of prayer
> And torture and delight
> Until my blood should ring the lamp
> And glisten in the light;
> I should arise your neophyte.[30]

Substituting the beloved, with her white gown, for the usual female focus of adoration, the Virgin Mary, the psychotic monk obsesses over the "curl" of her ears. His obsession reenacts Carrousel's erotic fixation on the curl of the Princess's hair: "Three times the barber curled a lock, / And thrice he straightened it again." In spite of these similarities, the Catholic element that plays such an important role in Eliot's poem seems to be absent from Beardsley's "The Ballad of a Barber," at least until we consider the illustration that accompanies the poem (Figure 3.2).

Beardsley's illustration places the viewer in the position of the barber's mirror prior to the horrendous act. Carrousel seems to contemplate his greatness while leering over the shoulder of the virginal Princess, and they share the scene with one other figure. The diagonal line that cuts almost uninterruptedly through the middle of the drawing and aligns the foregrounded pair finds its pinnacle at the crown of the statue of the Virgin and Child. Although they form three distinct figures, Carrousel, the Princess, and the Virgin Mary share a triangular unity of line that suggests an essential link, a curious trinity. At the same time, the interrupting line of the shelf on which the statue rests also produces a contrast between two pairs: mother and child in the background, murderer and victim in the foreground. The statue stands out especially in the illustration because it

Figure 3.2 Aubrey Beardsley, *The Coiffing* (1896). Used with the permission of the Harry Ransom Center, The University of Texas at Austin.

receives no mention in the poem. Its absence from the written text makes it all the more conspicuous in the visual one. Here, the mother of Christ becomes a witness to the rape-murder about to happen, standing in silent judgment over the decadent artist Carrousel. The subtle placement of a specifically Catholic icon in a position of contrast and judgment suggests once again that Beardsley's art does much more than glorify the grotesque and wallow in what Poe might term "the perverse." By juxtaposing the loving union of the mother and child with the barber's incipient act of violence against a young girl, Beardsley invites viewers to contemplate the sinister urges that may underlie and distort the pursuit of beauty through artifice. Similarly, the twisted devotion of Eliot's homicidal Saint Sebastian suggests that the urge to objectify and possess another human being through violence is a perversion of the martyr's act of self-sacrifice. Neither Carrousel nor Sebastian plays on pathos or begs for sympathy, unlike the speaker of Yeats's "He Wishes His Beloved Were Dead" (1899), yet another reimagining of Browning's "Porphyria's Lover." Instead, they stimulate their readers' and viewers' horror, revulsion, and titillation.

There is clear artistic sympathy in the sex-murder obsession in both "The Ballad of the Barber" and "Saint Sebastian," given the shared juxtaposition of Marian devotion and the erotics of homicide. But what of the flagellation that plays such an important role in Sebastian's sadomasochistic worship? ("I would flog myself until I bled.") Eliot's speaker promises to engage in a thoroughly un-modern form of self-abasement. Though some religious orders still engage in the practice, self-flagellation has not been widespread among European Catholics since the Middle Ages. Flagellant cults sprang up in the mid-thirteenth century in part as a reaction to plague and in part because of the millenarian fervor excited by the eschatological visions of mystics such as Joachim of Flora, who predicted the second coming of Christ some time around the year 1260.[31] The practice was popular. In its heyday, some processions of self-abusing penitents in Europe numbered as high as 10,000.[32] Fearing both the heretical and anarchical tendencies of this mass movement, the Church managed to suppress the practice for a time only to have it reemerge with greater intensity during the cataclysmic Black Death. After the late Middle Ages, public and private flagellation continued among smaller sects but became exceedingly rare among European Catholics. Among English Catholics, it was almost unheard of. That said, corporal punishment in British public schools and its entanglement with the *vice anglais* played an important role in the national predilection for whipping as a form of erotic expression well into the twentieth century.

Not surprisingly, flagellation held a special fascination for some British decadents. Swinburne set the tone when it came to flagellant fantasies. When the nineties generation and its inheritors followed suit, they consistently returned to the Catholic roots of the practice. For example, Frederick Rolfe's *Stories Toto Told Me* (1898) and *In His Own Image* (1901), collections of fanciful vignettes primarily about Catholic saints narrated by the catamite Toto to his priestly British patron "Don Friderico," make several references to whipping as a response to "naughtiness."[33] At one point, Don Friderico administers "a flagellation so sound and solemn ... as to impress Frat' Agostino [a Capuchin monk], who was present on the occasion in an official capacity, with the notion that we English regarded the function as possessing something of a sacramental nature."[34] Flagellation continued to play a role of importance for the modernist inheritors of decadent Catholicism. The British novelist Ronald Firbank (1886–1926), the modernist Wilde of the early twentieth century, picked up on the trend to comic effect and depicted whipping as an erotic pleasure under the guise of religious practice in novels such as *The Flower Beneath the Foot* (1923). Eliot's poem participates in this tradition by eroticizing this specifically Catholic form of self-purification, which is absent from "The Ballad of the Barber" but front-and-center in Beardsley's illustration of a fascinating but little-known decadent novel written by a Scottish poet.

John Davidson's (1857–1909) comic novel *A Full and True Account of the Wonderful Mission of Earl Lavender* (1895) is obsessed with flagellation. The narrative follows the debauched misadventures of two men under the adopted names of Earl Lavender and Lord Brumm, who are on the run from the burdens of married life. They band together to test Earl Lavender's confused theory of evolution by scouring London to find him the perfect female specimen with whom to mate. Lavender eventually settles on "the Lady of the Veil," an explicitly Marian figure and a senior member in an underground cult of celibate flagellants. In a prefatory note to the text, Davidson argues that flagellant cults are indicative of significant historic shifts and insists that the scenes described in his book are evidence of the reality of "the so-called *Décadence*":[35] "The Flagellant society to which the Lady of the Veil introduces Earl Lavender may therefore be taken as a sign of the times—a sign of an age of effete ideals."[36] Richard Le Gallienne emphasized the same idea in his 1896 review of the book: "As so often happens in imaginative literature, the most real scenes in the book are those which are ostensibly most unreal; for instance, the flagellation scenes in that underground Stevensonian world—an allegory, I suppose, of the tired taste and jaded sensibilities of our end of the century."[37] *Earl Lavender* is about more than whipping parties, but, given Davidson's fixation on flagellation as an indication of the decadence of the *fin de siècle*, Beardsley's *Frontispiece* (Figure 3.3) seems to capture the essence of the novel.

Figure 3.3 Aubrey Beardsley, *Frontispiece* (1895). Used with the permission of the Harry Ransom Center, The University of Texas at Austin.

As with all his "illustrations," Beardsley pulls out a central concern of the source text and weaves it into a wholly new artistic creation. Beardsley's Lady of the Veil looks more like a prostitute than Davidson's celibate acolyte, though the three thongs of her whip match the trinity of phallic candles on the mantle in a manner that suggests a spiritual practice. The pagan ritual described in Davidson's work is informed by Catholicism, and Beardsley plays up the Roman angle by dangling what looks like a monk's beads from Earl Lavender's robe. If we were to anticipate the content of Davidson's novel based on the frontispiece, we might expect a story about a wayward monk who, unsatisfied with self-flagellation, turns to a lady of the night for assistance.

Eliot never mentions *Earl Lavender* in his prose or letters, but he noted Davidson's poetic skill on several occasions. In a 1961 preface to a selection of Davidson's poems, Eliot placed "Thirty Bob a Week" (1894) on a par with Dowson's "Non sum qualis" and praised both for transcending the staid rhythm and poetic diction of their time.[38] Confessing a "reverence" for such early influences, Eliot traced his "debt" to Davidson back to his "formative years between sixteen and twenty."[39] Given his early and sustained interest in Davidson's poetry, it seems likely that Eliot would have been familiar with his prose as well. "Thirty Bob a Week" exposed Eliot to a new poetic diction and rhythm; *Earl Lavender* may have exposed him to flagellation—a practice entirely foreign to his Unitarian upbringing. Eliot produces something more serious and less farcical in "Saint Sebastian" than Beardsley and Davidson do in *Earl Lavender*. Still, the novel, its illustration, and its general fascination with flagellation as a decadent form of erotic expression anticipate Eliot's unusual poem in a manner that suggests, if not a direct influence, then at least a commonality of thought and expression. Those looking for more direct connections between Eliot and Beardsley must turn to Wilde.

***

The connections between the works of Beardsley and Eliot already explored in this chapter are based primarily on speculation concerning similarities of theme, tone, and subject matter. More direct connections between the two artists emerge when we trace Beardsley's influence through the medium of Wilde. When confronted with the drawings that Beardsley produced to accompany *Salomé*, Wilde expressed some fear that his text would end up "illustrating Aubrey's illustrations."[40] His sentiment proved prophetic as reviewers instantly singled out Beardsley's not-so-subtle satire on the author and the play's aestheticized reimaging of the martyrdom of a saint. In *Enter Herodias* (Figure 3.4), for example, Wilde's broad features appear in both the visage of the behemoth drag queen Herodias and the jester skulking in the corner and gesturing toward the trinity of phallic candles.

Figure 3.4 Aubrey Beardsley, *Enter Herodias* (1894). © The Victoria and Albert Museum, London. Image used with permission.

The illustration betrays an almost school-boyishly innocent fascination with all things naughty, including the poorly concealed erection of the monstrous attendant, the phallic candles, and the exaggerated, pneumatic bust of Herodias/ Wilde. Beardsley may even be depicting a thinly veiled caricature of the nubile, blond Lord Alfred Douglas staring adoringly up at the man who misguidedly entrusted him with the translation of *Salomé*, a job for which Beardsley had originally applied.

With few exceptions,[41] commentators agree that Beardsley took advantage of the opportunity to lampoon Wilde while making his own significant contribution to late nineteenth-century Salomania. Beardsley's biographer Matthew Sturgis, for example, argues that "in the illustrations for *Salomé* Beardsley made his most devastating assault upon Wilde."[42] According to Wilde's literary executor Robbie Ross in his study of Beardsley (1909), the artist "was too subjective to be an illustrator. Profoundly interested in literature for the purposes of his art, he only extracted from it whatever was suggestive as pattern."[43] In other words, Beardsley does not adorn texts with his art; he alters them. Wilde himself acknowledged the disparities between the two texts of *Salomé*. Considering the illustrations "too Japanese," he complained that they resembled the "naughty scribbles a pernicious boy makes in the margins of his copybook."[44] Acknowledging the many caricatures of Wilde in Beardsley's images, Maureen T. Kravec concedes that "Beardsley's audacious visual objectification of depravity ... may not match the deliberately crafted metaphors of remote, cold beauty that sustain Wilde's tragedy."[45] In spite of these disparities, she suggests that both the drawings and the text "satiriz[e] the folly of self-centered possessiveness."[46] To my mind, such a characterization more accurately represents Beardsley, whose often grotesque pictures satirically subvert a world dominated by perverse lusts and self-destructive, unchecked desires, than it does Wilde, whose fatal heroine more often fascinates and titillates than repels. To fall back on Lionel Johnson's formulation, Beardsley manifests as "satirist of vices and follies" in *Salomé*, while Wilde emerges as "a sentimental student of them for their curiosity and fascination's sake."

Beardsley's subversion of Wilde may have played a part in Eliot's later favoring the imp of the perverse over the arch dandy in his Clark Lectures. For Eliot, the "current of feeling" in the "devotional" Catholic verse of Crashaw finds its inheritors in people like Newman and Beardsley, but in Wilde's work the impulse becomes "degraded" and "popularized." Eliot certainly recognized Wilde's importance,[47] but he reprises this distaste for the man, at least in terms of the relationship between art and religion, in his 1930 essay "Arnold and Pater."

There, he lumps the decadent artist in with those who get "all the emotional kick out of Christianity one can, without the bother of believing it."[48] Whether Eliot's comments fairly or accurately represent Wilde's relationship with religion is of little importance in the current discussion. What matters is that Beardsley represents a far more fitting artistic precursor. As I have already hinted, paradoxical impulses toward the sacred and the profane in the work of Beardsley and Eliot find expression in the artists' fascination with sin as a negative road to the good.

This strange *via negativa*, with its obsessive fascination with evil, anticipates Eliot's reflections on the work of Baudelaire.[49] A decade before that well-known essay, Eliot referred to the poet as a "deformed Dante" and insisted on the essential role of morality in his work.[50] In a 1921 review titled "The Lesson of Baudelaire," Eliot writes that "all first-rate poetry is occupied with morality: this is the lesson of Baudelaire. More than any poet of his time, Baudelaire was aware of what mattered most: the problem of good and evil."[51] Eliot went on to develop this view further in his essay "Baudelaire" (1930), which argues that the godfather of decadence confirms belief in the possibility of salvation through his obsession with damnation:

> Baudelaire perceived that what really matters is Sin and Redemption.... the recognition of the reality of Sin is a New Life; and the possibility of damnation is so immense a relief in a world of electoral reform, plebiscites, sex reform and dress reform, that damnation itself is an immediate form of salvation—of salvation from the ennui of modern life, because it at last gives some significance to living.... it is this which separates him from the modernist Protestantism of Byron and Shelley. (*SP* 236)

Affirming sin as a metaphysical reality, Baudelaire found salvation from the ennui of a banal modern world. The fact that Eliot contrasts Baudelaire's recognition of "Sin" with "the modernist Protestantism of Byron and Shelley" suggests that, even after his 1927 conversion, Eliot disdained liberal Protestantism and considered himself part of the "one holy catholic and apostolic Church," as any good Anglican would. From Baudelaire, Eliot distilled the simple truth that "the sense of evil implies the sense of good" (*SP* 236). In other words, the modern artist finds the good by proving the existence of evil. Like Dante, who descends to the bottom of Hell in order to ascend Mount Purgatory, Beardsley and his modernist inheritor—deformed Dantes both—make sin and vice the material for a complex satire that insists on the existence of something nobler.

Beardsley's *Salomé* illustrations enact just such an interrogation of sin by replacing Wilde's eccentric, capricious, beautiful heroine with a viler and more perverse subject. Wilde's fascination with the figure of Salomé resonates less clearly with Beardsley's satiric drawings than it does with the musings of Des Esseintes, the decadent antihero of J. K. Huysmans's *À Rebours*, who spends countless hours reflecting on the disturbing and intoxicating sensuality of Gustave Moreau's famous depictions of the femme fatale:

> Here she was no longer just the dancing girl who extorts a cry of lust and lechery from an old man…. She had become, as it were, the symbolic incarnation of undying Lust, the Goddess of immortal Hysteria, the accursed Beauty exalted above all other beauties.[52]

Such reveries corrupt the mind of Wilde's own decadent antihero, Dorian Gray. The narrator of Dorian's morality tale calls *À Rebours* "a poisonous book" and attests that "one hardly knew at times whether one was reading the spiritual ecstasies of some medieval saint or the morbid confessions of a modern sinner."[53] Like Dorian, Wilde could never free himself from the influence of Huysmans's novel, and it informs his aestheticized vision of Salomé. While the description of Moreau's painting (Figure 3.5) in Huysmans's breviary of decadence matches the almost magically perverse and disturbingly enticing atmosphere of Wilde's *Salomé*, Beardsley's iconic princess in *The Climax* (Figure 3.6) represents something more akin to grotesque parody. Peter Raby argues that the drawings supply their own "visual commentary, which brought out something of the play's dramatic qualities, and at the same time hinted at and suggested other levels of meaning."[54] By subverting Wilde's profane retelling of the death of John the Baptist and highlighting the grotesqueries of the play rather than its cold beauty, Beardsley creates his own "levels of meaning" and reveals himself as a satirist of sin—a decadent Catholic who paradoxically pursues the sacred by immersing himself in the profane.

Moreau and Beardsley present us with radically different versions of the same figure. Moreau's *Apparition* fits the Young Syrian's description of Salomé at the beginning of Wilde's play: "She is like the shadow of a white rose in a mirror of silver."[55] Such sublime language hardly comports with the levitating witch of Beardsley's *The Climax*, with her protruding, twisted facial features and crazed stare. A reviewer for *The Times* described Beardsley's illustrations as "unintelligible for the most part and, so far as they are intelligible, repulsive."[56] The image of Salomé's climax certainly contains an attractive precision of line, but, as Chris Snodgrass insightfully suggests, Beardsley routinely "exposes evil

Figure 3.5 Gustave Moreau, *The Apparition* (*c.* 1876). © RMN-Grand Palais/Art Resource, NY. Image used with permission.

Figure 3.6 Aubrey Beardsley, *The Climax* (1894). © The Victoria and Albert Museum, London. Image used with permission.

while simultaneously trying to seal it in stylized elegance."[57] Such an assertion builds upon Arthur Symons's keen observation that "in those drawings of Beardsley which are grotesque rather than beautiful, in which lines begin to grow deformed, the pattern, in which now all the beauty takes refuge, is itself a moral judgment."[58] The subject of *The Climax* receives just such moral judgment. Salomé's intimate, necrophiliac longing for the medusa-like head of John the Baptist is so powerful that it causes her to float free of the ground, like a fallen angel, and the drawing highlights the intensity of her desire. As Richard Ellmann points out, even the lust of Herod for his stepdaughter pales in comparison to Salomé's desire for the severed head of the prophet.[59] Beardsley's art graphically portrays the horror, and perhaps even the bathos, of this desire by depicting Salomé as aged and ugly, especially when compared with Moreau's alluring young girl. Unlike the heroine of Wilde's text or Moreau's painting, Beardsley's Salome has been robbed of what should be her most defining trait, the very thing that grants her control over Herod, her beauty. To put it another way, Huysmans's hero Des Esseintes would find none of the sublime perfection of Moreau in Beardsley's work. He would find parody instead.

Eliot's work extends the reach of this parody by drawing on Beardsley for one of the most memorable images in "The Love Song of J. Alfred Prufrock," the pathetic speaker's renunciation of prophecy and martyrdom:

> Should I, after tea and cakes and ices,
> Have the strength to force the moment to its crisis?
> But though I have wept and fasted, wept and prayed,
> Though I have seen my head (grown slightly bald) brought in upon a platter,
> I am no prophet—and here's no great matter;
> I have seen the moment of my greatness flicker,
> And I have seen the eternal Footman hold my coat, and snicker,
> And in short, I was afraid. (*CPP* 6)

B. C. Southam attributes the allusion to a severed head to the story of John the Baptist's death in the gospels of Matthew and Mark, and he notes that Salomé plays a leading role in Laforgue's *Moralités légendaires*.[60] Lee Oser expands on this observation: "Besides the traditional motif of decapitation, Eliot seems to have adopted Laforgue's idea of a modernized treatment of the biblical tale."[61] The Laforgue connection makes a great deal of sense, given his explicit, pervasive, well-documented influence on the young poet. But the allusion invites other interpretations as well, as Oser affirms by linking the striking image to the figurative use of John the Baptist in nineteenth-century American national and Puritan rhetoric of evangelization and civilization. In fact, Beardsley's Salomé may resonate more with Laforgue's princess than with Wilde's femme fatale. In *Salome's Modernity* (2011), Petra Dierkes-Thrun captures the poignant contrast between the two literary depictions of Salomé: "Laforgue's 'Salomé' ironizes the princess to the point of utter absurdity. Wilde, by contrast, provides a prolonged dramatic profusion of Salomé's supreme bliss mixed with grief. She remains a strangely attractive figure at the end, putting forth, in this moment of perverse tenderness, an unsettling vision of self-fulfillment and personal triumph."[62] Beardsley's princess exudes some of the "personal triumph" that Dierkes-Thrun sees in Wilde's; however, his depictions of Salomé tend to follow the lead of Laforgue by ironizing their subject "to the point of utter absurdity."

Understandably, Wilde's play remains a popular source text for the image of Prufrock's head upon a platter. James Ledbetter forcefully claims that a "correct reading of Eliot's 'Prufrock' requires that one cite Wilde."[63] Other critics note this connection, albeit without Ledbetter's insistence on correctness,[64] but there is little reason to single out Wilde's text as a primary or exclusive source for the image. The disparities in diction between "Prufrock" and *Salomé* also deserve attention. With the incantatory choric repetitiveness common in Wilde's play, Salomé demands Jokanaan's head, "in a silver charger,"[65] six times in rapid succession. Granted, Eliot may have chosen "platter" for the simple reason that it rhymes with "matter," but such a swerve from a supposed source text might also imply that the poet's inspiration came from an image rather than a written text.[66] Beardsley's *The Dancer's Reward* (Figure 3.7) represents a hitherto unacknowledged extra-biblical source text for the allusion to John the Baptist's severed head in "Prufrock."

By inverting the color dynamics of *The Climax*, Beardsley suggests an essential disconnect between Salomé's dream vision of possessing and kissing the prophet's head and the gory reality of that empty possession. By creating an aura of bloody grotesquerie, he denies Salomé the status of captivating heroine and foregrounds the horror of her desires and actions. Rooted to the ground in this illustration, Salomé assumes an even more horrific appearance. Her hair has the form and color of the scaly clouds in the upper-left-hand corner of *The Climax*. Held up by the long arm of the executioner, the prophet's head in *The Dancer's Reward* oozes gore that matches its now black hair. This illustration haunts Prufrock, who is neither Prince Hamlet nor John the Baptist. For a man whose fear of death—both the little and the big—prevents any meaningful action in life, the phallic black arm and the severed head exist in his mind as dual symbols of his impotence and nonexistence.

After asking if he should find the strength "to force the moment to its crisis," Prufrock claims to have "seen" his balding head "brought in upon a platter." One of Prufrock's famous denials, "I am no prophet—and here's no great matter," follows this confession. His momentary, visionary projection of his own head on

Figure 3.7 Aubrey Beardsley, *The Dancer's Reward* (1894). © The Victoria and Albert Museum, London. Image used with permission.

Beardsley's gory platter seems to represent the pathetic summit of his ambition. This fleeting act of the imagination provides a brief glimpse of "the moment of my greatness," but Prufrock's cowardly self-consciousness cannot entertain the possibility of the gruesome martyrdom depicted in *The Dancer's Reward*. Death, the "eternal Footman," derisively snickers at this hollow man's transitory fantasy of meaningful action, a mockery that leaves Prufrock "afraid." Salomé would dance naked for the head of the prophet, but Prufrock's impotent love song fails to capture the attention of the women in his life, who "come and go / Talking of Michelangelo." Eliot's juxtaposition of an indecisive modern man with Christ's heroic forerunner poignantly satirizes soulless, banal modernity, just as Beardsley's horrific illustration satirizes the perverse beauty and moral nullity of Wilde's *Salomé*. By presenting evil in all its horrible variety, both "Prufrock" and *The Dancer's Reward* insist on the existence of something better. In so doing, they also hint at their creators' belief in, to borrow again from Eliot's essay on Baudelaire, "what really matters ... Sin and Redemption."

Gabrielle McIntire argues that this one allusion to Salomé's victim in "Prufrock" contains a strong suggestion of the poet's developing religious sensibility and "prefigures Eliot's own conversion to Anglo-Catholicism in 1927."[67] We might even, she argues, "think of the secular uncertainty and incessant philosophic questioning that shadows 'Prufrock' as forecasting Eliot's more fervent desire for answers that would culminate in his turn to the Church."[68] Just as Yeats, Symons, and Johnson saw intimations of Beardsley's Catholicism in his *fin-de-siècle* drawings, critics such as McIntire see hints of Eliot's "turn to the Church" in his earliest poetry. In the following section, I will demonstrate that this turn to the Church signals not a definitive turn away from decadence but a continuation and evolution of Eliot's own decadent Catholic sensibility.

[Decadent]-Catholic in Religion

Earlier in this chapter, I referred to Eliot's 1926 lecture on Crashaw, in which he treats the prominent British decadents of the 1890s (Johnson, Dowson, Beardsley, Thompson, Wilde) as part of an essentially religious literary tradition. As I have suggested, this lecture invites us to explore the poet's own place in a genealogy that leads from Crashaw to Wilde and extends into the twentieth century. Most scholars end the discussion of Eliot and decadence with his magnum opus, *The Waste Land*. In fact, several recent articles (my own included) barely venture beyond the manifestations of decadent influence in such early, unpublished poems as "The Love Song of Saint Sebastian," "Spleen," and "The Death of Saint Narcissus."[69] And, with the notable exception of Ronald Schuchard, who argues that Eliot "found his spiritual inheritance primarily in ... Johnson, Dowson, Thompson, and Wilde,"[70] few have suggested a serious relationship between Eliot's post-conversion poetry and the tradition of decadent Catholicism.

Schuchard does not bring his awareness of Eliot's *fin de siècle* spiritual inspiration to bear on *Ash-Wednesday* (1930). He does correctly identify the poem as more than a record of conversion, finding in it "a crucial nexus in Eliot's poetry" that draws on the spiritual paralysis of the early work and anticipates the "meaningful prayer" of *Little Gidding*.[71]

It is a long-standing critical habit to divide Eliot's corpus into pre- and post-conversion. The post-conversion poetry has often been treated as irreconcilable with and inferior to the earlier work. As early as 1942, George Orwell critiqued *Four Quartets* for not living up to the standard set by Eliot's early work: "It is clear that something has departed, some kind of current has been switched off."[72] Drawing a firm dividing line, he claims that "the later verse does not *contain* the earlier, even if it is claimed as an improvement upon it. I think one is justified in explaining this by a deterioration in Mr. Eliot's subject matter."[73] By "deterioration" in "subject matter," Orwell means Christianity. As evidence of Eliot's poetic decadence, his falling away from an earlier and higher standard, Orwell considers the conclusion of *The Dry Salvages*:

> And right action is freedom
> From past and future also.
> For most of us, this is the aim
> Never here to be realized;
> Who are only undefeated
> Because we have gone on trying;
> We, content at the last
> If our temporal reversion nourish
> (Not too far from the yew-tree)
> The life of significant soil. (*CPP* 136–7)

He compares it to a misquoted extract from Eliot's early poem, "Whispers of Immortality":

> Daffodil bulbs instead of balls
> Stared from the sockets of his eyes!
> He knew that thought clings round dead limbs
> Tightening its lusts and luxuries;
>
> He knew the anguish of the marrow,
> The ague of the skeleton;
> No contact possible to flesh
> Allayed the fever of the bone.[74]

While both poems deal with death, Orwell complains that the Christian note of resignation in *The Dry Salvages* is a paltry replacement for the pagan conception of death that characterizes "Whispers of Immortality." He conveniently ignores the fact that Eliot attributes the perspective on death in "Whispers of Immortality" to one of the greatest Christian poets of the English language, John Donne. Eliot's poem actually reads:

> Daffodil bulbs instead of balls
> Stared from the sockets of his eyes!
> He knew that thought clings round dead limbs
> Tightening its lusts and luxuries;
>
> Donne, I suppose, was such another
> Who found no substitute for sense,
> To seize and clutch and penetrate;
> Expert beyond experience,
>
> He knew the anguish of the marrow
> The ague of the skeleton;
> No contact possible to flesh
> Allayed the fever of the bone. (*CPP* 11–12)

The shocking, disorienting, and unacknowledged omission of John Donne and the middle stanza serves Orwell's larger purpose, namely, separating an inspired young pagan Eliot from a defunct old Christian Eliot.[75]

Orwell's justification for preferring the supposedly pagan conception of death in "Whispers of Immortality" to its Christian counterpart in *The Dry Salvages* is that he finds the latter uninspiring and cannot fathom that Eliot might feel differently: "However unsatisfactory [the pagan view of death] may be, if it is intensely felt it is more likely to produce good literature than a religious faith which is not really *felt* at all, but merely accepted against the emotional grain."[76] My point in dredging up Orwell's review is not to pick apart all of its misreadings and contradictions; my point is that Orwell's insistence on separating Eliot's religious and pagan verse is conceptually wrong. Others have adopted Orwell's position. The reasoning behind such arguments tends to be simplistic. It goes something like this: prior to his conversion in 1927 to that bastion of British propriety, the Anglican Church, Eliot was a brilliant luminary of the Modernist avant-garde; afterwards, he became an object of pity if not scorn, a religious poet. Even Untermeyer, whose insightful review comparing Eliot with the British decadents opens this chapter, mistakenly saw Eliot's conversion as a break from his earlier work and a retreat to a comfortable orthodox "haven."

Recent scholarship offers a much-needed corrective by insisting on an essential continuity between the seemingly disparate pre- and post-conversion poems. In *Poetry and Its Others* (2013), Jahan Ramazani concedes that Eliot's more explicit prayer-poems, *Ash-Wednesday* included, fit "neatly into the narrative of his 1927 conversion."[77] Resisting the tidiness of this narrative, Ramazani argues that Eliot's "early poetry often draws on the ritual energies of prayer while immobilizing them in an icy reserve—a distancing that persists ... even in the later, more obviously prayerful poetry."[78]

This suggestion that Eliot's early poetry contains the germ of the later, more overtly religious verse is in sympathy with a 1931 essay on *Ash-Wednesday* by the poet and critic Allen Tate: "The mixed realism and symbolism of *The Waste Land* issued in irony. The direct and lyrical method of the new poems is based upon the similar quality of humility. The latter quality comes directly out of the former, and there is an even continuity in Eliot's work."[79] According to Tate, Eliot's early mix of realism and symbolism finds voice in irony, which Tate later defines as "the arrangement of experience ... which permits to the spectator an insight superior to that of the actor."[80] The humility derived from irony, Tate argues, proceeds from a sense of human folly. It is this essential connection between irony and humility that creates continuity in Eliot's poetry. Such irony is the trademark of Eliot's pre-conversion poetry and a sign of his commonality with that "satirist of vices and follies," Beardsley. By accepting Tate's claim regarding the "continuity" of that irony and the most salient quality of Eliot's later verse, "humility," we might begin to see decadence as a lingering presence in his religious poetry. *Ash-Wednesday*, for example, presents a fuller engagement with the legacy of decadence than many modernist texts because it participates more directly with the religious tradition that defined most of the decadent movement.

Eliot never liked being identified as a "religious poet," a term that he describes in the essay "Religion and Literature" (1935) as generally indicative of "a variety of *minor* poetry" (*SP* 99). After publicly defining himself as "classicist in literature, royalist in politics, and Anglo-Catholic in religion" in 1928, he could hardly live up to his stated ideal by appearing "*unconsciously*" Christian (*SP* 100). In the search for a model for his new role as a Christian poet—one torn by the competing desires of the flesh and the spirit and born into an age of unbelief—Eliot turned to the most recent, and what must have seemed like the last, major religious movement in British literature, the decadent movement.

Long before he sat down to compose the poems that would become *Ash-Wednesday*, Eliot already thought of many of the "nineties" poets as poets of religious faith. In 1917 he delivered twenty-five lectures on Victorian literature at a suburban secondary school, one of which was devoted to "Poets of Religious Faith—Christina Rossetti, Francis Thompson, and Lionel Johnson."[81] The title of the lecture is noteworthy: Eliot refers to Rossetti, Thompson, and Johnson as "Poets of Religious Faith" rather than the more limited "religious poets." For Eliot, these figures are poets first. This subtle distinction indicates that Eliot saw more in the *Yellow Book* generation than the straightforward devotional fervor he identifies in his 1926 Crashaw lecture. He foregrounds his appreciation of the decadents as "Poets of Faith" as opposed to "religious poets" in his verbosely titled 1923 *Vanity Fair* article "A Preface to Modern Literature: Being a Conspectus, Chiefly of English Poetry, Addressed to an Intelligent and Inquiring Foreigner." An intelligent and inquiring foreigner himself, Eliot looks back to the decadents as radical social critics and opponents of insular Victorian culture:

> Here was a group of English people who had succeeded … in acquiring a high degree of emancipation from the worst English vices; which was neither insular, nor puritanical, nor cautious.… Wilde and his circle stood for something much more important than any of the individual members.… In general they represented urbanity, Oxford education, the tradition of good writing, cosmopolitanism.… The greatest merit of this group of people is … a moral quality apparent in the group as a whole: it had a curiosity, an audacity, a recklessness.[82]

Eliot appreciates the decadents, primarily, as iconoclasts, but he also praises a "moral quality" in their rebellion against English insularity. This veiled recognition of the source of their collective artistic power is accompanied by a coded nod to their shared Catholicism. By referring to "Wilde and his circle" as anti-puritanical and Oxford educated (a not uncommon epithet for Catholic sympathizer or Anglo-Catholic ritualist), Eliot subtly links their "audacity" and "curiosity" with religious sympathy. Eliot's writings regarding the British decadents, though few and far between, paint a consistent picture of an artistic movement at once essentially religious and vigorously avant-garde.

Eliot clearly feared becoming a purely "devotional" poet, that is, "not a poet who is treating the whole subject matter of poetry in a religious spirit, but a poet who is dealing with a confined part of this subject matter: who is leaving out what men consider their major passions, and thereby confessing his ignorance of them" (*SP* 99). Johnson, Dowson, and Thompson demonstrated that British, Christian poets might treat all the passions of poetry in a religious spirit. Their work provided a model for *Ash-Wednesday*—a poem as concerned with the passions as it is with pious devotion. Lionel Johnson comes naturally to mind when considering a model for Eliot in his post-conversion guise of "poet of religious faith." He shared many of Eliot's predilections. Aside from being a classicist, Johnson's adoration of Charles I marked him as a royalist. Though, like nearly all his compatriots, Johnson chose the Roman as opposed to Anglo-Catholic faith, his most overtly religious poems reveal a kinship with Eliot. Rather than indulging in purified ecstasy or pious devotion untainted by desire, Johnson's most powerful verses are those in which the speaker is most keenly aware not of goodness and hope but of evil and despair mitigated by only the slightest hint of beneficent providence. In his most anthologized and deeply personal poem "The Dark Angel" (1893), Johnson's speaker is tortured by a demon tempter who simultaneously embodies all of Johnson's vices and goads the sinner into repentance. Rather than confining itself to the comfortable subjects of religious devotion, Johnson's poem explores, in Eliot's phrase, the "major passions" of humanity. It plumbs the depths of the speaker's tortured psyche only to end in a state of tenuous hope and uncertainty.

Since I analyze "The Dark Angel" at length in Chapter 1, we might look here to its sister work, "Satanas" (1893),[83] one of several poems that Johnson, the consummate Oxford-educated classicist, composed in Latin:

> Quanto vitium splenderescit,
> Tanto anima nigrescit;
> Tanto tandem cor marcescit,
>   Per peccata dulcia.
> Gaudens mundi Princeps mali
> Utitur veneno tali,
> Voluptate Avernali;
>   O mellita vitia!
>
> (The more the sin begins to shine,
> The more the soul becomes black;
> The heart slowly begins to wither,
> At the hands of sweet sin.
> The Prince of this evil world rejoicing
> Uses such sorcery
> Such infernal delights;
> O honeyed vices!) (*CP* 123, translation mine)

"Satanas" represents a more contemporary model than the *Inferno* for Eliot's own serious contemplation of evil, sin, and corruption. Sin and vice are all too real for Johnson's speaker and all too attractive. They are the Devil's "veneno," the poisonous sorcery he uses to destroy his victim's soul. The speaker's obsession with damnation and evil recalls Eliot's 1930 essay on Baudelaire, quoted earlier in this chapter, in which he lauds the poet of diabolism for taking damnation seriously and rejecting the vacuous morality of the modern world. Johnson's affinity with Baudelaire is evident throughout his corpus. Ian Fletcher, who devoted a great deal of his substantial scholarly output to Johnson and helped save him from obscurity, was disturbed by the often uncompromising darkness of Johnson's poetic vision. He saw in it distinct affinities with Baudelaire: "Like Baudelaire, Johnson cannot reconcile what is positive in the secular world, material progress, the triumph of reason, optimism, with the realities of the spiritual world—suffering and evil."[84] We know that Eliot read Johnson and other British decadents before encountering Baudelaire. Johnson's demon-plagued writing provided Eliot with his first glimpses of the distinctly decadent Catholic poetic that he would later find in Baudelaire. For a more direct model than "Satanas" or "The Dark Angel" for Eliot's post-conversion prayer-poem, *Ash-Wednesday*, however, we should turn to Johnson's own poem of the same title.

Whether Johnson's "Ash Wednesday" (1893) directly inspired Eliot's poem is, like many questions of direct influence, unanswerable. Eliot knew Johnson's work, and that of the other nineties poets, before going off to college. Pound can be credited with keeping Johnson on Eliot's radar. Aside from writing the Preface to the 1915 edition of *The Poetical Works of Lionel Johnson*, Pound signed a copy of the book for Eliot in 1918. "Ash Wednesday" is just one of the many overtly religious poems in that collection, but its commonalities with Eliot's poem suggest that it may have functioned as a significant model:

Ashen cross across the brow!
Iron cross hid in the breast!
Have power, bring patience, now:
Bid passion be at rest.

O sad, dear, days of Lent!
Now lengthen your gray hours:
If so we may repent,
Before the time of flowers. (*CP* 76)

In the first two stanzas the speaker treats Ash Wednesday, the first of the "sad, dear days of Lent," as an opportunity to pacify his passion, cultivate patience, and find repentance. In these lines the speaker strives toward some reprieve from the dark angel and the influence of Satanas—praying for the grace to set aside desire and prepare his soul for Easter, "the time of flowers." Although Johnson describes the Church as imposing and severe, "Majestical, austere, / The sanctuaries look stern: / All silent! all severe!," he still acknowledges it as the repository of "Eternal Love" and a place of comfort: "Here is the healing place, / And here the place of peace: / Sorrow is sweet with grace / Here, and here sin hath cease" (*CP* 76–7). "Ash Wednesday" embodies Thornton's "decadent dilemma," which, as previously stated, he describes as the essential "failure to bring together the real and the ideal."[85] Decadent Catholic artists repeatedly depict their failure to reconcile their spiritual needs with fleshly desires. This same dilemma lies at the heart of Eliot's modernist prayer-poem.

If *Ash-Wednesday* can be said to have one, primary spiritual master, it is Dante. But Eliot's failed prayer, his imperfect devotional poem, does not tell the story of a soul's progress from a dark wood to the blinding empyrean; even the ecstatic moments are more fleeting and uncertain than Dante's glimpse of God in the *Paradiso*. Viewed liturgically, this disparity makes perfect sense. Dante's journey takes place during the Easter triduum, the three days that begin with the remembrance of Christ's passion on Good Friday and conclude with the celebration of his resurrection. Eliot and Johnson anticipate Easter but from the other side of the forty days of Lenten penance, of which Ash Wednesday is the first. The speaker of Eliot's *Ash-Wednesday*, like Johnson's, is reflecting on the day when Catholics (Roman and Anglo alike) are reminded of their mortality and compelled to contemplate and reject the destructive passions that make their time on Earth a testing ground for the spirit. The essence of the holy day is captured in the ritual of marking the faithful with ashes in the sign of the cross, when the priest says a version of either "Remember that you are dust and to dust you shall return" or "Repent, and believe in The Gospel." The ritual is a memento mori intended to drive believers into the confessional. Johnson reflects this call to the confessional in his "Ash Wednesday" when he prays for a cessation of passion so that he might find true repentance. Eliot's much longer prayer-poem asks essentially for the same things.

In the popular imagination, Eliot is so rarely associated with physical passion that many are unprepared to see a struggle with sexual desire at the heart of his poems, especially his "religious" poems. The attempt to reconcile spiritual needs and physical desires plays out in a less obvious fashion in Eliot's poetry than it does in such decadent Catholic poems as Johnson's "Dark Angel" and Dowson's "Nuns of the Perpetual Adoration." But this struggle is present throughout *Ash-Wednesday*. In section IV, for example, Eliot's speaker depicts a seemingly innocent scene in which he and a saintly female figure walk through a garden full of violets; but this scene, however peaceful, is haunted by echoes of the sexual transgressions that mark his early poetry.

> Who walked between the violet and the violet
> Who walked between
> The various ranks of varied green
> Going in white and blue, in Mary's colour,
> Talking of trivial things
> In ignorance and in knowledge of eternal dolour
> Who moved among the others as they walked,
> Who then made strong the fountains and made fresh the springs
>
> Made cool the dry rock and made firm the sand
> In blue of larkspur, blue of Mary's colour,
> Sovegna vos. (*CPP* 64)

Here Eliot returns to a recurring sight of sexual transgression from his earlier poetry and uses it as the setting for a vision of a Marian figure. Like the speaker of "Dans le Restaurant" who meets his young lover under a willow tree and the consciousness in *The Waste Land* that recalls a failed rendezvous with the hyacinth girl, the speaker of *Ash-Wednesday* walks with an unidentified female figure through a garden. Unlike the earlier scenes of sexual tension in Eliot's poetry, however, the walk among the violets in *Ash-Wednesday* is chaste and peaceful. The old transgressions have undergone a sea change, but their echoes still linger. In the walk "between the violet and the violet," for example, we hear traces of the "violet hour"—the hour of assignation for "the young man carbuncular" and the typist—in the third movement of *The Waste Land*. The female figure in *Ash-Wednesday* is an undefiled reincarnation of the typist. Rather than stockings, slippers, camisoles, and stays, she wears "Mary's colour," thus representing the antithesis of most of the women in Eliot's early poetry. Rather than tempting the poet to sin or reminding him of corruption, she inspires veneration, which the speaker voices in section II in the guise of a Marian litany:

> Lady of silences
> Calm and distressed
> Torn and most whole

Rose of memory
Rose of forgetfulness
Exhausted and life-giving
Worried reposeful. (*CPP* 62)

Again, those looking for poetic precedent for such a litany might be tempted to turn to Dante or some other medieval figure. The decadents provide a more contemporary reference point for this type of liturgical imitation in lyric poetry.

In his "A Descant upon the Litany of Loretto," Johnson invokes the many names of Mary to stave off the shadow of fear and evil that Eliot embodies in his famously enigmatic "three white leopards"—the phantoms that cause him to invoke his holy lady.

> Ah, Mother! whom with many names we name,
> By lore of love, which in our earthly tongue
> Is all too poor, though rich love's heart of flame,
> To sing thee as thou art, nor leave unsung
> The greatest of the graces thou hast won,
>   Thy chiefest excellence!
> Ivory Tower! Star of the Morning! Rose
> Mystical! Tower of David, our Defense!
>   To thee our music flows,
> Who makest music for us to thy Son.
>   So, when the shadows come,
> Laden with all contrivances of fear!
>   Ah, Mary! lead us home.... (*CP* 109–10)

Johnson's litany employs the traditional names of Mary—"Ivory Tower" "Star of the Morning"—and addresses her directly. The litany in *Ash-Wednesday* is inconsistent with any formal Catholic prayer, which is appropriate since the speaker is addressing a Marian devotee and not the Virgin herself. Nevertheless, both poets are compelled "by lore of love," as Johnson says. The praise of human song is "all too poor," but the singer is bound by his love of the Virgin to make a raid on the inarticulate using what shabby tools he has at his disposal. Eliot weaves the traditional act of naming Mary into his own desperate prayer-poem.

In spite of all this veneration, Eliot's "Lady" is not Mary. She is an untouchable ideal, yes, but also an intimate friend with whom to pass the time in small talk. She and the speaker talk "of trivial things / In ignorance and knowledge of eternal dolour," but a voice from the past intrudes in the midst of their walk. The intrusive murmur "Sovegna vos" alludes to Arnaut Daniel's valedictory

"Sovegna vos a temps de ma dolor" ("be mindful in due time of my pain"), from Dante's *Purgatorio*. Daniel, Dante's troubadour master, suffers among the purifying flames that consume the lustful near the summit of Mount Purgatory, and he admonishes the poet-traveler to remember the price of lust. But the next line from Dante, a line absent from *Ash-Wednesday* but present in the final stanza of *The Waste Land*, qualifies Daniel's warning with a reminder of his guaranteed purification and salvation—"poi s'ascose nel foco che gli affina" ("Then dived he back into the fire which refines them"). Eliot's speaker has no sacred, purifying fire except for guilt and the painful desire not to return to the scene of his past lusts—the willow bower, the hyacinth garden. Like Johnson in "Ash Wednesday," he conveys a longing that old passions might "be at rest" so that he might repent "before the time of flowers." Dante's epic journey takes place over the course of the few days leading to Easter, "the time of flowers." By contrast, Eliot and Johnson walk the road into the desert that Christ inhabited for His forty days of fasting and prayer. Central to this preparation is the act of confession and repentance that Johnson captures masterfully in "The Dark Angel."[86] *Ash-Wednesday* is likewise concerned with the confession of past sins as a means of overcoming passion, however fleeting the victory. Its concluding plea to Mary, "Suffer me not to be separated / And let my cry come unto Thee," expresses the same aspirational and imperfect victory over sin that occurs so often in Johnson's poetry and decadent Catholic poetry in general.

Of course, Eliot's poetry of religious faith is not simply imitative. As Hanson points out in *Decadence and Catholicism*, Eliot's brand of "modernist Christianity … may be seen paradoxically as both a rejection and an elaboration of the work of the aesthetes and decadents of the fin de siècle."[87] Grasping the ways in which Eliot participates in the tradition of decadent Catholicism as both satirist, in the manner of Beardsley, and poet of religious faith, in the tradition of Johnson, is an important first step in understanding the multiple ways in which he elaborated on decadent Catholicism in the age of modernism.

George Moore and James Joyce: Decadent Anti-Catholicism and Irish Modernism

For decadent artists such as Wilde, Dowson, Johnson, and Beardsley, who were born into an insular and respectable Anglicanism, Catholicism provided a source of new artistic color and spiritual quickening. For the novelists George Moore (1852–1933) and James Joyce (1882–1941), who were born into the notoriously Jansenistic Irish Catholic tradition, the Church became a primary source of personal and national intellectual paralysis. So stultifying was its influence that a young Moore, the son of well-to-do landed family in County Mayo, felt compelled to flee to France as soon as he came into his majority in 1873. There, he studied art and sought out the company of Impressionists such as Manet and Renoir as well as such members of the literary elite as Zola and Mallarmé. Eventually he made a considerable name for himself as the author of Zolaesque naturalist novels such as *Esther Waters* (1894), his most enduring novel, but Moore began his literary career as a rebellious and virulently anti-Catholic decadent poet and novelist. He created quasi-autobiographical protagonists who were drawn to the cosmopolitan aesthetics of continental decadence but opposed to the religion that helped define the literary movement in both France and England. In this endeavor, Moore was a forerunner of both Joyce and the decadents of the 1890s, a role he relished playing. Naughty before the nineties, he published two decadent bildungsromane before Wilde produced *Dorian Gray*. Though inspired by Baudelaire and Huysmans, French decadents with strong Catholic proclivities, Moore developed his own decadent anti-Catholic style.

Near the turn of the century, Joyce found himself in the role of reluctant pupil and enthusiastic critic of Moore, who was his precursor in several ways. Like Moore, he fled Ireland for the Continent in search of inspiration; also like Moore, he found in decadence a means of articulating his combative relationship with Irish Catholicism. But Joyce was no mere imitator. His replication of Moore's fugitive aesthetic was balanced by a satirical genius. This complicated literary relationship contributed significantly to the creation of one of the central characters of high modernism, Stephen Dedalus—the decadent, anti-Catholic protagonist of *A Portrait of the Artist as a Young Man* and parts of *Ulysses*.

Decadence and Cosmopolitanism

The late Victorian period was a watershed moment in the history of British cosmopolitanism, one of the profounder and more contentious legacies of modernity. Nearly all recent treatments of this subject accept a priori that nationalism and imperialism were troubling key components of nineteenth-century cosmopolitanism;[1] we can, however, resist the urge to throw out the baby with the bathwater by denouncing cosmopolitan desires as unredeemable extensions of imperialist mechanisms.[2] Decadent authors in particular deserve positive attention, in part because they sought to escape the nationalist insularity of English culture.

For English and Anglo-Irish artists of the nineties generation, decadence and Catholicism were essential to the development of cosmopolitan identity. Together they facilitated the cultivation of aesthetic, political, and spiritual distance from dominant Victorian culture. As we saw in the previous chapter, T. S. Eliot's praise of "Wilde and his circle" had much to do with their emancipation from insular Englishness. Eliot recognized the essentially cosmopolitan nature of British decadence and associated it with the group's laudable "recklessness." That this cosmopolitan drive never carried the decadents much further than France should come as no surprise. Both decadence and Catholicism were inextricably linked with France in the imaginations of such artists as Wilde, Johnson, and Dowson. *Salomé*, Wilde's decadent Catholic masterpiece written in French, embodies the distance from "Victorian propriety" that its author cultivated. Likewise, Johnson's "Our Lady of France," examined in Chapter 1, evinces its author's belief that he and Dowson had achieved a semi-alien status by embracing the religious and artistic forms of another country. This attempt by decadent authors to distance themselves from mainstream British culture, which seems less than revolutionary when taken by itself, played an important role in the development of modernism.[3]

For George Moore, whose experiments in decadent literature pre-date Wilde's, and for Joyce, whose earliest attempts at poetry are inflected by the *mal du siècle*,[4] Catholicism promised none of the cosmopolitan inspiration that it offered to English and Anglo-Irish decadents such as Johnson and

Wilde. Rather than offering an aesthetic, possibly exotic, and productively archaic means of opposing the rise of mass culture, Irish Catholicism *was* mass culture. The Church was the nation; the insular Irish vice; the disease, not the cure. Joyce and Moore's anti-Catholicism is central to their writings. Not surprisingly, Joyce's crusade against Rome owed a great deal to Moore.[5] Among the members of the Irish literary revival, Moore was the most vocally anti-clerical. His opposition to what he called the "Roman" church appears most notably in *The Untilled Field* (1903), a collection of short stories about rural Ireland that emphasize the moralistic despotism of local priests. As a whole, the collection focuses on the spiritual and intellectual stagnancy of Irish culture in a way that anticipates the central trope of paralysis behind *Dubliners*. Despite their shared indictment of Irish Catholicism, the two writers were notoriously antipathetic. Incapable of appreciating what he saw as Joyce's appropriation of his own aesthetic, Moore accused the younger man of inferior imitation. Likewise, Joyce repeatedly berated Moore's *The Untilled Field*.[6] The critical consensus over the past century has confirmed Joyce's superior artistic status—a fact much lamented by some scholars who champion the older novelist—but, as we will see, the decadent anti-Catholicism with which Joyce plays in *Portrait* is part of an intertextual dialogue with Moore's early poetry and novels.[7]

Stephen Dedalus has long been acknowledged as a counterpart to Edward Dayne, the protagonist of Moore's partially autobiographical novel, *Confessions of a Young Man*.[8] *Confessions* follows Dayne's flight from Ireland to Paris, where he fails as a painter and decadent poet but eventually discovers his vocation as a novelist. The Moore/Joyce relationship bridges *fin-de-siècle* and modernist literature. Although the biographer Adrian Frazier argues for Moore as a modernist in his own right, he elsewhere points out that by 1922, the annus mirabilis that witnessed the publication of both *Ulysses* and *The Waste Land*, Moore saw the "blossoming of Modernism" as "no more than the decay of forms."[9] The elder novelist received little enough respect from the younger generation of artists. When Eliot learned that the *Dial* had paid Moore £100 for a short story, almost three times the amount they offered for *The Waste Land*, he complained to Pound that it was about time publishers learned to "recognize Merit instead of Senility."[10] While Moore's writings certainly contain some of the stylistic attributes of modernism, Joyce's novels embody and define the period in a manner that distinguishes him from the older author's late Victorian naturalism. Far more than issues of style or form, decadent anti-Catholicism represents an essential component of the Moore/Joyce relationship.

Both authors depict would-be artists who must either escape the nets of "priest-ridden Ireland" in favor of cosmopolitan decadence or else submit to the stultifying provincialism of the Church.[11] Where Moore takes the position of the educated man of the world looking down with disdain on his homeland, however, Joyce's Catholic nostalgia and appreciation for "dear dirty Dublin" allow him to become both distanced critical observer and sympathetic countryman. As we will see, Moore's decadent anti-Catholics in exile, Edward Dayne and Mike Fletcher, look back at Ireland with contempt, and *The Untilled Field* is a catalog of Irish backwardness relieved only occasionally by softening irony or humor. A close reading of these texts reveals the imperialist strain that sometimes inflects the cosmopolitan impulse. After reconsidering Moore's early, decadent texts, it becomes easier to notice how Joyce both participated in and critiqued his predecessor's project. Stephen Dedalus, Joyce's broken doppelgänger, contributes to the indictment of Ireland and its Church by proclaiming his own decadent art in opposition to the Jansenist religion of his youth; but his critique is tempered by Joyce's self-parody and appreciation for the quotidian, humorous, human aspects of Irish culture.

Moore's Rebellion

By 1929, when Joyce and Moore met for the first time, both authors were established enough and had enough false modesty to grant each other the title of first man of European letters. Aside from insisting on the other's preeminence, the two spoke of their shared love of Paris and their common friends, and, according to Moore, they agreed that their careers "were not altogether dissimilar."[12] Moore commented on this similarity during one of their conversations; he also took the opportunity to bring up Joyce's penury in a backhanded compliment: "I have been only a revolutionary, while you have been a *heroic* revolutionary, for *you* had no money."[13] Joyce, always keenly aware of the difference in their financial situations, had taken a dig at Moore in his satirical broadside "Gas from a Burner" (1912), in which he refers to the play *The Apostle*: "Written by Moore, a genuine gent / that lives on his property's ten per cent." The line represents Joyce's resentment of Moore's landed pedigree. In what looks like a subtle riposte to the backhanded compliment about penniless revolutionaries, Joyce then offered to send Moore a French edition of *Ulysses*. The French edition seems like a comment on Moore's notorious early posturing as a cosmopolitan sophisticate living in Paris and refined to the point of forgetting his native language. Sensing a possible insult in the gift, the elder novelist felt compelled to remind his reluctant protégé that he could also "read English."[14] This passive-aggressive exchange may reveal more about the authors' personalities than their art, but it also suggests the extent to which Moore's early pose as a Parisian dandy defined him well into his career.

After fleeing Ireland to study painting in Paris, Moore entered the orbit of some of the greatest artistic minds of his time. He became acquainted with Degas, Monet, Renoir, and Manet. Much to Moore's delight, Manet (according to Moore) insisted on painting him because of his agreeable complexion and blond hair (Figure 4.1).[15] Moore later used the portrait as the frontispiece for his

Figure 4.1 Édouard Manet, *George Moore* (1873–79). © Metropolitan Museum of Art/Art Resource, NY. Image used with permission.

largely anecdotal, critical work *Modern Painting* (1893). The portrait presents a young aesthete with the disheveled hair of a bohemian. An unsympathetic contemporary critic, less taken with the subject's pasty complexion than Moore was, referred to the work as "Le Noyé repêché" (the drowned man fished out of the water).[16] Moore's limited talent as a painter was even more unfortunate than his appearance; the skill of his new Parisian circle never rubbed off. Abandoning painting in the late 1870s, he next tried his hand at imitating Baudelaire in English. Like Joyce, he began his literary career as an unsuccessful decadent poet. His first volume of poetry, *Flowers of Passion* (1877), elicited a mixture of censorious disgust and patronizing disdain, as seen in this anonymous review from *The Examiner*:

> "Flowers of Passion" is a feeble imitation of all that is silly and vicious in contemporary verse. There is scarcely an eccentricity or defect in the poetry of the day that is not copied in these poems.... Like some of the poets whom the author of "Flowers of Passion" parodies, he tries his best to create a startling effect by the use of the disagreeable and the disgusting; unlike them, he only succeeds in being ridiculous.[17]

His next collection, *Pagan Poems* (1881), garnered a similar response. Ashamed and frustrated by this second false start, Moore suppressed the two books, reportedly going so far as to demand that his publisher destroy all copies of *Pagan Poems*.[18] Consequently, both collections are hard to come by. The back-cover page of the copy I examined in the archives of the Harry Ransom Center bears this neat handwritten assessment: "The rare first edition."

Flowers of Passion is an excellent example of the decadent book as art object: the gilt cover design (Figure 4.2) depicts the poet's skull, crowned with laurels and supported by a lyre overgrown with ivy. Though it hardly compares in originality or delicacy, the cover art anticipates the work of Althea Gyles, who decorated the early volumes of Dowson and Yeats.

Not surprisingly, given their unpopularity and scarcity, *Flowers of Passion* and *Pagan Poems* have received little critical attention. Frazier brushes them aside as "confections of morbid, exotic, French decadence."[19] In the most recent of the two extant articles on the subject, Mark Llewellyn concludes with a dismissive evaluation of their merit: "Moore is not a great poet or even necessarily a good poet, but he is interesting nevertheless."[20] The fifty-seven poems in these two volumes are more than mediocre compositions by a man who would go on to write good novels; they are part of what makes Moore interesting. To understand the decadent anti-Catholic protagonists of his more successful early novels, we

Figure 4.2 George Moore, *Flowers of Passion* (1878). Used with the permission of the Harry Ransom Center, The University of Texas at Austin.

must return to the author's early attempts to shake off his provincial Irish identity and adopt the style of French decadence.

Catholicism was as important to the early French decadents as it was to their Anglophone inheritors in the nineties. Thus, Moore had the difficult task of squaring his imitations of Baudelaire, Gautier, and others with his own abhorrence of Rome. The title of *Pagan Poems* underscores his position on Christianity, but in *Flowers of Passion* Moore expresses his anti-Catholicism in more subtle ways. For the most part, the speakers of *Flowers of Passion* avoid direct allusion to the Church, with its rich storehouse of mystical and erotic symbolism, and concern themselves with looking back on old passions and contemplating death. In "The Corpse," for example, the speaker describes the decaying body of his beloved: "Wondering I gaze upon each lineament / Defaced by worms and swollen with decay, / And watch the rat-gnawed golden ringlets play / Around the sunken outline, shriveled, bent / In hideous grimace."[21] This poem participates in a long tradition of heart-broken men eroticizing female cadavers. It bucks the trend by dwelling on the hideous realities of bodily decay and refusing to mitigate perverse desire. Unlike the pristine bones of the chaste lovers in Donne's "The Relic," which are taken from the ground and presented to the local bishop as holy objects, this corpse is not miraculous or sacred. Unburied, it lacks even the final ritual sacraments that Baudelaire grants to his beloved in "Une Charogne." Moore's corpse is "defaced by worms," "swollen with decay," and "rat-gnawed," but the gruesomeness of decomposition doesn't prevent the speaker from picking up the body for a parting kiss. The poem's concern with remembered passion and the sexual fascination with decay is representative of the volume as a whole. Fittingly, the beloved's skull, with its hideous grimace, mirrors the memento mori on the cover of *Flowers of Passion*.

For a man as sexually predictable as Moore (necrophilia certainly would have earned a passing mention in Frazier's detailed biography), *Flowers of Passion* is surprisingly preoccupied with erotic perversity. Moore's fascination with traditionally aberrant forms of sexuality seems less tied to his own appetites than to one of the most consistent themes of his later prose—the desire to liberate himself from Christian morality. Aside from writing about desirable corpses, he also indulges in a voyeuristic lesbian fantasy. His poem "Hendecasyllables" plays with the idea of Sapphic love in the relatively difficult eleven-syllable falling meter of Catullus. Tennyson once used the same form in his much tamer "Hendecasyllabics" (1864), a masterful send-up of reviewers: "O you chorus of indolent reviewers, / Irresponsible, indolent reviewers, / Look, I come to the test, a tiny poem / All composed in a metre of Catullus."[22] The reviewers are supposedly too indolent to notice the use of a difficult meter without being told, but once informed, the speaker maintains, they should recognize the poet's skill. Moore's attempt to impress his reviewers is less witty and less adept than Tennyson's:

Here we wandering through the gardens moon-lit,
And faint bowers of odour laden roses,
Sing songs womanly speaking sweetest passion,
Such as Lesbians, over-smitten lyres
Kissing sister-ward leaning o'er the chosen,

Sung to feverish under-tunes in list'ning
To the fluctuant breathing of the ocean. (*FP* 108)

The poem is rather painful to read, with its lines straining to meet the demands of the meter with odd syntax ("Sing songs womanly") and the poet employing such awkward diction as "sister-ward." Nevertheless, Moore is characteristically daring in his deconstruction of sexual norms. Abjuring his role as seducer, the male speaker adopts a position of radical sexual equality with his female beloved. By reimagining their moon-lit professions of love as songs sung by lesbian lovers, he casts himself as a smitten damsel. This imaginative gender subversion is not only a poorly crafted imitation of Baudelaire's lesbian poems; it is an attack on the foundational sexual ethics of Moore's homeland; it is decadence wielded against Catholicism.

For all its daring, *Flowers of Passion* is largely unoriginal in its content, except when Moore indulges in subversion of the religion he openly denounces in later works. In the first stanza of the opening poem, "Dedication: To L—," the poet promises to fashion his verses into a replacement for the central sacramental of Marian devotion, the rosary:

Lean meward, O beloved! let me crown
Thy brows with chaplet. Votive wreath I twine
Of symbol flowers, and therein weave for sign,
From graft of passion, roses that have grown
Bitter as frothing of blood; yet cast not down
As worthless weeds, but set upon Love's shrine
In vase full filled with memories of mine,
These bloomless blossoms of a time long flown. (*FP* 1)

Here the speaker proposes to crown his beloved with a wreath made up of the bitter roses of his former passions—presumably the poems contained in *Flowers of Passion*—and urges her not to cast it away. But by referring to this "votive wreath" as a "chaplet," he plays on the word's secondary meaning, rosary,[23] and thereby proposes his collection of poems as an alternative to traditional prayer—a pagan rosary to be recited as a votive offering to the god of "Love." The "bloomless blossoms" on the wreath, presumably closed because of a lack of light, resemble beads more than flowers. (They also suggest "Roses of Midnight," the title of a book of verse composed by Edward Dayne, one of Moore's later fictional personae.) This symbolic substitution of poetry for prayer signals Moore's rejection of Marian devotion in favor of art and earthly passion. He elaborates on this rejection in the next stanza of the poem:

Fair fledglings of heart-hidden memories,
Pale passion flowers I bring to thee, my sweet,
As Mary brought her offerings of white doves;
No greater gifts have I to give than these
Of seeds we sowed. I lay them at thy feet;
For they are thine, and being thine are Love's. (*FP* 2)

Here the roses of midnight, the poems still to come, are directly compared to the doves that Mary brought to the temple as part of the ritual presentation of the infant Jesus to his heavenly father (Luke 2:24). In an act of gender-defying blasphemy, the poet metaphorically equates himself with Mary, usurping her status as *Theotokos* (Mother of God). Whereas Baudelaire typically portrays the Virgin Mary as a symbol of perfection against which his speakers might measure their lusts, Moore attempts to undermine Mary's perfection and moral authority by supplanting her and substituting his poetry for her sacrificial offering. With a final blasphemous twist of the poetic knife, the speaker transforms his beloved into "Love" itself, granting her the status of both heavenly Father and incarnate Son. Lacking sympathy with a Baudelairean Satanism that, as Eliot would later argue, paradoxically affirms the reality of a Christian God, Moore resorted to a second-rate blasphemy that seeks to jettison God altogether and supplant the divine passion with its human counterpart.[24]

Moore's foray into decadent anti-Catholicism may have started with *Flowers of Passion*, but with the publication of his early exercise in semiautobiographical mythmaking, *Confessions of a Young Man* (1886 in French, 1888 in English), he began in earnest to construct his dandified, cosmopolitan, decadent fictional self. This loosely autobiographical novel, referred to by George Schoolfield as Moore's "fling at Huysmanian decadence,"[25] follows Edward Dayne, the son of a landed Catholic family, who claims to have entered the world "with a nature like a smooth sheet of wax, bearing no impress, but capable of receiving any" (*CYM* 49). Equally suited, as he tells us, to the role of Pharaoh, pimp, and archbishop, Dayne finds himself drawn by chance to art and moves to 1870s Paris to pursue his calling by embracing a decadent lifestyle.[26] Aside from worshiping Swinburne and Rossetti and composing imitations of Baudelaire's work in a collection entitled, shockingly, "Roses of Midnight," Dayne enjoys such strange pastimes as tying live mice to Louis XV furniture and watching his python, Jack, devour them. Munira Mutran compares Dayne's immersion in the decadent Parisian lifestyle to the experience of Walter Pater's Marius in Rome: "Following his arrival, he savors the decadent life of the end of the century, end of an age, and end of an Empire."[27] Unlike Marius and the British decadents of the 1890s, however, Dayne despises Catholicism and feels no sympathy for the "eunuch-like, dirty, and Oriental" religion (*CYM* 109). His aversion to Rome complements his aversion to Ireland. In spite of his claim to be free of "original qualities, defects, tastes," Dayne identifies two "dominant notes" in his otherwise mercurial character: "an original hatred of my native country, and a brutal loathing of the religion I was brought up in" (*CYM* 109). His sentiments reflect the open disdain for all things Irish that defines Moore's earlier semiautobiographical book, *Parnell and His Island* (1887). Originally written in French for a French audience and later adapted for English readers, this vitriolic travel narrative presents an extended examination of all the defects of the Irish populace, from the exploitative landlords and priests to the subhuman peasants. Moore's contempt for his homeland anticipates the pernicious side of the cosmopolitanism that emerges in his *Confessions*. Caught up in the attempt to emancipate himself, the narrator of *Confessions* embraces an anti-Catholic and anti-Irish rhetoric reminiscent of that employed by the English imperialists then ruling Ireland. The language used to describe his "native" faith, "eunuch-like, dirty, and Oriental," also suggests an orientalist perspective in which Irish Catholicism and Eastern religion are both treated as unmanly, alien, and, even worse, unhygienic.

In the 1904 "Preface" to an English edition of *Confessions*, Moore charges that Catholicism "robs a man of the right of free will" and "takes the edge off the intellect" (*CYM* 39). He further asserts that "since the Reformation no born Catholic has written a book of literary value," a good example of the kind of stupid generalizations that earned the ire of G. K. Chesterton, who devoted an entire chapter of *Heretics* (1905) to Moore. *Confessions*, a key text in the literary history of decadence, expresses an open hostility to Catholicism that seems to contradict Ellis Hanson's claim that all the great decadent texts are stories of conversion (though apostasy might function paradoxically as a form of conversion from belief to disbelief).[28] Moore's early novels demonstrate that the relationship between decadence and Catholicism is not exclusively positive or generative. Dayne makes his opposition to Catholicism clear in both his prose and his poetry, of which we get a small sample. His poem "Nostalgia," for example, looks back to "the dreamful days of old" when shepherds wooed maidens on languorous summer afternoons and men were not "haunted and terrified by creeds." In Dayne's poem, Moore makes overt his nostalgia for a pagan past and disgust with the influence of Catholicism:

The future may be wrong or right,
The present is distinctly wrong,
For life and love have lost delight,
And bitter even is our song;
And year by year grey doubt grows strong,
And death is all that seems to dree.
Wherefore with weary hearts we long
For the old days of Arcady. (*CYM* 132)

The speaker suggests that although the future may yet be "right," the present remains bitter and loveless. The stanza calls to mind the opening of Yeats's "The Song of the Happy Shepherd,"[29] in which "Grey Truth" is the empty sustenance of a bleak present: "The woods of Arcady are dead, / And over is their antique joy; / Of old the world on dreaming fed; / Grey Truth is now her painted toy" (*WBY* 74). Moore appears to have read Yeats for the first time in 1894 when, in preparation for their first meeting at the Cheshire Cheese, he browsed a copy of *The Countess Kathleen and Various Legends and Lyrics* and was much impressed.[30] The collection did not include "The Song of the Happy Shepherd." If it had, Moore might have sensed a kindred spirit or even suspected a bit of theft. Then again, both poets might have borrowed from Wilde's villanelle "Pan" (1880):

O Goat-foot God of Arcady!
    Cyllene's shrine is grey and old;
This northern isle hath need of thee!

No more the shepherd lads in glee
    Throw apples at thy wattled fold,
O Goat-foot God of Arcady![31]

If there is evidence of poetic theft, at least each successive Arcadian poem improves upon its predecessor. "Goat-foot God of Arcady" becomes more painful with each refrain. All three poems affirm that for art to flourish the modern world must return, at least in spirit, to a pre-Christian spring of inspiration. Moore's decadent novels that follow *Confessions of a Young Man* reaffirm his belief in the rupture between art and Catholicism.

Nowhere is this dichotomy more pronounced than in Moore's novel *Mike Fletcher* (1889). After focusing on the condition of women in *A Mummer's Wife* (1885) and *A Drama in Muslin* (1886), Moore wrote his "Don Juan" trilogy about a group of young men who capture the essence of their age. *Mike Fletcher* is the final novel in the trilogy. Published a year before *The Picture of Dorian Gray* (1890), *Mike Fletcher* was also clearly inspired by Huysmans's "breviary of the decadence,"[32] *À Rebours*, and it anticipates many of the concerns of Wilde's own "poisonous book." In spite of its provocative nature and captivating prose style, *Mike Fletcher* has received less serious attention than it merits, given the undeniably important role it plays in the history of decadent literature in English. The novel follows Fletcher, a young Irish dandy, as he obsesses over a beautiful novice nun, contributes decadent poetry to a literary periodical, gains a fortune by seducing a rich old dowager, and eventually renounces everything by committing suicide. Though Fletcher is the primary focus of the novel, its opening chapter largely concerns another character who experiences the tension between art and religion. John Norton, Fletcher's friend and confidant, shares his poetic vocation and attraction to the pessimism of Schopenhauer, which they appreciate somewhat simplistically for its rejection of the "will to live" and disdain for human procreation. This interest in Schopenhauer marks both characters as modern and decadent. In his preface to *The Case of Wagner* (1888), Nietzsche relates his attempts to transcend the decadence of the modern age and identifies Schopenhauer as the philosopher of decadence.[33] Schopenhauer's apocalyptic negation of the fundamental desirability of life made his philosophy a natural complement to the terminal myths and decadent sense of entropic time best captured in the companion phrases *fin de siècle* and *fin du globe*. Nietzsche repeatedly links Schopenhauerian pessimism not only to modern decadence but also to what he sees as the life-denying nihilism of Christianity.[34] Moore, who had no direct knowledge of Nietzsche's work in the late 1880s, almost seems to imitate it by making Schopenhauer the muse of both the decadent Fletcher and the pious Norton. For Fletcher, rejection of the will to live means freedom from the restrictions of morality. For Norton, a fervent Catholic, Schopenhauer's pessimism becomes part of his own eschatological understanding of what he sees as Christ's rejection of life. Both men are steeped in the philosophy of decadence, but it leads them down the divergent paths of hedonism and asceticism.

Fletcher is Des Esseintes without the Catholic nostalgia born of a Jesuit upbringing; Norton is a would-be decadent with a hypertrophied religious sense. A lay celibate whose "aphorism 'Let the world be my monastery'" reflects an ascetic attempt to be in the world but not of it, Norton appears several times in Moore's early fiction. It is generally accepted that Moore modeled this fascinating character on his distant cousin and sometime collaborator Edward Martyn (1859–1923).[35] Martyn, the last inheritor of Tulira (an estate in County Galway not far from Coole Park), bankrolled the Irish Literary Theatre and collaborated with Moore, Yeats, and Lady Gregory. Throughout all of this literary activity, he lived a celibate life marked by devotion to both Catholicism and art. Moore's depiction of Martyn as the repressed Norton shows that he saw such dual loyalty to Christ and the muses as irreconcilable. As if to demonstrate the inescapable sympathy between decadence and Catholicism, however, Moore depicts Fletcher and Norton as kindred souls. Early in the novel, the melancholic Catholic and wanton sybarite are "thinking and writing the same thoughts" (*MF* 6). We never see any of Norton's poetry, but we do learn that it shares in the same Schopenhauerian pessimism and disgust with human reproduction that informs Fletcher's poetry and eventual suicide. Their ideas are mutually sympathetic; their beliefs are wildly at odds. Norton's poems contain all he considers best in the world, but his art is at odds with his faith. Though he shares Fletcher's desire that "the unspeakable spectacle of life might cease forever," Norton lives in awe of the Church and concludes that it is "far better that [his poems] should burn and he should save his soul from burning" (*MF* 7). Driven by a vision of a "medieval hell full of black devils and ovens" that seems to anticipate Fletcher's momentary glimpse of hell before his suicide (as well as Stephen Dedalus's traumatic vision of eternal torture), Norton seeks the counsel of a priest. The dim-witted old confessor, full of platitudes about the consequences of sin and the sacrifice of Christ, is completely ignorant of any thinker but Newman, and Norton can only bend his head "before the sublime stupidity of the priest" (*MF* 10). Rather than submitting his poems for review and approval by the clergy, he decides to burn them.

Moore opens his novel with this literary holocaust, a figurative artistic suicide,[36] in order to reiterate his deeply held conviction that no true artist can flourish under the yoke of Catholicism. Although Fletcher's decadent lifestyle and philosophic convictions eventually lead him to suicide, his life and art are free from the controlling influence of religious dogma and scruples. Compared with that of Norton, who sacrifices his intellectual and artistic ideals out of a belief in damnation, Fletcher's fate is admirable. His combination of pessimism and hedonism allows him to live up to the decadent ideal established in Pater's "Conclusion" to the *Renaissance* by indulging in sensual and spiritual experimentation. In comparison, Norton's decision to destroy his poems illustrates Moore's assertion in *Confessions* that Catholicism "robs a man of the right of free will" (*CYM* 39). No vision of the relationship between Catholicism and art could be more different from those of Johnson, Dowson, Beardsley, and Wilde. The institution that drew in the decadents of the nineties with promises of new substance and color for their art promised Moore only intellectual stagnation.

Mike Fletcher is, perhaps, best understood as Moore's fantasy alter ego—a self-made man who sacrifices everything for his art. The son of an Irish peasant and a French maid, Moore's decadent antihero lacks the breeding of Des Esseintes and Dorian Gray. Fletcher looks back on his adolescence in Ireland with a distaste that reflects Moore's own sentiments: "I could not endure the place. Every day was so appallingly like the last" (*MF* 19). His time in Ireland bored Fletcher and, even worse, constantly reminded him of his Irishness. Every time he saw the Anglo-Irish gentlemen and ladies of Cashel, the young Fletcher recalled his family's decline. Though he insists that his ancestors were originally pure English stock, his life in Ireland was that of a peasant, albeit a sensitive and ambitious peasant. When we first meet Fletcher as a young man in London, he has mostly shaken off his Irish identity and established himself as a dandy and a notorious Casanova. Fletcher is Dorian Gray with no need of a Lord Henry. First among the rabble-rousers and aesthetes of 1880s London, he has ruined hundreds of young women. He "brings an atmosphere of sensuality wherever he goes, and all must breathe it; even the most virtuous are contaminated" (*MF* 4–5). Yet Catholicism has a superficial fascination for Fletcher.

The first exploit that the novel depicts is his attempted seduction of a nun. Nuns play a significant role in decadent literature, but Moore taps into a longer tradition of anti-Catholic literature that plays with the idea of the potentially explosive, repressed sexuality of the female religious. This tradition predates but finds its most potent expression in Denis Diderot's novel *La Religieuse* (*The Nun*) (1796), in which a young woman is forced into a convent and reveals its shocking sadistic and lesbian secrets in a series of letters. Hanson finds examples of this genre in Wagner's *Parsifal* (1882), Villiers de l'Isle-Adam's symbolist drama *Axël* (1890), and Beardsley's unfinished erotic novel *Under the Hill*. For the most emblematic manifestation of this genre, he turns to Moore's companion novels *Evelyn Innes* (1898) and *Sister Theresa* (1901). Together, the two books tell the life story of a beautiful opera singer who rejects fame and passionate love affairs to become a nun. These neglected classics of the nun fiction genre found several avid readers in their own day, including James Joyce, who had two copies of each novel in his Trieste library. As with many of the books in the collection, they contain long lines of red crayon in the margins with large red Xs next to passages that seem to have particularly intrigued Joyce.[37] *Evelyn Innes* is sparsely annotated except for those sections dealing with the heroine's conflicted feelings about the relationship between sexuality and religion. Two sentences highlighted in the margin with a thick red line and large red X seem to have been particularly important to Joyce: "The restriction of sexual intercourse is the moral ideal of Western Europe; it is the one point on which all Christians are agreed; it is the one point on which they all feel alike."[38] Evelyn goes on to reflect on the artificiality of sexual restriction as well as the inescapable hold this moral fiction has on her conscience. There is no room in this chapter to explore Joyce's annotations in depth, but it is worth noting that he found attractive the ideas about sexual liberation in Moore's decadent-inflected nun fiction. It is also worth recalling the pornographic picture of a "nun" that Molly Bloom finds in her husband's desk drawer.

Even Hanson, who rightly identifies *Evelyn Innes* and *Sister Theresa* as major texts in the history of decadent Catholic nun fiction, overlooks the fact that a decade prior to the publication of *Evelyn Innes* Moore depicted an eroticized nun in *Mike Fletcher*. The novel's narrator implies that Fletcher has conducted several successful seductions in the past. His attempted conquest of the aptly named Lily Young proves more difficult. At first, he is convinced that she has left the convent before making her final vows in order to provide him with a new and exciting conquest. Much to Fletcher's chagrin, she proves more conscious of his carnal motives than her sheltered upbringing suggests. The furnishings of Fletcher's apartment make it clear that the two view religion quite differently. Surprised to see a medieval crucifix and a statue of Mary in her would-be seducer's bedroom, Lily asks him about his faith. He assures her that the Catholic trinkets are merely ornamental and that he appreciates only the "picturesque" qualities of the crucifix (*MF* 26). For Lily, Christ is far more than picturesque: "Christ is very beautiful. When I prayed to Him an hour passed like a little minute" (*MF* 26). Considering their theological conversation an elaborate form of foreplay, Fletcher attempts to coax Lily into bed. Rather than falling into his arms, however, she lectures him about the true nature of love:

> "Men do not mind whom they love; even in the convent we knew that."
> "You seem to have known a good deal in that convent; I am not astonished that you left it."
> "What do you mean?" She settled her shawl on her shoulders.
> "Merely this; you are in a young man's room alone, and I love you."
> "Love! You profane the word." (*MF* 29)

The interaction is fascinating in part because Moore refuses to endorse either character's point of view explicitly. Fletcher is depicted as a superficial dandy, but Lily's Christian idea of love and devotion to the crucified Christ is also suspect. For her, love can only be found "in contemplation and desire of higher things …

in thought and not in violent passion" (*MF* 33). Lily is certainly wise to deny Fletcher, especially given his history of fathering and then denying illegitimate children; but, from Moore's perspective, her sexless notion of love and attraction to a man she can never touch, Christ, must have seemed somewhat more ludicrous than Fletcher's hedonism. Instead of establishing Lily as the embodiment of an ideal chastity, Moore uses her to represent the Catholic perversion of love into a purely spiritual phenomenon that scorns the flesh. Unsurprisingly, she leaves Fletcher without capitulating to his increasingly vehement, almost violent advances. Briefly shocked by the rejection, Fletcher soon enough regains his composure and moves on to the next amusement.[39]

When not attempting to seduce nuns, Fletcher composes decadent poetry that celebrates hedonism and death. In "The Ballad of Don Juan Dead," he laments that future generations of women will be denied his charms:

> O happy moths that now flit and hover
> > From the blossom of white to the blossom of red,
> Take heed, for I was a lordly lover
> > Till the little day of my life had sped;
> > As straight as a pine-tree, a golden head,
> And eyes as blue as an austral bay.
> Ladies, when loosing your evening array,
> > Reflect, had you lived in my years, my prayers
> Might have won you from weakly lovers away—
> > My love was stronger and fiercer than theirs. (*MF* 14)

Upon hearing the poem, a friend rebukes Fletcher for its artificiality and the "meretricious glitter" of his style (*MF* 14). It would seem that Moore internalized some of the criticism of his own decadent poetry. With its Latinate syntax and rotting lover, Fletcher's ballad could have been included in one of Moore's early volumes. In fact, it closely resembles "Ode to a Dead Body" in *Flowers of Passion*:

> Thou hast no lover now. Why have they gone
> > And left thee here alone?
> Is there not one of all the hundreds who
> > Once kissed thee thro' and thro'
> In the deep silence of the summer night
> > In rapture and delight,
> Whose memory a little gold might crave
> > And give to thee a grave. (*MF* 5)

Moore's "Ode" treats the deceased Lothario as an object of semidetached contemplation. Fletcher identifies so completely with Don Juan that he speaks in the dead man's voice. In spite of the differences in perspective, the similarities between the two poems suggest that Moore sees Fletcher as another decadent alter ego, after the fashion of Edward Dayne.

In keeping with Moore's particular brand of decadence, Fletcher rejects Catholicism for a self-destructive blend of Schopenhauerian pessimism and hedonism. Fletcher imagines crafting his grand philosophic vision into a poem, which he describes to his colleagues at *The Pilgrim*, "a weekly sixpenny paper devoted to young men, their doings, their amusements, their literature, and their art" (*MF* 39). In the poem, he envisions a human race that has rejected "man's natural and inveterate stupidity (Schopenhauer calls it Will)" by embracing self-destruction (*MF* 52). Realizing the pointlessness and horror of endless procreation, humanity has accepted oblivion. Only one man remains. Isolation allows him to see "into the heart of things" and understand Christ as the "perfect symbol of the denial of the will to live" (*MF* 49). But this philosophical reconciliation with or appropriation of Christ does not translate into sympathy for the Catholic Church. The last man alive wanders the post-human wasteland reflecting on the follies of the old world, of which Rome is the symbol: "Rome is his great agony, her shameful history falls before his eyes like a painted curtain" (*MF* 48). While inspecting the ruins of the supposedly eternal city he finds a lone woman who blasphemously proposes that they continue the human race. Unable to escape the wiles of this *femme vitale* (a thinly veiled stand-in for that bastion of reproduction, the Catholic Church) the protagonist of Fletcher's poem, his Schopenhauerian artist-adventurer, commits one final act of salvific murder. This is decadence unimpeded by Catholicism, a belief in decay and the desirability of nonexistence that transcends all ties of tradition and nature. The opposition between the Church and the philosopher-artist that Fletcher establishes in his decadent retelling of the Adam and Eve myth harkens back to Norton's literary holocaust at the beginning of the novel. Following the path of Des Esseintes, Huysmans's paradigmatic decadent antihero, Fletcher finds in Schopenhauer's pessimism a corollary of what he perceives as the Christian disdain for the physical world without the false promise of mysterious providence and a just afterlife. Unlike Huysmans's protagonist, however, Fletcher follows his philosophical convictions to their logical conclusion by asserting his intellectual independence in defying the Church's injunction against suicide.

As I have suggested, Moore's deeply held belief in an essential opposition between Catholicism and art led him to disparage Ireland as a nation incapable of meaningful literary production. In *Ave*, the first volume of his memoir, *Hail and Farewell!* (1911), Moore recounts a conversation with his cousin Edward Martyn in 1894 on the cusp of what we now know as the Irish literary revival. At the time the two men lived in London in circumstances much like those of Fletcher and Norton:

> Standing before the carven porch, I thought what a happy accident it was that Edward Martyn and myself had drifted into the Temple, the last vestige of old London—"combining," as someone has said, "the silence of the cloister and the license of the brothel"—Edward attracted by the church of the Templars, I by the fleeting mistress.[40]

After working on *Esther Waters* or *Modern Painting* till midnight in a garret near the Temple, Moore would wander over to Martyn's equally humble lodging in Pump Court (the neighborhood inhabited by Norton in *Mike Fletcher*) and chat with him about art and literature until the early morning hours. On one such occasion, Martyn shared his desire to write plays in Irish. Moore guffawed at the idea: "I thought nobody did anything in Irish except bring turf from the bog and say prayers."[41] Martyn fell silent at this, but when pushed said simply, "You've always lived in France and England, and don't know Ireland." Unsettled by this indictment, Moore momentarily wondered if he had been wise to flee Ireland, but he soon reminded himself that "an Irishman must fly from Ireland to be himself."[42] Martyn, raised in Ireland and the Church, could see the artistic potential latent in his countrymen. Moore the cosmopolitan aesthete saw no promise of cultural rebirth, and his derisive comment about gathering peat and saying prayers anticipates his most scathing and unsympathetic depictions of Irish life.

The *Untilled Field* (1903), while not a decadent text in any obvious sense, contains Moore's most strident and concentrated critique of his native land. Not surprisingly, the Church is the focus. Written in the key of Zola, the book attempts to capture all that is wrong with Ireland in a series of short stories. The first, "In the Clay," reiterates a recurring idea in his earlier fiction: no artist can create art in Ireland. The story's protagonist, a sculptor with roots in Dublin who "should have been one of Cellini's apprentices,"[43] has his workshop ransacked by a group of boys put up to it, he suspects, by the parish priest. His final pronouncement leaves the moral of the story clear. Ireland, the artist concludes, "is no country for an educated man. It won't be fit for a man to live in for another hundred years. It is an unwashed country, that is what it is!"[44] The next twelve short stories are devoted to the same theme. Priests are depicted as domineering gossips who make bad marriages, oppose dancing, preach fire and brimstone, chase off young lovers, and generally bleed Ireland dry of both money and joy. Even the few partially sympathetic figures, such as the priest who composes a letter to Rome arguing for clerical marriages as a means of increasing the Irish population and stimulating local economies, are prevented by their superiors from enacting any positive change. Anyone with a spark of personality or individuality emigrates to America or the Continent, and those who return after time abroad can stand only a short visit to their native country. In the story "Home Sickness," for example, the central figure leaves his job as a barman in a Bowery slum to visit his hometown, a place unchanged by the passage of thirteen years and still repulsive in its backwardness:

> His eyes fell on the bleak country, on the little fields divided by bleak walls; he remembered the pathetic ignorance of the people, and it was these things that he could not endure. It was the priest who came to forbid the dancing. Yes, it was the priest.... He must go away from this place—he must get back to the bar-room.[45]

For Moore even a smoke-clogged Bowery tavern is preferable to the "bleak country" and its "pathetic ignorance." This collection of stories presents a potent critique of sexism, superstition, institutional abuse of power, and petty religious scrupulousness. At the same time, its almost unequivocally negative depiction of Ireland suggests that Moore's self-imposed exile produced in him more than the salutary distance necessary to critique the institutions and ideas of his people; it alienated him from his own culture to the extent that nearly everything about Ireland became abhorrent. Moore's decadent anti-Catholicism was inextricably entangled with a deep-seated anti-Irish prejudice. His inheritor, Joyce, took a somewhat different route.

Non Serviam: Stephen Dedalus as Decadent Anti-Catholic

In his 1935 essay "Religion and Literature," T. S. Eliot laments the secularization of the novel. He parses this decline into three phases. In the first phase, Christian faith was largely ignored as a subject because it was taken "for granted"; in the second, organized religion became something to be "doubted" or "contested" (*SP* 100). Dickens exemplifies the first phase and Hardy the second. The third phase, Eliot argues, belongs to "those who have never heard the Christian faith spoken of as anything but an anachronism." He includes "nearly all novelists" in this group, "except Mr. James Joyce" (*SP* 100). It is true that Eliot signals nothing in this remark except that Joyce grew up among people of religious faith. He does not claim closet Christianity for his Irish contemporary, though some critics have been tempted to make claims that are nearly as untenable.[46] Instead, Eliot singles Joyce out as a man, to borrow Pound's phrase, "out of key with his time." Like the decadents of the nineties, whom Yeats portrayed as artists born during the wrong phase of the moon, Eliot views Joyce as an artist born out of step with the secular movement of literary history. He is the only novelist who experienced faith as anything other than "an anachronism." By implication, Joyce, somewhat like Eliot himself, *is* an anachronism, a modern writer whose earliest impressions were inflected by religion. Joyce firmly renounced his faith, but Catholicism already had a hold on his art and received at least some of his sympathy.

Such was not the case for Moore, whose post-adolescent life was so completely defined by atheism that he can hardly be said to have renounced his faith; it was never his. Even his eventual conversion to the Church of Ireland had nothing to do with spiritual matters. Enraged at being called a Catholic in a review of *The Untilled Field* and angry with the bishops of Ireland for hosting Edward VII, Moore saw joining the Church of Ireland as both an act of public protest and the only way to separate himself definitively and publicly from Rome. The Reverend Gilbert Mahaffy met with Moore several times to discuss his motivation for joining the Anglican Communion. It was a difficult assignment. Unable to admit to belief in the divinity of Christ, Moore attempted to find common ground by denigrating Catholicism:

> I began to describe a new Utopia—a State so well ordered that no one in it was allowed to be a Papist unless he or she could prove some bodily or mental infirmity, or until he or she had attained a certain age, which put them beyond the business of the world—the age of seventy, perhaps, the earliest at which a conversion would be legal. "A sort of spiritual Old Age Pension Scheme" I said; and a picture rose up before my mind of a crowd of young and old, all inferior, physically or intellectually, struggling round the door of a Roman Catholic Church, with papers in their hands, on the first Friday of every month.[47]

Reverend Mahaffy was more disturbed than amused by Moore's utopian vision, but he eventually managed to shepherd his charge through the conversion process. When, in the wake of this farce, a reporter asked Yeats how devout a Catholic Moore had been prior to his apostasy, the typically somber and serious poet could barely stifle his laughter.[48] Joyce, by contrast, had the faith necessary for renunciation. A devout youth, he grew up with a strong sense of and appreciation for the intellectual and aesthetic elements of Catholicism. Acknowledging the importance of his education, he once told a friend that he should properly be identified not as a Catholic but as a Jesuit. A student of Aquinas and Dante, among others, with a keen love of ritual, Joyce understood the religion of Ireland from the inside. Because of what Mary Lowe-Evans dubs "Catholic nostalgia,"[49] Joyce managed to balance his scathing critique of Irish Catholicism with a sympathy, or at least a self-ironizing humor, that is absent from Moore's work and resembles what William Empson terms "double irony."[50] Joyce was more than happy to heap aspersions on Ireland and himself, but he refused to exclude either from his imaginative largesse. Nowhere is this balance more in evidence than in the narratives concerning Stephen Dedalus, the descendant of Moore's decadent characters. Joyce undermines Stephen, the young decadent anti-Catholic, as a way of asserting distance between himself and Moore's unironic and vehemently anti-Irish form of cosmopolitanism. By creating ironic distance between himself and his creation, Joyce simultaneously provides a critique of Moore's decadent anti-Catholicism and insists on a more humane cosmopolitanism. Joyce's modernist fiction evinces the lasting influence of Moore's decadent anti-Catholic vision, as articulated in *Confessions* and *Mike Fletcher*, but it also rejects the more malignant elements of his cosmopolitanism by tempering detached satire with genuine sympathy and a love of the ordinary life of Ireland.

A Portrait of the Artist as a Young Man participates to an extent in the tradition of Moore's *Confessions of a Young Man* and thereby acts as a bridge between decadence and modernism.[51] Both are largely autobiographical accounts of young Irish men who, inspired by Byron and Shelley, reject their religion as they try to assert themselves as artists. They make this assertion by imitating decadent poetry (a point on which I will elaborate shortly) and fleeing Ireland in favor of France. Moore never publicly accused Joyce of literary theft. He did repeatedly assert the superiority of *Confessions* in his private correspondence. Joyce never denounced *Confessions* as vociferously as he did *The Untilled Field* and other works by Moore. Instead, he used the similarities between Stephen Dedalus and Edward Dayne to create an intertextual conversation with Moore, one that repeatedly satirizes the older novelist. Resemblances between Stephen (Joyce's ironic alter ego) and Dayne (Moore's fantasy self) allowed Joyce to assert salient differences between himself and his precursor.

The most immediately noticeable difference between *Confessions* and *Portrait* is how they begin. Devoting only a few pages to his life before leaving Ireland, Edward Dayne essentially starts his narrative as an exile and student of French painting and decadent manners. Joyce who, unlike Moore, has no interest in writing Ireland out of his protagonist's intellectual and spiritual background, devotes significantly more time to Stephen's early development. Stephen never sets foot outside of Ireland in *Portrait*; in *Confessions* Dayne barely mentions his homeland or his upbringing. The young man on the streets of Moore's Paris already carries his prejudices on his sleeve, including a pronounced aversion to his country and its religion. He is already in pose when he first appears. Joyce's narrative depicts Stephen's earliest experiences as they impress themselves on the smooth wax of his childhood mind. The first words in the book are those of Simon Dedalus telling the story of a moocow and baby tuckoo, an experience of paternal love never repeated and soon replaced by wet bedsheets, bad smells, and Stephen's proto-poem inspired by Dante's horrifying assertion that boys who don't apologize have their eyes plucked out by eagles: "*Pull out his eyes, Apologize, Apologize, Pull out his eyes*" (PA 20). Of course, the most pronounced influence on young Dedalus is the Church. A rereading of his youthful encounter with religion reveals those elements of specifically decadent Catholic rhetoric that emerge at the genesis of Stephen's self-realization as an artist.

Unlike Dayne's, Stephen's story is not that of a well-to-do young man from backward County Mayo who finds himself forging an artistic identity on the civilized continent. His narrative is Irish, not Parisian. Yet his earliest youthful manifestations of an artistic sensibility bear the unmistakable marks of decadence. As a child in the chapel at Clongowes, he finds comfort and stimulation in the "holy smell," and while suffering from fever and contemplating death in the infirmary, he experiences his first Paterian reverie:

> He could hear the tolling. He said over to himself the song that Brigid had taught him.
>
> > *Dingdong! The castle bell!*
> > *Farewell, my mother!*
> > *Bury me in the old churchyard*
> > *Beside my eldest brother.*
> >
> > *My coffin shall be black,*
> > *Six angels at my back,*
> > *Two to sing and two to pray*
> > *And two to carry my soul away.*
>
> How beautiful and sad that was! How beautiful the words were where they said *Bury me in the old churchyard!* A tremor passed over his body. How sad and

> how beautiful! He wanted to cry quietly but not for himself: for the words, so
> beautiful and sad, like music. (*PA* 35–6)

In his feverish state, the boy experiences his first moments of aesthetic
perception. The words of the ditty are "beautiful and sad"; they send a "tremor"
over his body; and he almost weeps because the words are "like music." Stephen
instinctively shares Pater's idea that all art aspires to the condition of music, and
the words offer his first taste of the sad beauty of poetry.

Later, after hearing from Wells that some "fellows in the higher line" had
been caught with wine on their breath, Stephen daydreams about an even more
"terrible sin": "Perhaps they had stolen a monstrance to run away with it and
sell it somewhere" (*PA* 57). Fantasizing about the titillatingly "strange" and
"great sin," he imagines the boys sneaking into the sacristy under the cover of
darkness to "steal the flashing gold thing into which God was put on the altar
in the middle of flowers and candles at benediction while the incense went
up in clouds" (*PA* 57). The beautiful sights and smells of the altar accentuate
this imagined transgression. When Stephen's mind returns to the actual theft
of the wine, he discovers that "the word [is] beautiful: wine"; it makes him
think of "dark purple because the grapes were dark purple that grew in Greece
outside houses like white temples" (*PA* 57). Stephen only entertains a classroom
daydream; nevertheless, his tendency to fantasize about sin and to take strange
pleasure in imaginatively constructing blasphemous acts anticipates the later
corruption of his mind and development of his art. Here we see the first signs
of the troubled but potentially fecund artistic relationship between Stephen, his
faith, and his language.

Once "cold and cruel and loveless lust" stirs in Stephen's soul (*PA* 104), his
youthful reveries are overshadowed by more wanton imaginative pleasures.
Burning to "appease the fierce longings of his heart," he becomes, at least in
his own mind, a sort of Dorian Gray figure, indulging in "mortal sin" at night
and putting on "a tissue of subterfuge and falsehood" in the light of day (*PA*
107). Rather than fantasizing about absconding with holy objects taken from
their place on the altar, he imaginatively selects "demure and innocent" female
faces and transforms them "by a lecherous cunning" into materials for the "dark
orgiastic riot" of his evenings (*PA* 107). Like Ernest Dowson's poetic persona,
whose lusts are both abated and fueled by the persistent image of an ideal, pure
girl, Stephen thinks back on visions of his "holy encounter" with his romantic
ideal woman, Mercedes from *The Count of Monte Cristo*, whenever the "wasting
fires of lust" momentarily abate (*PA* 108).

Soon, imagined transgressions no longer suffice. Prowling the streets of Nighttown, Stephen enters his Baudelairean phase.[52]

> He had wandered into a maze of narrow and dirty streets. From the foul laneways he heard bursts of hoarse riot and wrangling and the drawling of drunken singers .... The yellow gasflames arose before his troubled vision against the vapoury sky, burning as if before an altar. Before the doors and in the lighted halls groups were gathered and arrayed as for some rite. He was in another world: he had awakened from a slumber of centuries. (*PA* 108)

The laneways resounding with the sounds of debauchery give way to a street on which gas lamps burn "as if before an altar." Celebrants of a perverse liturgy, prostitutes and their customers array themselves "as for some rite." The narrator's description does not juxtapose the ideal and the debased; it conflates the two. It employs similes dependent on the language and images of Catholicism, as if by making Nighttown the holy ground of "another world" the narrative voice might sanctify Stephen's fall from grace and elevate the experience of paying for sex to the status of a sacramental rite. The description is suggestive of decadence because it never strays far from one of the central obsessions of the movement, Catholicism. Even Moore's patently decadent characters share in this fascination. Mike Fletcher despises the Church, but his one persistent love interest captures his attention because she is a novice at a convent. Joyce's narrator participates in this tradition and anticipates Stephen's later imitation of decadent art—his villanelle—by describing his initiation into the rites of sex using the language of decadent Catholicism. By the time Stephen becomes a young man, he, like Mike Fletcher, is drawn to a decadent form of self-expression that depends on Catholicism for its metaphorical language. Once we appreciate that Stephen's Catholicism is an essential element of his decadence, it becomes easier to reconcile the dominant aspects of his character: fearful, pious child and brazen *fin-de-siècle* young man.

Following his pseudo-sacramental sexual awakening at the end of Chapter II, Stephen realizes the impossibility of reconciling his sexuality and his faith, but his narrative continues to enact a transitory, perverse unity between the two. At first, Stephen's "pride in his own sin" paired with a cold indifference to and "loveless awe of God" temporarily inure him to the desire for reconciliation with his stifling deity (*PA* 112). Yet, even in this state of separation from God, the cult of Mary dominates his mind. The Blessed Virgin plays an integral role in the dialectic of sin and grace at the heart of decadent Catholicism. In John Gray's imitation of Baudelaire, "À une Madone" (discussed in Chapter 1), sadomasochistic desire for the lover blends with sacred longing for the Mother; however, Mary's own immutable purity is enhanced, not diminished by the poet's exposed lust. As a focal point for the poet's shame—his "recognition of the validity of Christian virtue despite [his] own spiritual abjection"—Mary forces the poet to reveal himself as "an artist of the despicable."[53] Enticed by the sensuality of the little office[54] he leads every Saturday morning as a prefect in the sodality of the Blessed Virgin Mary, Stephen takes perverse delight in the hypocrisy of praying to this symbol of purity. Joyce's narrator represents Stephen's thoughts as if they were a decadent Catholic prose poem:

> The glories of Mary held his soul captive: spikenard and myrrh and frankincense, symbolising the preciousness of God's gifts to her soul, rich garments, symbolising her royal lineage, her emblems, the lateflowering plant and the lateblossoming tree, symbolising the agelong gradual growth of her cultus. When it fell to him to read the lesson towards the close of the office he read it in a veiled voice, lulling his conscience to its music. (*PA* 102)

In spite of, or perhaps because of, his sexual awakening at the end of Chapter II, Stephen experiences a new and somewhat disturbing attraction to the figure of Mary. Initially, her glorious odors and vestments are complemented by the lesson of the office, which drowns his shame in soothing music. Soon, however, the words of the office blend with the lingering residue of sin:

> If ever he was impelled to cast sin from him and to repent the impulse that moved him was the wish to be her knight. If ever his soul, reentering her dwelling shyly after the frenzy of his body's lust had spent itself, was turned toward her whose emblem is the morning star, *bright and musical, telling of heaven and infusing peace*, it was when her names were murmured softly by lips whereon there still lingered foul and shameful words, the savor itself of a lewd kiss.
>   That was strange. (*PA* 113)

Strange indeed. Stephen's ritual naming of Mary brings about a momentary desire to repent, but mixed with this desire is a tendency to revel in the erotics of ritual devotion. Stephen finds himself most liable to be "turned" by his prayers when their music is mixed with the lingering savor of "shameful words" and "a lewd kiss." Whether or not Joyce experienced this attraction to the same degree, he, like Dante, understood the potential erotic implications of Marian devotion. In his 1909 letters to Nora he recognizes how the devout child is father to the man: "You have been to my young manhood what the ideal of the Blessed Virgin was to my boyhood."[55] He also anticipates Stephen's conflation of the ideal and debased in explicit terms:

You are mine, darling, mine! I love you. All I have written above is only a moment or two of brutal madness. The last drop of seed has hardly been squirted up your cunt before it is over and my true love for you, the love of my verses, the love of my eyes for your strange luring eyes, comes blowing over my soul like a wind of spices. My prick is still hot and stiff and quivering from the last brutal drive it has given you when a faint hymn is heard rising in tender pitiful worship of you from the dim cloisters of my heart.[56]

Joyce seems to separate sexual desire and love. Only after the spasm can he achieve a post-coital euphoria in which his "worship" of Nora rises from the "dim cloisters" of his heart. The physical ejaculation leads to the spiritual one. Joyce's letter describes a more explicit version of what Stephen experiences in *Portrait*—murmuring Mary's name after "his body's lust had spent itself." Stephen's fleeting experience of the interdependence, or at least interrelatedness, of sex and mysticism evokes in his mind the unsettling erotic conflation of virgin and whore that is prevalent in the work not only of Baudelaire but also of Gray, Wilde, and Dowson.

Up to this point, I have focused on the movement from Stephen's earliest aesthetic reveries to his reenactment of the decadent dialectic of sin and grace. This use of a Catholic register of images and impressions in the service of decadent expression reaches its climax in the young artist's only completely represented act of poetic production. Dredged up from Joyce's earlier poetic essays, Stephen's first artistic creation is a decadent knockoff that captures, in Ellmann's words, "Stephen's contraposed urges (from Chapters II and III), first towards the prostitute, then towards the Virgin Mary."[57] "The Villanelle of the Temptress" could be indebted to any practitioner of its eponymous verse form, but among the decadents Dowson stands out as the master of the form and a clear source of this poem's inspiration. Critics have demonstrated Joyce's debt to Dowson,[58] but we know surprisingly little about Stephen's literary education. He claims Byron as his poetic master, then writes like an 1890's decadent. We never see him reading or citing Baudelaire, Pater, Wilde, or Dowson. Nevertheless, his experiences are shaped by their work. The decadent bildungsroman—*À Rebours, Confessions of a Young Man, The Picture of Dorian Gray*—typically follows its protagonist's education with great care. Moore in particular takes pains to identify and discuss the decadent poets and artists who form Dayne's consciousness and artistic sensibility. Unlike Stephen, Dayne does not simply start sputtering decadent verse in a fit of post-masturbatory inspiration. Granted, both young men begin their poetic education with Shelley and Byron, but Dayne provides the reader with an explicit description of his induction into the amoral world of French decadence:

Belief in humanity, pity for the poor, hatred of injustice, all that Shelley gave may never have been very deep or earnest; but I did love, I did believe. Gautier destroyed these illusions. He taught me that our boasted progress is but a pitfall into which the race is falling, and I learned that the correction of form is the highest ideal, and I accepted the plain, simple conscience of the pagan world as the perfect solution of the problem that had vexed me so long; I cried, "ave" to it all: lust, cruelty, slavery, and I would have held down my thumbs in the Colosseum that a hundred gladiators might die and wash me free of my Christian soul with their blood.

The study of Baudelaire hurried the course of the disease. No longer is it the grand barbaric face of Gautier; now it is the clean shaven face of the mock priest, the slow, cold eyes and the sharp, cunning sneer of the cynical libertine who will be tempted that he may better know the worthlessness of temptation. "Les Fleurs du Mal!" beautiful flowers, beautiful in sublime decay. What a great record is yours, and were Hell a reality how many souls would we find wreathed with your poisonous blossoms. The village maiden goes to her Faust; the children of the nineteenth century go to you, O Baudelaire, and having tasted of your deadly delight all hope of repentance is vain. (*CYM* 80–1)

Interestingly, Dayne finds only darkness, temptation, and damnation in the work of Baudelaire. For Moore, the French poet's path is not a circuitous road to the Cross (as Eliot would later argue) but a straight road to a fictional Hell, one paved with his own verses.

Joyce provides no such clear-cut source text for Stephen's decadent poetry. Dorian needs a Mephistopheles and a poisonous book to guide him into decadence, but, like Huysmans's archetypal degenerate sybarite Des Esseintes, Stephen requires only a Jesuit education, a healthy sexual appetite, and the Catholic Church. With no clear precedent for his villanelle in the narrative of *Portrait*, with no obvious source to imitate, Stephen's poem appears to be a genuine epiphany. While composing his villanelle, Stephen takes on the role of "priest of the eternal imagination" and reflects on the act of artistic creation as one of consecration: "The radiant image of the eucharist united again in an instant his bitter and despairing thoughts, their cries arising unbroken in a hymn of thanksgiving" (*PA* 223). He performs a sort of artistic transubstantiation, the process of conversion whereby the substance of Christ's flesh is made present literally under the accidents (outward appearances) of unleavened bread. Stephen's arousal, his initial source of inspiration, undergoes such a complete transformation that it becomes almost unrecognizable in his finished poem.

True source of inspiration aside, the poem is confusing and ambiguous: "Are you not weary of ardent ways, / Lure of the fallen seraphim? / Tell no more of enchanted days" (*PA* 225). Whom is the speaker addressing? The poem, as it appears in *Portrait*, has no title, so the "temptress" remains an ambiguous "you." The addressee is feminized in later stanzas:

And still you hold our longing gaze
With languorous look and lavish limb!
Are you not weary of ardent ways?
Tell no more of enchanted days. (*PA* 225)

Satan caused the fall of one-third of the angels by tempting them with his delusions of grandeur, but he never seduced them with languorous looks and lavish limbs, such carnal enticements having, we suppose, little attraction for incorporeal beings. At this point in the poem, Stephen's subject seems to be an amalgam of all the women he has lusted after in his youth, including his current love-object, Emma. Not surprisingly he articulates his desire for this supreme fleshly temptress by linking her metaphorically to his greatest spiritual temptress—the Virgin Mary:

Gabriel the seraph had come to the virgin's chamber. An afterglow deepened within his spirit, whence the white flame had passed, deepening to a rose and ardent light. That rose and ardent light was her strange wilful heart, strange that no man had known or would know, wilful from being the beginning of the world: and lured by that ardent roselike glow the choirs of the seraphim were falling from heaven. (*PA* 219)

Stephen's dream vision conflates the Annunciation, the fall of Satan's angels, and his own sexual desire in a manner redolent of decadent Catholicism. In this strange epiphanic vision, Gabriel brings the "white flame" of the Holy Spirit to impregnate Mary. Rather than encountering the humble virgin of the Bible, who asks only that God's will be done, Gabriel is confronted by a woman whose "wilful heart" draws all the "choirs of the seraphim" from heaven. The impregnation of the virgin in the poem instigates a second fall and the incarnation simultaneously. This perverse vision of the Annunciation, with its dual portent of miraculous birth and great destruction, undergirded by the sexual desire of a divine being for a human woman, has more in common with Yeats's "Leda and the Swan" (which was originally titled "The Annunciation") than it does with any biblical text. In spite of the highly sexualized nature of the poem, Stephen's temptress retains Mary's virginity ("no man had known or would know"). He cannot bring himself to blaspheme the virginity of Mary even as he fuses her with the subject of his poem—the unnamed temptress. This insistence on preserving Mary's virginity is a potent reminder that neither Stephen nor Joyce ever felt comfortable crossing certain lines. Joyce hinted at the limits of his rebellion some years after the publication of *Portrait* when he famously refused to toast to sin while drinking with William Carlos Williams. Yet despite Stephen's adherence to the idea of Mary's dogmatically protected virginity, his poem associates her with an object of lust capable of engendering sexual desire even among the angels. This is the Mary of Chapter III, the chaste virgin queen whom Stephen reveled in worshiping with unclean lips.

Aside from indulging in the decadent habit of expressing sexual desire in relation to specifically Catholic icons, "The Villanelle of the Temptress" owes a more formal debt to decadence. In the introduction to a recent anthology of decadent verse, Caroline Blyth refers to the villanelle as the fixed form most associated with "the 'Nineties and the *fin de siècle*."[59] Given Joyce's familiarity with the decadent villanelles of Wilde, Gray, and especially Dowson, and his interest in satirizing Stephen's grand artistic ambitions, it is hardly surprising that "The Villanelle of the Temptress" reads like an imitation of such poems as Dowson's "Of His Lady's Treasures" (1893):

> I took her dainty eyes, as well
> As silken tendrils of her hair:
> And so I made a Villanelle!
>
>   ....
>
> I took her whiteness virginal
> And from her cheeks, two roses rare:
> I took her dainty eyes as well.
>
>   ....
>
> I said, "It may be possible
> Her image from my heart to tear."
> And so I made a Villanelle.[60]

At first, Dowson's poem seems quite superficial. Having conquered his beloved and taken her "whiteness virginal," the poet must tear her image from his heart and preserve her physical "treasures" in a fittingly artificial vessel—the villanelle. But, unlike Stephen's poem, Dowson's is artfully self-conscious. The content revels in the frivolity of the form. In its own poetic present, Dowson's poem justifies the speaker's composition of another villanelle that he "made" at some point in the past. The poem could almost be titled "Villanelle in Defense of a Villanelle."

Conversely, Stephen's choice of the form seems not only random but also ill-advised. There are examples of unironic and lofty villanelles, but near the turn of the century one could hardly choose a form less well suited to Stephen's grand expression of passion. Even when applied to its original pastoral subject matter in Wilde's "Pan" (1880), the form reflects ironically on the content: "And Thine our English Thames shall be, / The open lawns, the upland wold, / O Goat-foot God of Arcady, / This northern isle hath need of thee!"[61] Wilde entreats Pan to bring antique pagan vitality to dull English literature, but he does so in a seventeenth-century French verse form, as if to stress the nation's "need" of inspiration. Stephen writes in the same antique form and immediately in the wake of a literary movement that loved the villanelle primarily for its frivolous artificiality. Given the context of its bizarre framing narrative, Stephen's mystical vision seems especially poorly suited for the form he chooses and more akin to such strange but serious devotionals as Johnson's "Before the Cloister" (1896): "Come, vestal lady! In my vain heart light / Thy flame, divinely white! / Come, lady of the lilies! blaunch to snow / My soul through sacred woe!" (*CP* 150) or Wilde's "San Miniato" (1876): O! crowned by God with thorns and pain, / Mother of Christ, O! mystic wife, / My heart is weary of this life, / And over-sad to sing again" (*P* 40). But whereas these speakers express some submission to the moral economy of the Church, Stephen's poem appropriates the language of the Church in a failed attempt to transcend the shame and guilt that dominate the devotional verses of Johnson and Wilde.

> Our broken cries and mournful lays
> Rise in one eucharistic hymn.
> Are you not weary of ardent ways?
>
> While sacrificing hands upraise
> The chalice flowing to the brim,
> Tell no more of enchanted days. (*PA* 225)

Like the narration of lust in Chapter II, in which Nighttown becomes parodic of the scene of a specifically Catholic rite, Stephen's poem couches his yearning for his temptress in the language of the central sacrament of Catholicism, Holy Communion. He joins in mournful choir, singing a "eucharistic hymn," while priestly hands raise a "chalice flowing to the brim." Cries of passion form the litany of a new rite in which the virgin's vagina replaces the sacramental vessel containing Christ's blood, and sexual guilt is replaced by ecstasy. Thus the poem self-consciously perverts a Catholic sacrament. For Stephen, as for some of the decadents of the 1890s, the rituals of Communion seem suggestive enough to invite such perversion.

In composing "The Villanelle of the Temptress," Stephen proclaims his rebellion against his nation's faith as well as his dependence on it as the material for his art. When he sets out at the novel's conclusion to undergo "for the millionth time the reality of experience" (*PA* 253), he is preparing both to follow in the footsteps of Moore's exiled decadent anti-Catholics and attempting something new. Unlike Dayne, for whom escape to Paris meant rejecting all things Irish in order to forge a new cosmopolitan identity, Stephen sets out with the hope of forging the "uncreated conscience of [his] race" (*PA* 253). His intentions, though naïve, differ significantly from those of Moore's protagonist in *Confessions*. Unfortunately, for Stephen, his grand vision proves illusory.

When Stephen reemerges in *Ulysses* (1922), he does so as a failed poet living in the shadows of successful literati such as AE and George Moore. He is not a cosmopolitan dandy come back to chronicle the lives of the backward inhabitants of his backward home and lead a literary revival. Having found little inspiration and no artistic success in Paris, Stephen returns as a failed artist and a failed apostate. On the sixteenth of June 1904 he still walks the streets of Dublin bearing the cross of his religion. His rebellion has stalled. As Buck Mulligan points out to Haines, Stephen is held back from artistic creation by the "visions of hell" that began haunting him in *Portrait* (*U* 10.1072). The decadent poets whom Stephen imitates in *Portrait* found inspiration in Catholicism, even in its visions of Hell. Moore managed to use his opposition to Catholicism as inspiration for his work. Stephen's imagination is paralyzed by the Church. Unable to transcend his religion by making its rituals and symbols his own, as he attempts to do in "The Villanelle of the Temptress," he languishes and allows others to usurp his vocation as Ireland's "priest of the eternal imagination" and blasphemous artist.[62] His failure to liberate his imagination from its Roman master is compounded by his failure as a poet. Stephen's one poem in "Proteus" is incomplete and derivative. An overeducated, eccentric, penniless outsider, Stephen finds himself incapable of producing art and excluded from the circle of Dublin's literary elite. His one desperate attempt to gain favor with his more accomplished literary peers fails. The *Hamlet* speech in "Scylla and Charybdis" meets with objections from AE, then something even worse: bored silence. Eventually AE checks his watch and gets up to leave, but before he can go John Eglinton asks if he will be in attendance at a soiree hosted by George Moore:

A tall figure in bearded homespun rose from shadow and unveiled its
cooperative watch.

—I am afraid I am due at the *Homestead.*

Whither away? Exploitable ground.

—Are you going? John Eglinton's active eyebrows asked. Shall we see you at
Moore's tonight? Piper is coming.

—Piper! Mr Best piped. Is Piper back?

Peter Piper pecked a peck of pick of peck of pickled pepper.

—I don't know if I can. Thursday. We have our meeting. If I can get away in
time. (*U* 9.269–78)

Moore's get-together is negligible to AE, who will come only if he can "get away
in time" from his commitments at the Hermetic Society. For Stephen, exclusion
from the event is a crisis. He may well have hoped that his lecture on *Hamlet*
would impress his audience enough to garner an invitation to the event. Joyce
quickly pours salt in the wound of this failure by having Eglinton reveal that Buck
Mulligan and Haines have been invited by Moore himself: "Malachi Mulligan is
coming too. Moore asked him to bring Haines" (*U* 9.305–6). At the conclusion
of *Portrait*, Stephen wishes to write Ireland's national epic. In *Ulysses* it seems far
more likely that "Monsieur Moore," "lecturer on French letters to the youth of
Ireland," will be the man for the job: "Our national epic has yet to be written, Dr.
Sigerson says. Moore is the man for it" (*U* 9.1101–2; 9.309–10). The irony of all
this failure is that Joyce's record of Stephen's humiliation and shame is also his
greatest assertion of a new vision for literature. In *Catholic Emancipations* (2007),
Emer Nolan suggests that Joyce "debunks the notion of a flight from Ireland to a
more 'advanced' culture" and thereby signals his "rejection of a key trope of Irish
naturalist fiction" established by Moore.[63] In *Ulysses* Joyce drags Moore's young
man, the exiled decadent anti-Catholic Edward Dayne, back to his homeland
not as a successful cosmopolitan rebel but as a confused youth still bound by the
invisible chains of his religion and incapable of artistic creation. Out of this raw
material, Joyce creates a groundbreaking novel about an artistically impotent
Irish decadent.

We as readers know that Moore never writes the national epic of Ireland; that
honor goes instead to the author of *Ulysses*. In the very writing of this iconic
modernist novel, Joyce both exorcises the ghost of his phantom self, the failed
decadent anti-Catholic, and eclipses the work of Moore.

Evelyn Waugh: Decadent Catholicism Revisited

On the surface, Evelyn Waugh appears out of place in a study of decadence and modernism. The naughty nineties were long gone when he began his university education in 1922, the year when both *Ulysses* and *The Waste Land* were published. Waugh reached adulthood during the heyday of modernism, but his mature novels—*A Handful of Dust* (1934), *Scoop* (1938), *Brideshead Revisited* (1945), and the *Sword of Honour* trilogy (1952–61)—seem almost antimodernist. These novels contain an implicit disdain for the subjective element of modernist fiction, with its emphasis on the unreliability of perception and the relativity of once-fixed notions of morality. In spite of the influence of prominent modernists such as T. S. Eliot, allusions to whose work abound in Waugh's corpus, he opted, by and large, for a traditional realism of style familiar to readers of Charles Dickens but foreign to literary modernism. Still, to the extent that several modernist authors are defined by their interaction with the phenomenon of decadent Catholicism, Waugh undoubtedly fits in the age of modernism.

As we have seen, the art of Yeats, Pound, Joyce, and Eliot is all, to a greater or lesser extent, inflected by decadent Catholicism. More than any of these authors Waugh produced art that embodies the spirit of this artistic phenomenon. The most notable example is *Brideshead Revisited: The Sacred & Profane Memories of Captain Charles Ryder* (1945). The novel opens in the midst of the Second World War. Charles Ryder, a jaded, middle-aged painter turned ineffectual army captain, moves with his battalion into temporary quarters in the English country estate of Brideshead. This unanticipated return to an important place from his past casts Charles into a reverie from which he narrates the story of his life and his relationships with the now-scattered inhabitants of Brideshead Castle. Charles's narrative begins in 1920s Oxford and follows his youthful affair with the eccentric and beautiful Lord Sebastian Flyte. Their romance ends when Sebastian, tortured by the competing demands of his flesh and his Catholic faith, descends into alcoholism, flees the country, and eventually finds a home at a

Tunisian monastery. Several years later Charles begins an adulterous affair with Sebastian's sister, Julia. The two are prepared to divorce their current spouses and remarry, in flat contradiction of Julia's Catholic upbringing, until the deathbed reconversion of her apostate father inspires Julia to choose faith over love by breaking things off with Charles. The novel concludes where it began. Captain Ryder, inspired by his own act of recollection and revelation, experiences his own conversion in the family chapel at Brideshead.

Brideshead Revisited is one of the most important and influential Catholic novels in the English language. It is also one of the queerest novels of its time. Doubtless *Brideshead*'s continued relevance in the twenty-first century springs largely from this dual fascination. Catholic critics can enjoy the novel's essential orthodoxy while playing down its queerer moments; queer critics can enjoy its romantic depiction of homoerotic love while still decrying Waugh's orthodoxy as reactionary and dated. I would like to suggest that the fascination with *Brideshead* shared by these seemingly divergent discourse communities stems at least in part from the novel's ability to traverse the mine-strewn no-man's-land that divides long-established Catholic moral teaching from more recent secular orthodoxies concerning the freedom of sexual expression.

Before 1945, Waugh wrote mostly satire. Soon after its publication, influential reviewers such as Edmund Wilson singled out *Brideshead* as different; it was a "serious" novel, a "Catholic tract."[1] For decades critics treated it as a straight (in both senses), if somewhat sentimental and baroque, conversion narrative and either ignored or denied Waugh's complicated representation of homoeroticism. Not until the early 1990s did we begin to see articles with titles such as David Bittner's "Sebastian and Charles—More than Friends?" that sound somewhat naive today. As critics began taking the homoerotic elements of *Brideshead* for granted, many continued to treat the relationship between Charles and Sebastian as a sort of erotically charged but sexually chaste friendship.[2] Even Leon Higdon, who denounced Bittner and others as peddlers of homosexual panic in his article "Gay Sebastian and Cheerful Charles: Homoeroticism in Waugh's *Brideshead Revisited*" (1994), continued to insist upon a homo-heterosexual binary that largely misses the point of the novel's complex attitude toward sexuality. Since then, Catholic publications have tended to explain away the affair between Charles and Sebastian as, at worst, a sort of felix culpa on each character's road to redemption.[3]

In the last ten years, queer theorists have largely redefined the critical conversation by arguing that the novel's representation of homosexuality indirectly or inadvertently undermines what they depict as the author's otherwise stifling and inescapable orthodoxy. Such critics are typically happy to disavow

Waugh the doctrinaire papist while simultaneously laying claim to his creation, *Brideshead*, by accentuating its queerness. Francesca Coppa, in her contribution to the collection *Catholic Figures, Queer Narratives* (2007), elevates the aesthete Anthony Blanche from the role of supporting character to that of queer *agent provocateur*. Blanche, she insists, "escape[s] from the totalizing Catholic discourse which takes over *Brideshead*" and in so doing "provides the thin wedge for a reinterpretation of the novel."[4] Coppa's reinterpretation relies on reversing the thrust of the novel's main conversion narrative by reading the book as "a look back towards a lost pagan Arcadia" dominated by the romantic Sebastian Flyte.[5] Ultimately, this reading requires a conscious decision to reject the novel's Catholic discourse. Likewise, in "Homosexuality in *Brideshead Revisited*" (2011), Peter Christensen argues that the novel "treats homosexuality sympathetically instead of condemning it" and thereby challenges dogmatic Catholicism with "a more generous and *catholic* spirit."[6] Both Coppa and Christensen make valuable contributions to our understanding of the nature and function of homoerotic desire in *Brideshead*; however, they also return predictably to the firewall that separates Catholic orthodoxy from queer sexuality. What these critics fail to appreciate is that Waugh's novel participates in a decadent Catholic literary tradition that had already done a great deal to hack such firewalls, in part by appropriating a specifically Catholic form of lay celibacy that defied the expressive hypothesis inherent in the gay-straight dichotomy, which itself emerged partly in reaction to the Wilde trials.

Brideshead problematizes easy divisions between queer identity and Catholic faith in two ways familiar to those acquainted with decadent Catholic texts. First, it presents queer desire—and homosexual experimentation in particular— as part of an imperfect but potentially *enriching* element in a process of spiritual maturation. Second, the novel's conclusion eschews any simple return to compulsory hetero-normative modes of sexuality. Waugh's drama of conversion offers no simple progression from sinful sexual experimentation to more-or-less wholesome Catholic family life. Instead, the conclusion of *Brideshead* commits its central characters to a form of sexuality that is at once patently orthodox and potentially queer: celibacy. In *Celibacies: American Modernism and Sexual Life* (2013), Benjamin Kahan produces a history of celibacy as a positive mode of sexuality that often subverts more normative expressions focused exclusively on marriage and reproduction. Calling into question what conventionally qualifies as sex, Kahan focuses on the myriad ways in which celibacy "unsettles the familiar repression/liberation and normal/queer binaries."[7] Though his book builds on the foundational work of theorists such as Leo Bersani and Eve Sedgwick as well as the more recent work of Heather Love and Jack Halberstram, Kahan argues that practitioners of queer theory often fail to treat celibacy as a "coherent sexual identity rather than a 'closeting' screen for another identity."[8] Conventional queer readings of texts assume an "expressive hypothesis" that leaves "no room for sexuality that does not aspire to normative sexual acts."[9] Within the bounds of this hypothesis, the absence of sex is typically conceptualized as repression. For Kahan, celibacy "falls within the penumbra of the queer"; it exists on the outer edges of queerness but also contains some of its own hermeneutical possibilities because "celibate and queer readings overlap without being coextensive."[10] Since a celibate reading can simultaneously cooperate with and operate outside of queer models, such a reading may provide a way to illustrate points of overlap in Catholic and queer readings of *Brideshead*. As much as it might disconcert Kahan, who explicitly asserts his interest in "wrestling celibacy back from the political Right,"[11] the queerness of Waugh's celibates—their ability to operate outside of and even subvert culturally sanctioned notions of sexual normality while also pursuing or adhering to an orthodox morality—may help us to understand better the queerness of one of Catholicism's canonical novels.

By revisiting *Brideshead* without the common assumption that it simply plays at being gay before reasserting the straight sexual orthodoxies of mid-twentieth-century England, we may begin to see how the novel, if not necessarily the author, invites us to momentarily set aside gay-straight, queer-Catholic binaries in favor of a more nuanced vision of the possibilities of sexual-spiritual interpenetration. But, in order to appreciate this accomplishment, we must first acknowledge that Waugh's tenuous reconciliation of seemingly opposed discourse communities is not a wholly original endeavor. Looking back to the decadent school of the 1890s, we can understand better Waugh's appropriation of the art and myths of the queerest Catholic movement in English literary history. Recent scholarship has demonstrated Waugh's artistic debt to decadence,[12] but critics have yet to explore the relationship between decadence and Catholicism in his corpus. As a young writer, Waugh consciously modeled his craft on the work of the most overtly decadent novelist of the early twentieth century, the queer convert Ronald Firbank. When, in middle age, he composed his first overtly "Catholic" novel, Waugh drew on both the art of Aubrey Beardsley and the story of Oscar Wilde's deathbed conversion, vital sources of inspiration that critics have heretofore overlooked. He used this decadent material to construct his own distinctly queer conversion narrative. In doing so, he established *Brideshead* as part of a longer decadent tradition that implicitly troubles the divide between Catholic literary modernity and queer theory.

"Firbank Is Baroque"

A somewhat anomalous figure in British literature of the 1910s and 1920s, Ronald Firbank (1886–1926) embodies much of the spirit of *fin-de-siècle* decadence in works of fiction that have all the formal qualities of modernism. His invariably short novels combine the nonlinear narrative style and cinematic quality of texts like Ford's *The Good Soldier* (1915), Eliot's *The Waste Land* (1922), and Faulkner's *The Sound and the Fury* (1929) while still maintaining a blithe humor largely alien to such dour texts. Though still relatively unknown in modernist studies, Firbank has long maintained a devoted following among other novelists. Alan Hollinghurst, of whom we will hear more in the coda, devoted part of his doctoral thesis to Firbank and made him a central figure in his 1988 novel *The Swimming-Pool Library*. Harry Mathews, author of *Tlooth* (1966), once hailed Firbank as "*the* great formal innovator" and credited him with playing a larger role than Joyce in inventing modernism.[13] Hyperbole aside, Firbank was an innovator, and his example inspired Waugh.

Never quick to pay homage, Waugh openly acknowledged the older novelist's influence. Looking back on his early development as a writer in a 1962 interview, he admitted to flagrantly stealing from Firbank in one of his earliest novels, *Vile Bodies* (1930): "[*Vile Bodies*] was secondhand.... I cribbed much of the scene at the customs from Firbank."[14] The scene to which Waugh alludes was taken from Firbank's unfortunately titled *Prancing Nigger* (1924).[15] Here is the exchange that begins his customs scene: "'Have you nothing, young man, to declare?' '... Butterflies!' 'Exempt of Duty. Pass.'"[16] And here is Waugh's: "'Have you anything to declare?' 'Wings.' 'Have you wore [*sic*.] them?' 'Sure.' 'That's all right, then.'"[17] Firbank's dialogue plays subtly with the famous, and perhaps apocryphal, incident in which the young Oscar Wilde told an American customs official that he had nothing to declare but his genius.[18]

Unlike so many of his contemporaries, who worked hard to distance themselves from the legacy of the 1890s, Firbank wore the influence of Wilde, Beardsley, and Frederick Rolfe on his sleeve. He was the last dandyish holdover from a different age. The second son of a conservative MP and grandson of a self-made railway contractor, he inherited his family's money but none of its economic savvy and political ambition. A shy, effeminate, affected homosexual, Firbank embodied a decadent trope established by Huysmans in *À Rebours*: he was the supposedly "degenerate" male scion of a formerly prosperous family. He was also, not surprisingly given his decadent allegiances, a convert to Catholicism.

While studying at Cambridge in 1907, Firbank converted to Catholicism and was accepted into the Church by Mgr. Robert Hugh Benson, a literary man with his own connections to decadent Catholicism. Following in the footsteps of Cardinal Newman, Benson left the Anglican clergy in 1903 and became a Catholic priest in 1904. After taking his vows, Benson shared an intimate correspondence with the decadent novelist and would-be priest Frederick Rolfe (Baron Corvo)—so intimate that the letters were destroyed soon after his death.[19] Benson never became a household name, but Catholic publishers still regularly release new editions of his writings, especially his sensational dystopian fantasy *Lord of the World* (1907), a copy of which can be found in Waugh's library. In this proto science-fiction novel, a lowly British priest living in the near future ascends to the papacy and combats his doppelgänger, the Antichrist, who leads the forces of militant secular humanism in an attempt to wipe out the Catholic Church. *Lord of the World* has little of decadence about it, but it bears some resemblance to Rolfe's *Hadrian the Seventh* (1904), in which a failed English priest is unexpectedly elevated to the papacy only to be assassinated by a Scotsman. Most of Benson's work was less sensational. *The Conventionalists* (1908), a semiautobiographical novel published a year after *Lord of the World*, follows Algy Bannister, a fictionalized and idealized version of Firbank, through his conversion under the tutelage of a fictionalized Benson. Bannister eventually becomes a novice at a Carthusian monastery in Sussex; Firbank himself led a very different life after his conversion. He left Cambridge without a degree and spent years wandering the continent and traveling to more exotic locales, such as Haiti, Havana, and Barbados, all seemingly on a whim. This cosmopolitan streak surprised Firbank's British contemporaries, including Osbert Sitwell, who at first knew him only as an effeminate and shy eccentric.

Sitwell described the "unrivalled butterfly" as a man outside the regular social order of literary London:

> With a thin frame, long head, and a large aquiline, somewhat chinless face, the cheekbones prominent and rather highly coloured, showing that he was ill, he had something of the air, if one can imagine such a combination, of a witty and decadent Red Indian. And on to this stock had been grafted, too, a touch of priest, and even of curate. I have never seen anyone who in the least resembled him in looks.... This stranger haunted the background of my favorite scenes for me, just as those of Greco's pictures are frequented by a gaunt and spectral saint.[20]

Firbank, in this description, seems like a being from another world. A strange mixture of saint, savage, and priest, he hovers around the peripheries of modern

London like a specter, one marked by the same air of sickness and frailty that attended many artists of the nineties. Sitwell weaves this frailty into his own decadent mythmaking in a manner that resembles Arthur Symons's posthumous reflections on Dowson and Beardsley. According to Sitwell, "The angel of death ever hung over him [Firbank]. Moreover, he was much given to fortune-tellers, crystal-gazers, and givers of Egyptian amulets, and the soothsayers, seeing him, prophesied evil."[21] Indeed the angel of death claimed Firbank at an early age. A slight chill caught while visiting Rome was all that it took to kill this delicate aesthete at the age of thirty-nine. Framing Firbank's death as an almost natural extension of his vanity, Sitwell notes that the young dandy managed to avoid the age of forty, "the thought of which he so much disliked."[22] Firbank's body spent a short time interred in Rome's Protestant Cemetery along with Keats and Shelley before the officials realized their mistake and moved his Catholic remains to the Campo Verano. This final farcical turn could almost have been taken from one of Firbank's novels. Satirical in tone and notoriously lacking in plot, they are all concerned with the absurdities of human fate, and several engage with Catholicism and queerness in a patently decadent manner that Waugh would later imitate.

Nowhere is the influence of decadent Catholicism more evident in Firbank's corpus than in his novel *Concerning the Eccentricities of Cardinal Pirelli* (1926), which is partly a caricature of continental Catholicism. Pirelli, the Cardinal-Archbishop of Clemenza, is everything that British anti-Catholics could wish him to be. Licentious, power-hungry, and frivolous, he embodies the decadence that the Anglican Church deprecated. The only action in the story occurs in the first and final chapters. At the novel's outset, Pirelli presides over the baptism of a Duquesa's beloved Alsatian puppy, a baptism performed with crème de menthe instead of holy water. His animal instincts undisturbed by the sacrament, the puppy leaps from his doting owner's arms and proceeds to ride her unfortunate husband's leg. Unbeknownst to the Cardinal, a papal legate has witnessed the entire scene of bestiality and blasphemy. After news of the incident finds its way to Rome, the pontiff summons Pirelli for defrocking. This incident of sacramental abuse found its way back into the public eye in 2013 when Pope Francis excommunicated an Australian priest for, among other things, allowing a communicant to administer Communion to an Alsatian.[23] Pirelli manages to avoid punishment by dying of a heart attack while chasing a choirboy through his cathedral, in the nude.

Unfortunately, most commentary on *Concerning the Eccentricities of Cardinal Pirelli* stops after recounting these incidents, as if such shocking camp speaks for itself. But settling for paraphrase is a mistake because Firbank's wit, the thing that inspired Waugh the most, reveals itself only under the pressure of close reading. In an otherwise uneventful middle chapter, for example, Pirelli flees to the countryside to compose a defense of his actions:

> Standing amid gardens made for suffering and delight is the disestablished and, *sic transit*, slowly decaying monastery of the Desierto. Lovely as Paradise, oppressive perhaps as Eden, it had been since the days of the mystic Luigi of Granada a site well suited to meditation and retreat. Here, in the stilly cypress-court, beneath the snowy sierras of Santa Maria la Blanca, Theresa of Avila, worn and ill, though sublime in laughter, exquisite in beatitude, had composed a part of the *Way of Perfection*, and, here, in these same realms of peace, dominating the distant city of Clemenza and the fertile plains of Andalucia, Cardinal Pirelli, one blue mid-day towards the close of summer, was idly considering his Defence. "*Apologia*, no; merely a defence," he mused: "merely," he flicked the ash-tip of a cigar, "a defence! I defend myself, that's all! ..."
>
> A sigh escaped him.[24]

The garden of Pirelli's monastery refuge is "made for suffering and delight," a masochistic combination common in decadent Catholic texts. Firbank paradoxically calls this earthly paradise "oppressive as Eden." Oppressive, perhaps, because the venal cleric would be unsatisfied with the pleasures afforded by God's relatively austere earthly paradise. Surely, he would take little delight in Eve. In this place where Saint Teresa, "worn and ill, though sublime in laughter, exquisite in beatitude," composed her famous mystical treatise, Pirelli drafts his own defining document. His preference for the term "defence," "merely a defence," rather than "*Apologia*," implies that he sees himself not as a man who must explain his actions but as an unjustly persecuted defendant. Unlike the saintly Cardinal Newman, Pirelli clearly feels no need to write an elaborate explanation of his life. In fact, he seems to find the exercise tedious. As the ash falls from the tip of his cigar, he sighs at the ennui of justifying his ways to men.

Ultimately, Pirelli is a caricature created for the novelist's delight. Firbank's story reveals a fascination with corruption that can be realized only when a Cardinal, a prince of the Church, degenerates into a tired voluptuary. Such fascination is akin to that expressed by Gautier in his poem "Carmen" when the Archbishop of Toledo sings Mass at the feet of the iconic decadent femme fatale. Like Gautier, Firbank appreciated the farcical register of decadent Catholicism, and his tendency to juxtapose the sacred and profane for comic effect clearly attracted Waugh. For example, when Catholicism emerges as a subject of discussion in the first book of *Brideshead,* Firbank's influence is palpable. After Sebastian first introduces the topic of his faith into conversation, Charles is understandably dubious:

> "Oh dear, it's very difficult being a Catholic." ...
> "Well, I can't say I've noticed it. Are you struggling against temptation? You
>   don't seem much more virtuous than me."
> "I'm very, very much wickeder," said Sebastian indignantly.
> "Well then?"
> "Who was it who used to pray, 'O God, make me good, but not yet'?"
> "I don't know. You, I should think."
> "Why, yes, *I* do, every day. But it isn't that." He turned back to the pages of the
>   *News of the World* and said, "Another naughty scout-master." (*BR* 95)

Nearly one hundred pages into the novel, this conversation brings Catholic guilt into Charles's queer Arcadia for the first time. But the pathos of Sebastian's situation, his reflection on the painful struggle contained in the words taken from St. Augustine's *Confessions* (*c.* 397), is undercut by his interest in the tabloid naughtiness of the world. In *Brideshead,* Waugh employs this diversionary tactic repeatedly as a means of slowly introducing religion without allowing it to dominate the narrative or drown out the camp romance of decadence. When Charles attempts to draw out the conversation, Sebastian checks him with annoyance and reinforces his own ethos of cavalier frivolity: "Oh, don't be a *bore,* Charles. I want to read about a woman in Hull who's been using an instrument."

Waugh derived this tendency to juxtapose the sacred and profane to comic effect directly from Firbank and, by extension, Wilde; yet he insisted that Firbank's wit expressed a complexity, skill, and even seriousness that Wilde lacked. Waugh understood Firbank as an artist who absorbed and transformed Wildean decadence, elevating it from a state of ornamental frivolity to something more artistically sound:

> Those who delight in literary genealogy will find his ancestry somewhat obscure. He owes something to *Under the Hill* [Aubrey Beardsley's unfinished erotic novel] and Baron Corvo [Frederick Rolfe], but the more attentively he is studied, the more superficial does the debt appear.... His raw material, allowing for the inevitable changes of fashion, is almost identical with Oscar Wilde's—the lives of rich, slightly decadent people set against a background of traditional culture ... but Wilde was at heart radically sentimental. His wit is ornamental; Firbank's is structural. Wilde is rococo; Firbank is baroque.[25]

This excerpt from the essay "Ronald Firbank" (1929), written the year before Waugh's conversion, traces Firbank's "literary genealogy" and paints him as both decadent acolyte and modern innovator. Beardsley, Rolfe, and Wilde are obvious influences and models, but his debt to them is "superficial." Wilde and Firbank share the same "raw material," including "slightly decadent people"; Firbank, however, outdoes Wilde in terms of wit. To support this assertion, Waugh contrasts the eminently quotable Wilde with his twentieth-century counterpart, whose humor is rarely if ever found in one-liners or clever turns of phrase. There are no jokes in Firbank's work; instead, subtle details of the narrative coalesce into humorous moments. The distinction seems true enough, and the metaphorical contrast of rococo and baroque carries greater meaning than Waugh is willing to spell out explicitly. First, the chronology is inverted. The flamboyant, ornamental, asymmetrical rococo style grew out of the baroque, but Waugh makes Firbank's innovation a reversion to an earlier, only slightly less florid form. Second, the baroque association with the Catholic Counter-Reformation and the rococo association with secular superficiality suggest a shift in focus from Wilde's epigrammatic wit to a slightly more austere, religious perspective. To put it another way, Waugh depicts Firbank as an artist who arose from a gaudy Louis XV chair in Paris and settled into a pew at the Gesù in Rome. The two settings and styles are undeniably related, and elaborately decorative, but the traveler's progress is a movement away from decadent style and toward something equally ornate but more disciplined and more Catholic.

Charles Ryder is also baroque. Waugh makes this point explicit when Charles discusses the role of Brideshead Castle in his aesthetic development:

> Since the days when, as a schoolboy, I used to bicycle round the neighboring parishes, rubbing brasses and photographing fonts, I had nursed a love of architecture, but, though in opinion I had made that easy leap, characteristic of my generation, from the puritanism of Ruskin to the puritanism of Roger Fry, my sentiments at heart were insular and medieval.
>
> This was my conversion to the Baroque. Here under that high and insolent dome, under those coffered ceilings; here … I felt a whole new system of nerves alive within me, as though the water that spurted and bubbled among the stones, was indeed a life-giving spring. (*BR* 90)

Before he came to Brideshead, Charles's love of architecture was a paradoxically heterogeneous mix of modern "puritanism" and "insular" medievalism. Under the influence of Sebastian's family home, he experiences a conversion that awakens a new artistic sensibility. The water that flows from the castle's baroque fountain becomes something sacred in this metaphor of aesthetic conversion and baptism. Immediately following this transformative experience, Charles finds the box of oil paints that he will use in his first major artistic project. This aesthetic awakening is the first of the two conversions that Charles experiences on the Marchmain family estate, and it explicitly anticipates the second in a manner that suggests that Waugh never ceased associating baroque sensibility with Catholicism.

Again, what separates Wilde and Firbank, in Waugh's estimation, is the ornamental rococo superficiality of the former and the sound baroque structure of the latter. Wilde almost seemed to anticipate such a critique in *De Profundis* while contemplating the necessary evolution of his style after his experience of suffering in prison: "Something must come into my work, of fuller harmony ... of simpler architectural order, of some aesthetic quality at any rate."[26] Waugh's critique bears its subject's stamp of approval. In his haste to disavow or explain away the obvious marks of decadent artifice in Firbank's writing, however, Waugh seems to miss the ironic fact that the baroque always already contains and anticipates the rococo. Like Firbank, Waugh knowingly engaged with decadence without fully participating in it. As early as 1919, while attending Lancing College, Waugh took an interest in decorative book binding (a potentially decadent preoccupation, as he was fully aware): "I have just thought," the young Waugh writes, "what an excellent binding could be made of half black morocco, and half cloth of gold, but I have only enough of it to do a very small book and it would only be suitable for certain sorts, such as Oscar Wilde."[27] Though clearly drawn to decadent style, Waugh recognizes that a book produced in this style might only be "suitable for certain sorts." His texts engage with decadence in a similar manner. *Brideshead* in particular reveals an attraction to the queerer elements of decadence that is never wholly subdued by or subsumed into orthodox Catholic belief. Like the works of Firbank, many of Waugh's texts amalgamate the queer spirit of the rococo with the more explicitly Catholic moral structure of the baroque.

Aubrey Beardsley's Decadent Arcadia

Firbank played a key role in helping Waugh develop his signature satirical wit. To furnish the queer Oxonian Arcadia of his first "serious" novel, however, the author of *Brideshead* returned to the world of 1890s decadence. Among the leading personalities of *fin-de-siècle* decadence—such as Lionel Johnson, Beardsley, and Wilde—Waugh discovered artists who found in the Catholic

Church a beautiful storehouse of myths and symbols as well as a theology that invited them to reconceptualize their queer desires within the framework of a demanding but potentially salvific sacramental economy. Wilde's initial attraction to Catholicism peaked during his Oxford years, when he wrote shame-ridden paeans to the Virgin Mary and narrowly dodged formal conversion. Following this early and seemingly earnest fascination with Rome, Wilde went on to all but define the persona of the modern homosexual while simultaneously complicating the emerging cultural conception of a neat divide between so-called normal and aberrant modes of sexual expression. Other decadent figures troubled this easy binary even further by seemingly refusing to make use of their genitals at all. Hanson links the decadent distaste for actually having sex to a preference for artistic and spiritual ecstasies: "Huysmans, Rolfe, and Gray took vows of chastity, while others, like Pater, Beardsley, and Johnson, might as well have.... The ecstasies of art and religion are infinitely superior to the physical spasm of sex because they are a spiritualization and an intensification of desire. Even Wilde would have agreed."[28] The case of Beardsley is especially intriguing in light of his influence on *Brideshead*, a matter previously unexplored in Waugh studies.

Beardsley's eventual conversion to Catholicism owed a great deal to his patron Marc-André Raffalovich, whose *Uranisme et Unisexualité* (1896) challenged the inherent moral superiority of heterosexuality and praised what he called unisexuality. Raffalovich also insisted that love between men should exclude physical intercourse and focus instead on artistic expression and celibate friendship. In the same year that he published this important work of queer cultural criticism, Raffalovich joined the Catholic Church. He chose the baptismal name Sebastian, sometimes signing himself "Your most loving brother, Sebastian" when corresponding with the love of his life, the decadent poet John Gray.[29] Beardsley carried on regular correspondence with both men and often addressed Raffalovich as "My dear Mentor." The address was partly flattery of a generous benefactor; nevertheless, Raffalovich presented Beardsley with a vision of sexuality that embraced both the schoolboy naughtiness of his erotically charged art and the fervor of his developing Catholic faith. Waugh made use of the art and myths of decadence throughout his career, but one illustration by Beardsley played an essential role in his decadent drama of conversion, *Brideshead*. With the help of evidence from Waugh's library, we can see how he turns a subtle allusion to Beardsley into the central symbol of the first book of *Brideshead*. Only by appreciating Waugh's appropriation of Beardsley can we begin to understand his novel as a self-conscious participant in a longer

Catholic literary tradition, one especially concerned with the relationship between aesthetics, theology, and non-normative sexuality.

In Book One, "Et in Arcadia Ego," Charles attempts to find his place in the homosocial wonderland of 1920s Oxford. When he first arrives, his respectable cousin Jasper attempts to steer him clear of High-Church "sodomites": "You'll find you spend half your second year shaking off the undesirable friends you made in your first.... Beware of the Anglo-Catholics—they're all sodomites with unpleasant accents. In fact, steer clear of all the religious groups; they do nothing but harm" (*BR* 27). Charles promptly ignores this advice and finds himself in the company of two charmingly queer Catholics, Lord Sebastian Flyte and Anthony Blanche. Soon after falling under Sebastian's spell, Charles begins an aesthetic transformation that manifests itself most immediately in a seemingly superficial alteration to the décor of his college rooms. Upon arriving in Oxford, Charles had taken some pride in decorating his rooms with the avant-garde art of Van Gogh, Roger Fry, and McKnight Kauffer. But his exposure to Sebastian's circle leaves him disenchanted with these masters of modernity:

> When at length I returned to my rooms and found them exactly as I had left them that morning, I detected a jejune air that had not irked me before. What was wrong? Nothing except the golden daffodils seemed to be real. Was it the [Fry] screen? I turned it to face the wall. That was better. (*BR* 35)

Sick of the avant-garde pretension represented by Roger Fry's Provençal landscape, Charles changes his environment to better match the aesthetic of Sebastian's baroque charm and Anthony's queer camp. By the time his respectable cousin Jasper comes to rebuke him for taking up with these "sodomites with unpleasant accents," Charles's room has "cast its austere winter garments, and, by not very slow stages, assumed a richer wardrobe" (*BR* 45). The transformed room no longer reflects its inhabitant's concern with following current artistic trends. It now reflects Charles's fascination with the luxuries of consumption: "the box of a hundred cabinet Partagas," "a dozen frivolous books," "a Lalique decanter and glasses" (*BR* 45). As far as we can tell from his final description of the room, visual art no longer has a place. No prints or screens or posters proclaim Charles's artistic allegiances. He has ceased airing his artistic pretensions, but Waugh has just begun airing his own.

At the center of Charles's decadent cell is an object that functions as the principal symbol of Book One of *Brideshead*: "A human skull lately purchased from the school of medicine, which, resting in a bowl of roses, formed, at the moment, the chief decoration of my table. It bore the motto '*Et in Arcadia Ego*' inscribed on its forehead" (*BR* 95). At first glance, the skull seems like an allusion to a much older memento mori tradition. The motto, "Et in Arcadia Ego," is typically linked to Poussin's painting *Les Bergers d'Arcadie* (1637),[30] in which the words appear on an ancient tomb, much to the consternation of a group of youthful shepherds. In alluding to Poussin, however, Waugh also evokes Aubrey Beardsley's satirical commentary on *Les Bergers d'Arcadie*, titled "*Et in Arcadia Ego*" (1896), thereby deepening the aura of decadence that surrounds Charles's youthful transformation.

Waugh maintained an interest in Beardsley from his early days at Oxford well into the 1940s. Though he never published anything substantial about the enfant terrible of the *fin-de-siècle* art scene, Waugh mentions Beardsley occasionally in his early prose,[31] most notably in his first book, *Rossetti: His Life and Works* (1928), in which Beardsley represents a definitive break with earlier traditions of pen-and-ink artistry. While discussing art since Rossetti, Waugh writes that "from Beardsley onward … to almost every black-and-white designer and illustrator living, there has been a new attitude to pen drawing based on the initial conception of a white page to be decorated with black lines, and the fewer lines, so long as they are significantly and rightly disposed, the better."[32] Waugh never idolized Beardsley, but he clearly grasped his importance as an innovator. Apart from this commentary on Beardsley's formal innovations, Waugh had little to say about the artist. Beardsley is, however, well represented in Waugh's library, now housed at the Harry Ransom Center at the University of Texas. For example, Waugh owned a complete bound series of the most substantial vehicle for Beardsley's early work, *The Yellow Book*. Since the books still bear his father's bookplate, it seems likely that Evelyn inherited them following Arthur Waugh's death in 1943, just before he began to write *Brideshead*. The elder Waugh published an essay on "Reticence in Literature" in the first number of *The Yellow Book* (1894) alongside some of Beardsley's iconic illustrations, and the two men may have crossed paths at one of Edmund Gosse's fashionable salons. These volumes of *The Yellow Book* are a potent reminder of the place of Aubrey Beardsley and decadence in the Waugh family's history. Evelyn's own bookplate appears in the extraordinary J. M. Dent and Co. 1893 edition of the *Morte d'Arthur*, which Beardsley illustrated. It can also be found in a bound copy of the first two issues of *The Savoy*, the periodical that replaced *The Yellow Book* once it became too conventional. This appreciation for Beardsley was obvious enough to those closest to Waugh. In a copy of *The Best of Beardsley*, Waugh's eldest daughter inscribed "Papa with lots of love Teresa." The book contains a reproduction of "Et in Arcadia Ego."

Beardsley's substantial presence in Waugh's library is matched by his obvious influence on Waugh's own illustrations and drawings. Though destined to become a novelist, the young Waugh was deeply interested in the visual arts. At the age of fourteen, he wrote a defense of cubism, published by the journal *Drawing and Design*. After leaving Oxford, he tried pursuing the same career path as Charles Ryder but soon found that he lacked the necessary skill and diligence. Despite abandoning painting as a career, Waugh produced a significant amount of visual art during his lifetime and preserved it for posterity. Among his many experiments from his time at Oxford are several Beardsley-esque pen-and-ink sketches. One, dated 1923, depicts a reclining satyr that seems to represent Waugh's own well-known devotion to debauchery during his Oxford years. Another drawing depicts a similar satyr sitting beside a tombstone that could fittingly bear the title "Et in Arcadia Ego" (Figure 5.1).

Figure 5.1 Evelyn Waugh, *Satyr with Tombstone*. Used with the permission of the Harry Ransom Center, The University of Texas at Austin.

Whether or not the sketches suggest Waugh's admiration for Beardsley, they reveal the influence of his distinctive style.

Aside from the fact that it bears the same title as the first book of *Brideshead*, Beardsley's *Et in Arcadia Ego* (Figure 5.2) provides a more contemporary point of reference than Poussin's *Les Bergers d'Arcadie* (*c.* 1638) (Figure 5.3).[33]

Figure 5.2 Aubrey Beardsley, *Et in Arcadia Ego* (1896). Used with the permission of the Harry Ransom Center, The University of Texas at Austin.

Figure 5.3 Nicolas Poussin, *Les Bergers d'Arcadie* (*c.* 1650) Musée du Louvre, Paris/ Art Resource, NY. Image used with permission.

Beardsley's illustration also has much more in common with the purely homosocial Oxonian paradise described in the first book of *Brideshead*. Poussin depicts a Virgilian pastoral landscape populated by three lusty shepherds and a beautiful maiden in classical garb contemplating a tomb that bears the cryptic inscription "Et in Arcadia Ego" ("I too in Arcadia").[34] The phrase is enigmatic and ambiguous in large part because of the unidentified "ego." The inhabitant of the tomb may have wished to convey a simple reminder, "I [the deceased] once lived in Arcadia," but the motto is conventionally understood as a warning about mortality: "I [death] am present even in paradise." The shepherds' confusion suggests that they inhabit a sort of prelapsarian earthly paradise in which death, represented by the mysterious tomb, remains both a yet-undiscovered terror and an ancient nemesis. Goethe adopted the motto as the epigraph to his *Italian Journey* (1816–17) but seemed exclusively interested in its nostalgic resonance (i.e., "I spent good days in Arcadia once"). He lends the phrase added significance by discussing the history of the Accademia degli Arcadi, the Roman literary academy founded in 1690, which took the Panpipe as its emblem and sought to save Italian poetry from rococo artificiality by returning to a simpler pastoral form of literary expression. The phrase eventually found its way into the history of British aestheticism through Pater, who, self-consciously following Goethe's lead, uses a slightly adapted version, "Et Ego in Arcadia Fui" ("And even in Arcadia, there I was"), as the epigraph to the final chapter of *The Renaissance*. In that chapter, which examines the life and work of archaeologist and art historian Johann Joachim Winckelmann (1717–68), Pater dwells on Winckelmann's time in Rome as a temporary escape from the "tarnished intellectual world of Germany" to a paradise of learning and beauty.[35] Like Goethe, Pater seems to adopt the phrase unironically as an expression of the nostalgia felt by northern European intellectuals for the classical beauty and sunny climate of the Mediterranean, which temporarily counteracts the *fatigue du nord*. Pater himself spent time in Italy, but his Arcadia was never in the present. He was always a tourist in classical Sparta or quattrocento Florence, a voyeur peering with fascinated intensity at the perfections of a bygone era.

Picking up on Pater's dual fascination with and isolation from an idealized past, Beardsley replaced the typical subjects of Arcadian art with what might be seen as a middle-aged British tourist. Instead of robust young shepherds Beardsley substitutes a slender, balding dandy complete with a lace cravat, pencil mustache, and a petite cane—a diminutive phallus that leaves something to be desired when juxtaposed with the shepherds' ample staffs. This aging fop is nothing like his predecessors. Clearly a creature of the *urbs artificialis*, this city-dweller seems wholly out of place in any natural surroundings. His pointed ballerina's feet seek to avoid full contact with the earth. He seems both fascinated and overwhelmed by the spectacle of the phallic tombstone penetrating the leafy pubis of the yew tree, traditional symbol of death, which stretches its limbs ominously above his balding head. Furthermore, his discovery of death is solitary. He has no one with whom to interpret the epitaph carved below the funeral urn, and his position as solitary interpreter is highlighted by the fact that Beardsley renders the phrase as "ET IN ARCADIA/EGO." The dandy reflects the isolated "I." This disciple of artifice is as much a foreigner in a Virgilian Arcadia as death. Poussin's shepherdess offsets the threat of death with the promise of new life, but one can hardly imagine Beardsley's dandy enjoying the company of any woman, especially a vigorous bucolic goddess. Chris Snodgrass captures the irony of the scene nicely in *Aubrey Beardsley, Dandy of the Grotesque* (1995):

> Beardsley makes the pathos of inevitable death doubly ironic, having the issue faced in his pastoral Arcadia by a virtual caricature of the urban artificial dandy ... The dandy's presumably youthful jauntiness, unruffled confidence, and pretentious elegance are undercut by his distinctly receding hairline; unusually

diminutive cane; contorted, vaguely satyric feet ... and by the fact that above and around the pedestal reach out the dark boughs of a yew tree.[36]

By the time the illustration was published in 1896, Beardsley's health was swiftly declining, and his work for *The Savoy* was, to a greater degree than usual, obsessed with the idea of impending death. *Et in Arcadia Ego* appeared in the eighth and final issue of the periodical,[37] the content of which was supplied entirely by Beardsley and his publisher Leonard Smithers. Compared to his *Salomé* drawings or his illustrations of the *Morte d'Arthur*, *Et in Arcadia Ego* receives relatively little attention in Beardsley criticism, but it left a lasting impression on Waugh.

Appreciating Beardsley's influence on Waugh and the allusion to *Et in Arcadia Ego* helps us to understand better the nature of the fragile paradise he constructs in Book One of *Brideshead*. The Arcadia that Waugh establishes is nothing like Poussin's Virgilian pastoral. Exclusively homosocial and covertly homosexual, Charles's Oxford has little room for simple shepherds and none at all for a buxom shepherdess. The noteworthy inhabitants of his world are queer Catholics, late-born decadents of the kind with whom Waugh spent his time at Oxford as a member of the Hypocrites' Club, a notorious clique of artists and hedonists. We know with certainty that the personalities and eccentricities of at least two members of this club inspired the creation of Anthony Blanche,[38] the playful devil animating Charles's queer Arcadia:

> He was tall, slim, rather swarthy, with large saucy eyes ... ; part Gallic, part Yankee, part, perhaps, Jew; wholly exotic.
>
> This, I did not need telling, was Anthony Blanche, the "aesthete" *par excellence*, a byword of iniquity from Cherwell Edge to Somerville. He had been pointed out to me often in the streets, as he pranced along with his high peacock tread; I had heard his voice in the George challenging conventions; and now meeting him, under the spell of Sebastian, I found myself enjoying him voraciously. (*BR* 34)

An "aesthete" and a "byword for iniquity," Anthony sets himself apart from his peers with his affected stutter and a "high peacock tread" that calls to mind the light step of the dandy in Beardsley's illustration.

For all his originality of appearance and wit, however, Anthony derives much of his character from Ambrose Silk, a Wildean artist from Waugh's earlier novel *Put Out More Flags* (1942). Ambrose has outlived his era and must slum it with the uninspired young members of the 1940's avant-garde. The bohemians with whom he associates consider him "a survival from the *Yellow Book*." He is painfully aware of how anachronistic he seems in "the new decade":

A Pansy. An old queen. A habit of dress, a tone of voice, an elegant, humorous deportment that had been admired and imitated, a swift, epicene felicity of wit, the art of dazzling and confusing those he despised—these had been his; and now they were the current exchange of comedians; there were only a few restaurants now, which he could frequent without fear of ridicule…. Beddoes had died in solitude, by his own hand; Wilde had been driven into the shadows, tipsy and garrulous, but, to the end, a figure of tragedy looming big in his own twilight. But Ambrose, thought Ambrose, what of him? Born after his time, in an age which made a type of him, a figure of farce.[39]

Because of his resemblance to Wilde, Ambrose has become a type and a figure of ridicule. Wilde at least expired as "a figure of tragedy looming big in his own twilight." Waugh's dandy is little more than an "old queen," except when we find him occupying one of the famous haunts of decadence: "The Café Royal, perhaps because of its distant associations with Oscar and Aubrey, was one of the places where Ambrose preened himself, spread his feathers and felt free to take wing. He had left his persecution mania downstairs with his hat and umbrella. He defied the universe."[40] Among the ghosts of Wilde and Beardsley, Ambrose momentarily casts off the depression of the living anachronism and feels at home. He allows time to "slip back to an earlier age than his own youth … when amid a more splendid décor of red plush and gilt caryatides *fin-de-siècle* young worshipers crowded to the tables of Oscar and Aubrey."[41] A decadent artist born too late to fawn over "Oscar and Aubrey" but too soon to ride the crest of the next artistic wave, he is out of place in the mid-twentieth century. In a last-ditch effort to assert his relevance in the twentieth century, Ambrose sets out to revive the dead aesthetic of the last century and cajoles a publisher into supporting a new magazine that will transcend the political strife of the Second World War and devote itself to art for art's sake. He envisions his magazine, the aptly named *Ivory Tower*, as "something like the old *Yellow Book*."[42] Its inaugural issue centers on an artistic celebration of the life of Ambrose's German lover, Hans—a former Nazi soldier destined to die in a concentration camp. Those familiar with *Brideshead* will notice the presentiment of Sebastian's less idealized lover, Kurt. Unfortunately, a bit of ill-advised editing turns Ambrose's homoerotic elegy in prose into what appears to be fascist propaganda. To escape incarceration, he flees to Ireland disguised as a Catholic priest. In a final farcical turn, Waugh sends the last of the decadents into exile in the garb of the Church. The tragicomic story of Ambrose Silk plays only a supporting role in *Put Out More Flags*, but it hints at the more serious engagement with decadence in *Brideshead Revisited*, in which Ambrose reemerges under another name.

If Anthony Blanche embodies all the transgressive dandyism of British decadence, then Sebastian captures its spiritual angst. When we first meet the enchanting young peer, he seems, like Anthony, to mimic the eccentricities of a past age. Aloysius, his pet teddy bear, for example, evokes Gérard de Nerval's pet lobster, Thibault, whom he claimed to have taken on numerous jaunts at the end of a blue silk leash. Significantly, Sebastian's toy takes on a life of its own as a symbol of the failure of his seemingly invincible innocence. Like his titular saint, Aloysius symbolizes youthful innocence and purity, as well as aristocratic prestige. Sebastian abandons the bear only after he enters the downward spiral of shame and self-destruction engendered by his pious mother's well-intentioned but disastrous attempts to control her son. As his name suggests, Sebastian is destined for a kind of suffering entirely alien to the childish Arcadias of the nursery and Oxford. Anthony's flirtatious comment—"My dear, I should like to stick you full of barbed arrows like a p-p-pincushion"—emphasizes that Waugh had the penetrated martyr in mind when he named Sebastian, whose surname, Flyte, might also be a phonetic reminder of the "flight" of arrows that pierced the saint's body.[43] Read this way, the full name hints at Sebastian's saintliness and self-torturing shame. It is also reminiscent of the name Wilde assumed after his release from prison, Sebastian Melmoth, a pseudonym that blurs the line between the saved and the damned by joining the name of the patron saint of athletes and soldiers (and homosexuals) with that of the Faustian protagonist of *Melmoth the Wanderer* (1820), a novel written by Wilde's uncle.

Richard Kaye, who has written extensively about the figure of St. Sebastian in nineteenth- and twentieth-century literature and culture, summarizes Wilde's infatuation with the saint:

> Oscar Wilde, enchanted with Guido's [Guido Reni's] rendition of Sebastian, which he saw on an 1877 trip to Genoa, embraced the martyr as a personal saint and in the process helped to turn Sebastian into specially homosexual property. The playwright's youthful fascination for the Catholic Church ... accounts for much of his interest in the symbolic trappings of Sebastian imagery (34). Dorian Gray, for example, owns a cloak which is starred with the "medallions of many saints and martyrs, among whom was St. Sebastian" (114).... Adopting the accouterments of Roman martyrdom as a badge of honor, Wilde chose the name of "Sebastian Melmoth" as his nom de voyage on departing for Paris after his 1897 release from Reading Gaol. Wilde's complex relation to Sebastian suggests the contradictory appeal of the martyr, whose arrows, recalling the *stigmata diavoli* of a Medieval Plague, denoted the visible markings of the homosexual outcast.[44]

Wilde did not discover Sebastian. For centuries, the saint served not as a feminized fleshly fetish but as one of the more masculine figures in the vast ranks of the beatified dead. Generations of English soldiers, archers especially, prayed to the saint for courage in battle and assistance eviscerating their enemies. Outside of England, however, Sebastian developed a different kind of following among artists who, perhaps bored with using the crucifixion to study and depict the male nude, took a special interest in the penetrated saint. But what inspired men like Guido in Italy repulsed many in England. As Kaye points out, respectable English intellectuals such as Charles Dickens spent a good deal of the early nineteenth century denouncing fleshly renaissance depictions of the saints in general and Sebastian in particular. Unsurprisingly, art that inspired disapprobation from men like Dickens became irresistible to more adventurous British artists. For Wilde, John Gray, "Michael Field," and Montague Summers, to name a few, Sebastian became an important symbol of same-sex desire.

By the time Waugh created his Sebastian, the saint was established as the most prominent figure in decadent Catholic hagiography, excepting the Virgin Mary. By appropriating this loaded name and bestowing it on a beautiful youth destined to a life of dissolution followed by a return to the Church, Waugh shows an understanding of the essential link between decadence and Catholicism, as well as a familiarity with the decadent conversion narrative established in the lives and art of men like Beardsley, Wilde, Gray, Johnson, Dowson, and Douglas. Anthony Blanche is a late-born decadent, but Sebastian Flyte is a late-born decadent Catholic, and his spiritual drama is uncannily familiar. Lionel Johnson turned to alcohol when his fleshly desires outstripped the moral demands of his faith. Wilde haunted the Vatican under the name Sebastian following his exile. Dowson wrote poems and short stories that express a longing for escape from the world in the sheltering alternative-reality of the cloister. Book One of *Brideshead* creates a seemingly ideal Arcadia, but the promise of its epitaph is inescapable: outside the sheltering walls of Oxford and the childish comforts of the nursery lies a life that demands suffering and ends in death.

Book Two, "Brideshead Deserted," casts Charles out of his queer Arcadia and into the modern wasteland. It fulfills the implicit promise of the epitaph "Et in Arcadia Ego," which is a reminder that nothing in this world is permanent. Wasted by alcohol, Sebastian falls out with everyone around him and retreats to North Africa. As Sebastian's influence on the story wanes, Rex Mottram comes to the foreground as the representative force of the modern world, and Charles leaves youth, romance, and religion in Oxford and at Brideshead: "'I have left behind illusion,' I said to myself. 'Henceforth I live in a world of three dimensions—with the aid of my five senses'" (*BR* 195). He abandons his Arcadia, begins an artistic career as the last documenter of the great houses of a crumbling aristocracy, and leaves the Flytes in a state of slow collapse. The modern world he enters is Rex's world, one clearly contained in three dimensions and circumscribed by five senses. In this world, neither refined decadence nor sincere Catholicism has a place. When Rex imitates Huysmans's decadent protagonist Des Esseintes by gifting his fiancée Julia with a live tortoise bearing her initials on its shell in diamonds, he simultaneously reveals his material wealth and his aesthetic fatuity. When he attempts to take instruction in Julia's faith, Rex is equally unsuccessful; he leaves his Jesuit priest frankly baffled. Though his charge is dead set on joining the Church, the instructor, despairing of ever reaching him, complains that Rex "doesn't seem to have the least intellectual curiosity or natural piety.... he doesn't correspond to any degree of paganism known to the missionaries" (*BR* 221). After her marriage deteriorates, Julia seconds this assessment: "He isn't a real person at all; he's just a few faculties of a man highly developed." The reasoning behind Waugh's indictment of Rex is familiar among Christian writers of the era. T. S. Eliot repeatedly accused modernity of producing incomplete individuals worthy of neither salvation nor damnation, a point he makes most notably in his essay on Baudelaire (1930). C. S. Lewis similarly foretold the rise of one dimensional "men without chests" in *The Abolition of Man* (1943). If Book Two of *Brideshead* moves away from the fascinating decadence of the *fin de siècle* and into a soulless modernity, then the final section of the novel offers a complex alternative to both.

G. K. Chesterton provides the metaphoric vocabulary for this alternative. Book Three takes its name, "A Twitch upon the Thread," from one of Chesterton's Father Brown detective stories, an allusion that Waugh imbues with special significance over the course of the novel. Chesterton's story first appears in the text during the early crisis of Sebastian's descent into alcoholism. In one of the ghastlier scenes in the book, Lady Marchmain attempts to ease her mind and distract the family from her son's behavior by reverting to her old practice of reading to the children after dinner: "It was the custom ... always to ask Lady Marchmain to read aloud on evenings of family tension.... That night she read part of *The Wisdom of Father Brown*" (*BR* 150). One gets the sense that such readings were common during her estranged husband's bouts of drunkenness. Waugh uses the incident to plant the seed of what will slowly develop into the novel's main theme. Following Lady Marchmain's death and the closing of the chapel, both metaphors for the family's spiritual decline, Cordelia draws on Chesterton as a source of comfort and hope:

Anyhow, the family haven't been very constant, have they? There's him [Lord Marchmain] gone and Sebastian gone and Julia gone. But God won't let them go for long, you know. I wonder if you remember the story mummy read us the evening Sebastian first got drunk—I mean the *bad* evening. "Father Brown" said something like "I caught him" (the thief) "with an unseen hook and an invisible line which is long enough to let him wander to the ends of the world and still to bring him back with a twitch upon the thread." (*BR* 254)

Curiously, the story Cordelia references does not come from the collection *The Wisdom of Father Brown* (1914), which Charles recalls Lady Marchmain reading on "the *bad* evening." The idea of the twitch upon the thread comes from the short story "The Queer Feet," which appears in *The Innocence of Father Brown* (1911). This slight textual incongruity could be an invitation to question the accuracy of Charles's memories, or Waugh may have simply wished to associate his allusion to Chesterton more with wisdom than innocence; or maybe he simply forgot. Either way, at the family's nadir, Cordelia foreshadows the conclusion of the novel's spiritual drama by suggesting that divine grace might still draw all the children of Brideshead back to their ancestral religion. Such foreshadowing may seem heavy-handed, but Waugh moderates Cordelia's omniscience by having her overlook the possibility of Charles's own conversion. During their conversation he asks if she is still attempting to convert him, and she replies, "Oh, no. That's all over, too" (*BR* 254). The capitulation is significant in a girl who once attempted to convert the Kaiser through prayer; it allows Waugh to imply that even the pious Cordelia may underestimate the power of divine grace. This same grace snares Charles early in life, but the twitch upon the thread that draws him to Catholicism comes only through an act of remembrance sparked by a coincidental return to Brideshead during the Second World War. In this way, Chesterton's fishing metaphor becomes central to Waugh's entire project.

Waugh was conscious of his debt to Chesterton, as he once made clear in a memo to producers at MGM studios, who were considering a film adaptation of *Brideshead*. Hoping to elucidate the novel for the philistines in Hollywood, Waugh drew their attention to the important source text:

The Roman Catholic Church has the unique power of keeping remote control over human souls which have once been part of her. G.K. Chesterton has compared this to the fisherman's line, which allows the fish the illusion of free play in the water and yet has him by the hook; in his own time the fisherman by a 'twitch upon the thread' draws the fish to land.[45]

Waugh knew Chesterton from an early age,[46] and the old champion of orthodoxy clearly had a profound influence on *Brideshead*. In the novel, Chesterton emerges as a purveyor of sage wisdom and a voice speaking a different language than the dialect of either the *fin de siècle* or the modern era. Chesterton was both a serious critic of modernity and a trenchant adversary to the decadent nineties. *The Man Who Was Thursday* (1908) is, among other things, an explicit attack on what Chesterton saw as Oscar Wilde's obsession with decay, moral corruption, and art-for-art's-sake.[47] The novel opens with a verse dedication to a like-minded friend, Edmund Clerihew Bentley; the poem begins with a condemnation of the Schopenhauerian pessimism that informed much of late Victorian decadence:

> Life was a fly that faded, and death a drone that stung;
> The world was very old indeed when you and I were young.
> They twisted even decent sin to shapes not to be named:
> Men were ashamed of honour; but we were not ashamed.[48]

Chesterton contrasts his honorable, vigorous youth with the cult of decay and spiritual corruption that defined the art of the era. He goes on to evoke Whitman as an artistic ally against Wildean decadence: "And the *Green Carnation* withered, as in forest fires that pass, / Roared in the wind of all the world ten million *leaves of grass*."[49] The verse is not Chesterton at his best, and the irony of enlisting Whitman as an ally of straight orthodoxy seems a rather innocent touch. Chesterton believed that he was siding with Whitman's life-affirming and joyous vision against what he saw as a cult of decay. In short, he saw himself as a crusader against decadence.

But if Chesterton provides one of the keys to *Brideshead*, then what sense is there in Hanson's claim that the novel "may be seen as a modernist classic of decadent Catholicism"?[50] Those scholars sympathetic to what they see as Waugh's essentially orthodox worldview are often happy to accept, beneath the novel's exquisite style and biting humor, a fairly straightforward narrative movement from sin to salvation. Within the discourse community of the Catholic Church, the painful but theologically tidy conclusion feels both natural and good. Waugh, though titillating and savage at times, is theologically sound. More than Wilde and some other decadent Catholic writers of the late nineteenth and early twentieth centuries, Waugh was consciously concerned with maintaining orthodoxy in his art at all times. After reviewing *The Heart of the Matter* (1948), in which Graham Greene comes perilously close to justifying suicide, Waugh cautioned his friend about the dangers of allowing heterodox ideas to creep into his work:

> I think it will lead others astray. Indeed I saw a review by Raymond Mortimer in which he stated ... that you thought Scobie [the novel's protagonist] a saint. I think you will have a great deal of troublesome controversy in the USA. The bishops there are waiting to jump on decadent European Catholicism—or so it seemed to me—and I just escaped delation by sending everyone to heaven.[51]

Clearly Waugh was aware that European Catholicism had a strong reputation for decadence and heterodoxy, a reputation that he believed any Catholic author should try to avoid reinforcing. His final comment, "I just escaped delation by sending everyone to heaven," suggests that the seemingly tidy closure of *Brideshead* was partially informed by a desire to avoid "delation" (denunciation) by distancing the novel from the tradition of "decadent European Catholicism" and distracting readers from some of its queerer elements.

Brideshead certainly feels irreproachably orthodox. By the conclusion, everyone has either dropped his or her bad habits and found a place in the Church or, like Rex and Anthony, fallen out of the narrative. But the fact that Waugh believed himself liable to censure by Church authorities means that he understood that his novel was potentially scandalous. In fact, his letter to Greene characterizes the imaginative act of mass salvation at *Brideshead*'s conclusion as a sort of cover for the rest of the book. Hanson's identification of the novel as a "modernist classic of decadent Catholicism" invites us to consider that Waugh does more than simply lead his characters and readers on a circuitous spiritual journey from evil to good; he invites us to treat the novel as more than a morality play in prose. The Arcadia of Book One, for example, draws on the spiritual-sensual tension that defines many decadent Catholic texts, including that great morality tale, *Dorian Gray*, which also features a homoerotic relationship between a beautiful young dandy and a painter. Ultimately, Waugh is not content to cast his romantic vision aside or denounce it as forcefully as he does the modern world that dominates the rest of the text. He clearly favors the romance and allure of both decadence and Catholicism over the brave new modern world, the hollowness of which he embodies in both Rex and the youthful Lieutenant Hooper:

> Hooper was no romantic. He had not as a child ridden with Rupert's horse or sat among the camp fires at Xanthus-side; at the age when my eyes were dry to all save poetry ... Hooper had wept often, but never for Henry's speech on St. Crispin's day, nor for the epitaph at Thermopylae.... In the weeks we were together Hooper became a symbol to me of Young England. (10)

Waugh regularly poked fun at his own generation for putting on the romantic airs of another century. In *Brideshead*, he laments the loss of romance in the next generation. Chesterton offers an orthodox vision of grace to fling in the face of modernity, but Waugh never accepts his wholesale rejection of decadence. Charles's inclusion of "Rupert's horse" in his catalog of romantic childhood imagination calls to mind a time when, as a student at Oxford, Wilde attended a lavish ball dressed as the famous Royalist commander, Prince Rupert. Waugh and Charles have more in common with Wilde's generation than with their own. The splendor of Book One could not enchant as it does if the author felt no sincere nostalgia for a youth spent in conversation with, and imitation of, the nineties. Waugh's nostalgia is so intoxicating that he comes close to making that past seem and feel far more appealing than the lives of renunciation that lead his characters to a purer, more ascetic form of Catholicism. Of course, even this distinction between the book's Arcadian beginning and Catholic ending ignores the complexities of Waugh's narrative. The ending of *Brideshead* may seem straightforwardly orthodox, but even the climactic conversion of Lord Marchmain, the linchpin scene of the entire work, is inflected by the queerness of a more decadent Catholicism.

A Wild(e) Conversion

At its heart, *Brideshead* is a story of conversion. At a time when most authors writing about religion concerned themselves only with its loss, Waugh made an old man's act of reconversion to Catholicism the climax of his novel. When Lord Marchmain, Sebastian's obdurately lapsed father, returns to Brideshead and makes the sign of the cross only moments before his death, he inspires Julia to renounce her adulterous relationship with Charles and sets in motion Charles's eventual acceptance of the faith. Summarized in this way, the conclusion of *Brideshead* seems like a flat rejection of the decadent Arcadia of Book One; it justifies both Catholic critics' admiration and queer critics' scorn. But the neatness of this spiritual chain reaction belies the more complex nature of conversion in *Brideshead*. To grasp the potential queerness of the novel's denouement, we must first appreciate the queerness of its climax, a deathbed conversion that draws on the mythology surrounding Wilde's last-minute turn to Rome.

Wilde's deathbed drama is a popular legacy of the decadent nineties, one that Waugh knew well. Several members of the Wilde circle were still very much alive in the twenties. In a diary entry from 1928 Waugh recalls having lunch with Reggie Turner. One of the few members of Wilde's entourage to lend him support after his fall from grace, Turner nursed the ailing aesthete during his rather gruesome final illness and was present at his death. Waugh reports that Turner was "full of stories about Wilde and 'Bosie.'"[52] Such stories made their way into Waugh's imagination. Though critics have yet to fully appreciate the connection, Wilde's late profession of faith provided part of the inspiration for Marchmain's final moments. Naturally, most deathbed conversions are alike in some respects, conversion (as a turn or return to the Church) and death being the operative unifying forces. The bed itself is optional. Think of the good thief in the Gospel of Luke, who, on the threshold of oblivion and in the grip of great pain, repents his wickedness and finds redemption at the eleventh hour. Typically, critics treat the depiction of Lord Marchmain's last rites in *Brideshead* as a mixture of biography and fantasy. Waugh was present at and played an essential role in the dramatic deathbed conversion of his friend Hubert Duggan, an experience that directly informs the fiction. According to biographer Paula Byrne, Waugh used this experience as part of Marchmain's composite character.[53] Duggan partially inspired the conversion scene; William Lygon, 7th Earl Beauchamp, provided an important model for Marchmain's character. While at Oxford, Waugh carried on an intimate friendship with Lord Beauchamp's son, Hugh Lygon, who partially informed the character of Sebastian Flyte. Following the failure of his first marriage, the rootless Waugh became a sort of adopted sibling in the Lygon family and used their ancestral home, Madresfield Court, as the inspiration for Brideshead Castle. Aside from his pedigree, Lord Beauchamp seemingly has little in common with his fictional counterpart. In *Brideshead*, for instance, it seems clear that Lord Marchmain was never a particularly energetic or politically active figure. Beauchamp was quite the opposite. He worked vigorously as a public servant, held the distinguished title of Knight of the Garter, and spent his leisure time in artistic pursuits. He also had "exquisite taste in footmen."[54] Byrne asserts that Beauchamp's sexuality was common knowledge well before his eventual exile:

> When interviewing male staff he would pass his hands over their buttocks, making a hissing noise similar to that made by stable lads when rubbing their horses down.... The diplomat and diarist Harold Nicolson recalled a dinner at Madresfield when he was asked by an astonished fellow guest, "Did I hear Beauchamp whisper to the butler, 'Je t'adore'?" "Nonsense," Nicolson replied. "He said 'Shut the door.'" But Nicolson, bisexual husband of Vita Sackville-West,

knew that the other guest had indeed heard correctly.... At a certain exalted level of society, Lord Beauchamp's homosexuality had been an open secret for years.[55]

Such behavior had its consequences. In 1931, Beauchamp was sent into exile under threat of legal action after being outed by his brother-in-law to King George V. Ultimately, this banishment is the most salient connection between Beauchamp and Marchmain, as the former never experienced a dramatic conversion and the latter preferred the company of women, so long as he wasn't married to them. The deathbed conversion in *Brideshead* is an elaborate union of experience and imagination partially informed by the life of Lord Beauchamp, but Waugh also had another exiled homosexual at the forefront of his mind when he crafted the scene.

A good deal of what we know about Lord Marchmain comes from Anthony Blanche. In Book One, Anthony takes Charles to dinner with the transparent intention of seducing him away from Sebastian. Aside from plying Charles with food and drink, he carries on a long one-sided conversation about the eccentricities of the Marchmain family. Anthony describes Lord Marchmain as an indolent and Wildean sensualist with a Byronic edge:

> And Lord Marchmain, well, a little fleshy perhaps, but *very* handsome, a magnifico, a voluptuary, Byronic, bored, infectiously slothful, not the sort of man you would expect to see easily put down.... He daren't show his great purple face anywhere. He is the last, historic, authentic case of someone being hounded out of society. (*BR* 58)

Taken out of context, this description of a fleshy voluptuary "hounded out of society" could easily be applied to Wilde, though few found him particularly handsome. After establishing Lord Marchmain as a Wildean exile, Anthony goes on to describe his suffering at the hands of his pious, estranged wife, who has "convinced the world that Lord Marchmain is a monster" following Marchmain's wartime affair with a dancer. Lord Marchmain emerges as an unfortunate and undeserving victim of his wife's piety and charm. Anthony accepts this story, but he notes that it is unlike "a thousand such cases" in which the refusal to divorce "arouses sympathy for the adulterer." Marchmain stands apart from other adulterers because his wife has inexplicably convinced all of civilized society to turn its back on her husband and treat him like a man "wreathed in all the flowers of Sodom and Gomorrah" (*BR* 59).

Marchmain's exile, which Waugh clearly modeled on the life of Lord Beauchamp, also reminds us of Wilde's own expulsion from England for sexual offenses. More than his absence, the circumstance and manner of Marchmain's return home and his deathbed return to the Catholic Church invite us to consider Wilde as an inspiration. When the master of the house finally does return to Brideshead to die, he forgoes his regular rooms and requests rather unusual accommodations, the "Queen's bed" in the "Chinese drawing-room." Charles elaborates on the eccentricity of the orders at some length:

> The Chinese drawing-room was one I had never seen used; in fact one could not normally go further into it than a small roped area round the door … it was a splendid, uninhabitable museum of Chippendale carving and porcelain and lacquer and painted hangings; the Queen's bed, too, was an exhibition piece, a vast velvet tent like the *baldachino* at St. Peter's…. It came down the main staircase in pieces, at intervals during the afternoon; huge sections of Rococo, velvet-covered cornice; the twisted, gilt and velvet columns which formed its posts; … plumes of dyed feathers, which sprang from gold-mounted ostrich eggs and crowned the canopy; finally, the mattresses with four toiling men at each. Lord Marchmain seemed to derive comfort from the consequences of his whim. (*BR* 364–5)

The "Queen's bed" would have served as a more fitting deathbed for Wilde than the shabby one he actually occupied. Its name implies that the bed accommodated a royal visitor at some point, but the use of "Queen" as a slang term for homosexual also has a long history in British literature, dating back to the early eighteenth century. The *OED* cites Waugh's own employment of the term in *Vile Bodies* to refer to an Italian waiter who prowls Shepherd's Hotel in a pungent cloud of *Nuit de Noël*. Furthermore, as we have seen, Ambrose Silk refers to himself as an "old queen" in *Put Out More Flags*. Aside from its title, the rococo style of the Queen's bed provides another subtle nod to Wilde. Charles's comparison of the bed's "tent" with the grand baroque *baldachino* of St. Peter's seems to foreshadow a conversion, but, paired with its "Rococo" ornamentation, the bed becomes a strange edifice, at once queer and Catholic. The Queen's bed is perhaps the most important piece of furniture in all of Waugh's novels, and its distinctive style suggests a connection between Marchmain and a decadent aesthetic that both clashes with and embraces the grand, baroque style of the Catholic Counter-Reformation that defines most of Brideshead. This sense of the bed's strangeness is heightened by its relocation to the Chinese drawing-room, the only gaudy room in an utterly tasteful house.

In Brideshead, which Charles repeatedly associates with the baroque style, the Chinese drawing-room stands out as both exceptional and "uninhabitable." The Chippendale carving and porcelain are rococo and kitschy. Waugh disdains the room he has chosen for the realization of Marchmain's spiritual drama, as he makes clear later in the novel. When, in the epilogue, the army Quartering Commandant shows Charles around the estate he displays an unusual appreciation for the beauty of the house. Unlike the average soldiers who are always quick to deface and vandalize their surroundings, the Commandant makes special efforts to protect the house and even fences off the great fountain. Tellingly, he disparages the Chinese drawing-room, which now functions as the mess. He calls the room an "eyesore." Rather than covering the walls to protect them, as he does in the rest of the rooms, he leaves them exposed believing that, "it wouldn't matter much if [the room] did get damaged" (*BR* 397). In the Commandant's eyes, the setting of Lord Marchmain's last rites resembles "one of the costlier knocking-shops, you know—'*Maison Japonaise*'" (*BR* 397), a comparison that highlights the room's aura of sexual transgression and calls to mind both Beardsley's iconic *japonisme* and the "momentary Japanese effect" that, Lord Henry Wotton perceives in Basil Hallward's studio in the first lush paragraphs of *The Picture of Dorian Gray*. In short, the Chinese drawing-room resembles a brothel. Worse, it is a tawdry and vulgar relic of 1890s camp. Marchmain makes it even more so with the addition of frivolous Catholic bric-a-brac. Along with the Queen's bed, he also requests the silver basin and ewer from "the Cardinal's dressing room" (*BR* 367). Exactly which Cardinal gave the dressing room its name remains unclear, though the ghosts of Manning and Newman hover over the title. In any case, the specificity of the request makes the ewer and basin as integral to Marchmain's imagined deathbed scene as the bed and the wallpaper of the drawing-room. When the stage is finally set for his eventual demise, he reveals his aesthetic pretensions by suggesting that Charles paint the scene and call it "the *Death Bed*."

Marchmain is fulfilling a fantasy. His death is meant to be a spectacle. The room and its contents are the setting for his final refusal of God. It is a room inhabited by the ghost of Wilde and intentionally arranged to evoke the spirit of a more decadent age. But, seemingly unbeknownst to Lord Marchmain, the spirit of decadence is one of both excess and repentance. Lord Marchmain intentionally arranges his deathbed scene as a monument to Wildean frivolity. As Charles realizes in the novel's epiphanic conclusion, however, even the most tawdry art or architecture may serve a higher purpose never intended by the artist. Sitting in the family chapel that Lord Marchmain built for his wife and that the youthful Charles once identified as another monument to "the last decade of the nineteenth century" (the decade of decadence) the middle-aged Captain Ryder realizes that even a "beaten-copper lamp of deplorable design" can illuminate the tabernacle and inspire conversion (*BR* 402). Artists never know "the uses to which their work [will] descend." In the Queen's bed, surrounded by the decadent *japonisme* of a high-end brothel, Lord Marchmain returns to the Church he forsook. The climactic question of the entire novel is whether or not this Wildean outcast can be reconciled with the Church that has served as a frustrating antagonist his entire life. When he does, the courses of the lives around him change.

Marchmain's return disrupts everything. Julia's plan to divorce Rex and try another marriage to Charles crumbles beneath the weight of her renewed faith and his bourgeoning understanding of that faith. Unsure of what will come next but determined not to "set up a rival good to God's," Julia tries to articulate her decision to Charles: "It may be a private bargain between me and God, that if I give up this one thing I want so much, however bad I am, he won't quite despair of me in the end" (393). Charles claims to understand this decision. He doesn't, yet. Only after trying and failing to fill the void of love in his life by joining the Army, only after returning to Brideshead yet again, can he realize a mode of loving that was always available to the Flytes but newly available to himself. The rupture caused by the spectacle of Lord Marchmain's Wildean conversion allows Charles to discover a form of sexual identity stranger to modern sensibilities than that of either young homosexual lover or middle-aged adulterer.

Waugh's Queer Celibates

Unlike earlier Waugh novels, such as *Vile Bodies* and *A Handful of Dust*, *Brideshead* concludes with teleological equilibrium; all the main characters are moving toward their proper end, spiritually speaking. *Brideshead* represents Evelyn Waugh to so many readers that its deviation from his earlier work risks going unnoticed. The novel laughs at the conventions of popular narrative, especially Hollywood narrative, but the ending is more cathartic than farcical. By contrast *Vile Bodies* ends with the protagonist, lacking fiancée, friends, and prospects, in a broken-down car in the midst of a battlefield with only a drunken general and a reluctant prostitute named Chastity for company as the sounds of war rage about them. *A Handful of Dust* (1934) ends with Tony Last doomed to spend the rest of an already miserable life reading the complete works of Charles Dickens to his mad captor in a remote Brazilian village. The conclusion of *Brideshead* is more hopeful than either of these, though none of the characters is guaranteed anything like a happily-ever-after existence. Partly because of the novel's somewhat austere and pious conclusion, many readers prefer the romantic nostalgia of the first book, "Et in Arcadia Ego," to the rest of the text. And, though Waugh certainly toes the orthodox line by endorsing renunciation over romance, he grants the decadent past a splendor that he completely denies to the vacant, materialistic world of the modern helot Lieutenant Hooper and the soulless Canadian tycoon Rex Mottram. Rather than flatly rejecting his queer paradise of bachelors, Waugh draws it into his larger vision of humanity's properly oriented spiritual end. He uses Beardsley's "*Et in Arcadia Ego*" as part of the mise-en-scène of a drama that climaxes with a reimagining of Wilde's own turn to Rome. Appreciating this climax as more than a tidy conclusion to a provocative but ultimately tame twentieth-century morality play requires an understanding of Waugh's sympathy for Wilde, his complicated understanding of homosexual desire, and his fascination with perhaps the queerest form of human sexuality, celibacy.

First, we should note that Waugh criticized Wilde's imprisonment. In a 1930 article on the unfortunate reemergence of nineties' fashion, Waugh pokes fun at many of Wilde's artistic airs but also takes the time to publicly denounce his punishment: "He [Wilde] got himself into trouble, poor old thing, by the infringement of a very silly law, which was just as culpable and just as boring as the infringement of traffic or licensing regulations."[56] We might, at first, be taken aback by this sympathy, coming as it does from a champion of Catholic literary modernity. But, as others have pointed out, Waugh's treatment of homosexual activity was never flatly moralistic. In both his fiction and nonfiction he repeatedly treats romance between men as a potentially salutary phase in sexual and spiritual development. In *Brideshead*, for example, Charles voices sentiments in keeping with much of what Waugh wrote in his letters, diaries, and published prose. After acknowledging that his relationship with Sebastian involved "naughtiness" that ranks "high in the catalogue of grave sins," Charles employs an appropriately decadent metaphor to justify their youthful indiscretions:

> All the wickedness of that time was like the spirit they mix with the pure grape of the Douro, heady stuff full of dark ingredients; it at once enriched and retarded the whole process of adolescence as the spirit checks the fermentation of the wine, renders it undrinkable, so that it must lie in the dark, year in, year out, until it is brought up at last fit for the table. (*BR* 48)

Charles compares his sexual development to the process of producing port. The brandy added to the Douro prevents the sugar in the pure Portuguese wine from transforming into alcohol, as it would in the normal fermentation process. Similarly, homosexual experimentation temporarily prevents the young lover from reaching maturity. Until the brandy and wine have aged together in darkness for years and grown into a single entity, the "spirit" of queer love makes the lover unsuitable for "the table" (an unmistakable metaphor for the altar). What results is not simply delayed heteronormative love. Quite the opposite. The young man who goes through the process comes out the other end as a sweeter, more intoxicating drink than simple table wine. He is sexually transubstantiated into a being that dissolves simple gay/straight binaries in the process of maturation.

Such a reading may seem enigmatic unless we pay attention to one important but often neglected fact about the conclusion of *Brideshead*: none of the central characters is engaged in what most English readers at the time would consider normative sexual relationships. Nearly all have chosen a third way. Sebastian's youngest sister, the homely and saintly Cordelia, seems destined eventually for a religious order. After renouncing a life with Charles, Julia will live out her days as a separated woman unable to divorce and therefore celibate and single. Together, she and Cordelia will desert Brideshead and tend the wounded on the battlefields of the Second World War. Sebastian will live out his days with the brothers at the Tunisian monastery, never quite fit for a vocation but nevertheless tied to a homosocial community populated by celibate men who have consecrated their sexuality to the worship of an incarnate male God. Charles's conversion seems assured at the novel's close, yet his isolation from his former friends and lovers as well as his estranged children seems equally assured. Waugh leaves Brideshead (the place) deserted and its scattered Catholics committed to lives of voluntary celibacy. Peter Christensen notes this refusal to tie conversion to family and procreation, yet he insists that the novel's final resistance to compulsory heterosexual relationships demonstrates that Waugh unintentionally "pits two versions of Roman Catholicism against each other, the generous and the dogmatic."[57] My primary objection to such a reading is that it attempts to make *Brideshead* palatable from a queer perspective by turning it into an unwitting vehicle for heterodox Catholicism; it embraces the very oppositional sexual politics that *Brideshead* itself rejects. Rather than subverting orthodox Catholic theology, Waugh gives imaginative voice to an exceptionally if not uniquely Catholic expression of sexuality that verges on queerness. He commits his main characters to diverse forms of celibacy that function as coherent sexual identities, identities that subtly subvert cultural norms.

Here we return to the work of Benjamin Kahan, who argues that both inside and outside of clerical or religious contexts, celibacy has a long history of upsetting the status quo. Because Kahan distrusts those celibacies traditionally tied to conservatism and orthodoxy, his preference for more radical and overtly subversive expressions of celibacy results in an inadequate appreciation for the types of Catholic celibacy embraced by the characters in *Brideshead*. Indeed, Kahan has shockingly little to say about Catholicism. Other intellectuals who call for a reevaluation of the sexual politics of celibacy have invested more in the specifically Catholic manifestations of this potentially subversive mode of sexuality. One year after the publication of Kahan's book, the religious journal *First Things* published an article by Catholic theologian Grant Kaplan titled "Celibacy as Political Resistance" (2014). Building on the work of nineteenth-century theologian Johann Adam Möhler, Kaplan argues in part that the practice of clerical celibacy affects a form of political subversion by contending "with secular power for control of our public reality."[58] Synthesizing one of Möhler's central claims from *The Spirit of Celibacy* (1828), Kaplan writes:

> Celibacy is indeed useless to the state—which made it crucial for maintaining the Church's independence. Married life introduces responsibilities and inclines heads of household to become invested in the state's system of education and welfare, in addition to its economy. Celibacy disrupts this process of integrating men into the stream of family life and its responsibilities.[59]

Kaplan mainly concerns himself with clerical celibacy as a political and spiritual counterweight to the normalizing and utilitarian agenda of the modern nation state, but his argument also applies to cases of less visible but equally intentional lay celibacy. By drawing attention to matters of sexuality, he opens the door to a reconsideration of the queerness of all Catholic celibacy, priestly and lay. It has become normal to think of Catholicism and queerness as oppositional, at least in political terms. But if, as scholars like David Halperin have suggested, the future of queer theory depends on "reinventing its capacity to startle, to surprise, to help us think what has not yet been thought,"[60] then *Brideshead* should help us to do just that by hinting at the potential queerness of Catholic celibacy.

Both Kahan and Kaplan provide insights that may aid us in complicating the dichotomous queer-Catholic divide in Waugh scholarship. Kahan does so by highlighting the interpretive limitations of more conventional queer criticism while simultaneously situating celibacy "within the penumbra of the queer." If we assume the expressive hypothesis, as most queer readings do, then the host of celibate characters at the conclusion of *Brideshead* may be treated as little more than sexually repressed individuals separated from their genitals by their religion. Waugh acknowledged that Catholic celibacy, treated wrongly as cold chastity, could result in such repression or spiritual sterility. In his *Sword of Honour* trilogy (published between 1952 and 1961), the protagonist Guy Crouchback begins the narrative estranged from his unfaithful wife and stuck in a state of bleak chastity devoid of spiritual meaning: "Even in his religion he felt no brotherhood.... Lately he had fallen into a habit of dry and negative chastity which even the priests felt to be unedifying."[61] Because it is rooted in a positive desire for God, the celibacy on display in *Brideshead* has more in common with the homosexual love between Charles and Sebastian or the adulterous love between Charles and Julia than it does with Guy's "dry negative chastity." Waugh explicitly treats these sinful forms of sexual expression as, in Charles's words, "forerunners" to the love for God, a love expressed most perfectly, for Waugh, in virtuous but contranormative chastity.

The type of positive Christian celibacy envisioned in *Brideshead*, as well as its superiority to other forms of sexual expression (including married sex), has roots in the same texts traditionally used as the theological basis for priestly celibacy in the Catholic Church. Obviously, the example of Christ comes first. Not only did he live a celibate life, but also he challenged many norms regarding sex and family life. His disciples were commanded to leave their parents, wives, and children, and his Sermon on the Mount made clear that perfect Christians should abandon lust and devote all of their love to God and their neighbors by means of service to each. St. Paul was likewise demanding regarding marriage and sex among his followers. In 1 Corinthians he exhorts them to marry, if they must, but laments humanity's weakness: "I wish everyone to be as I am, but each has a particular gift from God, one of one kind and one of another."[62] Conceding some ground to normative sexual passion, Paul acknowledges that not all Christians possess the virtue to follow his chaste path. He quickly doubles down on the importance of celibacy by arguing that married people are distracted from pleasing God by the desire to please each other. This attitude toward celibacy reemerges in Augustine's writings, where he repeatedly and unequivocally affirms its superiority to marriage. Waugh does little in his fiction to directly praise celibacy. He prefers instead to demonstrate the inherent inadequacy of married sex. His most prominent examples of conjugal sex in *Brideshead* produce neither pleasure nor even lasting affection. Lord and Lady Marchmain, Julia and Rex, Charles and Celia, none seems to have benefited much from marriage. Charles especially seems to view marriage as an institution developed for the destruction of love and desire. His description of the mechanical sexual reunion with the hygienic Celia in Book Three is repulsive and helps to shed light on his early disparagement of marriage in the Prologue. After the loss of

Julia, Charles had temporarily found some sense of purpose in the Army. When his love for the institution fades, he naturally compares the disappointment to that felt by a disenchanted husband: "Here my last love died…. I was aghast to realize that something within me, long sickening, had quietly died, and felt as a husband might feel, who, in the fourth year of his marriage, suddenly knew that he had no longer any desire, or tenderness, or esteem, for a once-beloved wife" (*BR* 5–6). Were it not for the repeated emphasis on the sanctity of even a bad marriage in *Brideshead*, the novel would almost seem to disparage the institution and argue for the ultimate superiority of homosexual and adulterous love, which are at least enjoyable. Instead, it seems to follow the lead of Paul and Augustine in treating marriage as an institution devised for those who are incapable of realizing a celibate direction of their sexual energies toward the service of God.

To appreciate the queerness of the pious mode of sexuality espoused in *Brideshead*, we should turn briefly, before concluding, to another text that has traditionally exposed the intellectual fault lines separating queer and conservative modes of interpretation, Plato's *Symposium*. Given the notorious hermeneutical difficulty of the Platonic dialogues in general and *The Symposium* in particular, it is hardly surprising that what strikes one reader as a lengthy discourse on the beauty of homosexual love inspires another to proclaim Plato a defender of procreative marriage and opponent of the norms of Athenian pederasty.[63] As I have already argued, this same interpretive divide manifests itself in the conversation regarding sexuality in *Brideshead*. Neither text fits conveniently into expressive modes of hetero- or homosexual discourse because neither text ultimately grants pride of place to either conventionally queer or straight sex. Rehearsing Diotima's famous "ladder of love," Socrates acknowledges the necessity of beginning the work of philosophy with the love of beautiful male bodies. Just as in *Brideshead*, such adolescent *eros* potentially opens the young man to a desire for higher forms of love. Eventually, the lover may move beyond love of beautiful bodies, customs, and things to love of the immortal form of Beauty itself:

> This is what it is to go aright … into the mystery of Love: one goes always upwards for the sake of this Beauty, starting out from beautiful things and using them like rising stairs: from one body to two and from two to all beautiful bodies, then from beautiful bodies to beautiful customs, and from customs to learning beautiful things … so that in the end he comes to know just what it is to be beautiful.[64]

As if to affirm what Socrates has just said about the inferiority of love expressed through sex, as opposed to love shared between friends in the chaste pursuit of wisdom, the soon-to-be demagogue and traitor Alcibiades stumbles drunkenly into the gathering and bemoans Socrates' resistance to his sexual advances.

Roughly 2,500 years later, Waugh reimagined the ascent of the ladder of love by following Charles on an erotic quest that concludes when he embraces a celibate sexuality directed not at other bodies or things but at the ground of being itself. At Oxford, Charles learns to love beautiful bodies. Brideshead introduces him to beautiful customs. His art is absorbed with the beauty of human architecture. Each of these loves proves transitory, but each is essential to his eventual realization of immortal Beauty. Charles's final turn to God and acceptance of lay celibacy represent the realization of, rather than an escape from, his erotic development. If we reject the expressive hypothesis of sexual categorization and approach the celibacy of Waugh's characters as a coherent sexual identity that operates outside the realm of normative sexual acts, then its potential queerness becomes more apparent. Add to this Kaplan's emphasis on the subversive and contranormative aspects of specifically Catholic celibacy, and we begin to see *Brideshead*'s Catholic conclusion as potentially complementary to the decadent Arcadia of Book One. Rather than forcing a cast of sexually expressive characters to reject and repress their true natures in favor of cold orthodoxy, Waugh creates an imaginative space in which notions of sexuality dissolve and bleed into one another. In this space, conventionally taxonomized asexuals (Cordelia), homosexuals (Sebastian), bisexuals (Charles), heterosexuals (Julia), and others can all participate in a shared sexual identity similar to that of the simple, kind, profound Father Mackay, who ushers Lord Marchmain back into the arms of the Church. For several of the characters in *Brideshead*, conformity to Catholic moral teaching results in a form of celibacy that both complicates accepted categories of sexual expression and calls into question the simple binary between queer sexualities and Catholic teaching.

Alan Hollinghurst and DBC Pierre: Decadent Catholicism after Modernism

The century from 1880 to 1980 witnessed two distinct Catholic moments in the history of post-Reformation British literature. In the twilight of the *fin de siècle*, Catholicism played a pivotal role in both the lives and the literature of a generation of young British aesthetes. Roughly half a century later, England witnessed the beginning of another Catholic literary revival headed by a group of novelists including Evelyn Waugh, Graham Greene, and Muriel Spark. Of the three, Waugh drew the most direct and profound inspiration from the decadent nineties. Spark and Greene, though far subtler in their reactions to their artistic forerunners, deserve greater consideration as inheritors of the decadent Catholic legacy. Both write a good deal about bad Catholics in a manner that seems in sympathy with much of the art of the decadent nineties. Such debauched Catholic characters as Greene's "whisky priest," the nameless protagonist of *The Power and the Glory* (1940), lack any overt connection to the tradition of British decadence but share, for example, Johnson and Dowson's obsession with the penitent drunk, beloved by God because of his frightening nearness to the intoxications of spiritual rebirth. Greene himself, a dipsomaniacal, sex-addicted adulterer and convert who (to borrow Pound's quip about Dowson) "found harlots cheaper than hotels" and received the last rites under dubious circumstances, resembles a sinfully hypertrophied mixture of Wilde and "Baron Corvo," about whom Greene wrote a lengthy essay titled "Frederick Rolfe: Edwardian Inferno" (1934). Few characters seem less like this Christ-haunted hedonist-artists than Sparks's bathetically amoral schoolteacher, Miss Jean Brodie; nevertheless, *The Prime of Miss Jean Brodie* (1961) might be seen as a continuation of George Moore's Wagnerian fascination with the idea of a fallen woman turning to the convent. Suffice it say that Waugh was not the last artist to carry on the decadent Catholic project begun in the 1890s.

One aim of this book has been to establish decadence as the most profound Catholic literary movement in Britain since before the reign of Henry VIII—one on par with and partly responsible for the "revival" of the mid-twentieth century. Another has been to draw attention to the diverse manifestations of decadent Catholicism in the modernist literature that defined the early twentieth century. Admittedly, most literature written by Catholics in what would come to be known as the modernist period existed on the peripheries of that avant-garde movement. In the time between *The Picture of Dorian Gray* and *Brideshead Revisited*, G. K. Chesterton and Hilaire Belloc championed a muscular orthodoxy that treated the dandified nineties and the godless new century with similar distrust. This distrust did not stop Chesterton from writing one of the most underappreciated and formally innovative novels of the Edwardian period, *The Man Who Was Thursday* (1908). It did compel him to openly bash the decadent worship of artifice over nature in the book's epigraph. As the century progressed, at least one Catholic author with modernist sympathies emerged. David Jones managed to weave his faith into the narrative of his enigmatic war poem *In Parenthesis* (1937), which impressed T. S. Eliot but failed to gain him the broad recognition received by his modernist contemporaries. Another survivor of the First World War, J. R. R. Tolkien stands outside all camps. He wrote a new kind of literature that helped define a century but not a literary age.

In all of its various forms, what might be called "Catholic literature"—poetry and fiction concerned in some essential and usually positive way with the history, theology, sacramental worldview, rituals, symbols, and political realities of the Catholic Church—thrived in England from the 1880s until the 1980s. Though admittedly debatable and somewhat arbitrary, I would suggest one ending date for this century-long Catholic literary revival: 1982, when, after vacillating in his faith for decades and near the end of a life characterized more by moral transgression than orthodox piety, Graham Greene published his most devotional Catholic novel, the humorous and profound *Monsignor Quixote*. This date is both late and early: late because what is popularly termed "post-modernism" had already reasserted an essential opposition between art and organized religion, and early because a literary impulse that modernism could not kill seems almost destined to survive and remerge at some point in the twenty-first century.

But what of decadent Catholicism? What happened to this strange cultural phenomenon after *Brideshead Revisited*? I have argued that Eliot, Joyce, and Waugh continued to engage with decadent Catholicism in an artistically generative way well into the twentieth century. At first glance it may seem that this was the end of the road, but an attentive reader can still hear rare dying echoes of the phenomenon in literature of the last few decades.

Hollinghurst and the Ghost of Firbank

In his debut novel *The Swimming-Pool Library* (1988), Alan Hollinghurst (1954) repeatedly plays on the relationship between decadence and Catholicism. The novel follows the sexual adventures of a wealthy gay Lothario named William Beckwith as he navigates the homosexual subculture of modern London and explores the biography of the aged Lord Charles Nantwich, a closeted and persecuted dandy from another generation. Hollinghurst's novel shocked readers by dropping the innuendos and implied off-stage sexual antics of so much previous queer fiction and depicting same-sex desire (and actual sex) in a raw, unsublimated, unstylized light. It also proved that some vestiges of British decadence survived beyond the age of modernism. Surprisingly, Hollinghurst eschews Wilde as the obvious primary literary analogue for modern queer identity politics and instead turns to the novels of Ronald Firbank, the late-born decadent whom I discuss at greater length in Chapter 5.

Early in *The Swimming-Pool Library*, a more erudite and bookish friend puts Will on to Firbank's work, most notably the novels *Valmouth* (1919) and *The Flower Beneath the Foot* (1923). After a cursory first reading of *Valmouth*, Will manages to capture the amalgam of decadent extravagance and modernist difficulty that remains Firbank's hallmark:

> I had deferred reading him in the childishly stubborn way that one resists all keen and repeated recommendations, and had imagined him until now to be a supremely frivolous and silly author. I was surprised to find how difficult, witty and relentless he was. The characters were flighty and extravagant in the extreme, but the novel itself was evidently tough as nails.
>
> I knew I would not begin to grasp it fully until a second or third reading.[1]

Soon after this experience, Will begins reading the diaries of Lord Nantwich, who was, we discover, an acquaintance of both Waugh and Firbank. From that point on, Firbank becomes a sort of recurring character in the novel. At one point, we see a first edition of *The Flower Beneath the Foot* (1923) trampled under the steel-toed boot of a young skinhead. At another, the novel's main characters gather to watch a newly discovered video fragment showing Firbank near the end of his life leading an impromptu parade of peasants through the streets of an Italian village south of Rome. Lord Nantwich's diary recounts meetings with Firbank, who is introduced as a writer of "the most wonderful novels ... all about clergymen, & strange old ladies, &–& darkies."[2] As Nantwich recalls, Firbank was an awkward man who drank too much and "combined the futile caution of the drunkard with a true instinct for elegance—if of a somewhat decadent kind."[3] In spite of Firbank's profound presence and the general aura of *fin-de-siècle* decadence that pervades the novel, Catholicism plays a relatively small role in the narrative. The only overt allusion to the relationship between decadence and Catholicism comes in the guise of the familiar patron saint of late Victorian aesthetes, St. Sebastian.

At their first formal meeting over lunch, Lord Nantwich introduces Will to the middle-aged photographer Ronald Staines, an uninspired Beardsley with a camera whose eccentricities identify him as a holdover from the nineties. Staines's primary occupation is the production of low-budget pornography. In his more ambitious moments, Staines also produces kitschy homoerotic "art," which he describes to Will at their first meeting:

> "They're a new departure, newish anyway, and rather religious and full of feeling. One's a kind of *sacra conversazione* between Saint Sebastian and John the Baptist. The young man who modeled Sebastian was almost in tears when I showed it to him, it's so lovely."
>
> "How did you do the arrows?" I interrupted, remembering Mishima's arduous posing in a self-portrait as Sebastian.
>
> "Oh, no arrows, dear; it's before the martyrdom. He's quite unpierced. But he looks ready for it, somehow, the way I've done it."
>
> "How can you tell it's Sebastian, then," said Nantwich emphatically, "since the only thing that identifies Se-bloody-bastian is that he's got all those ruddy arrows sticking up his arse?" This seemed a fair criticism, but Staines ignored it.[4]

The farcical humor of this dialogue recalls the comic style of both Firbank and his self-identified imitator, Waugh. As I point out in Chapter 5, Waugh credited Firbank with dropping Wilde's flamboyant aphorisms and memorable one-liners in favor of less-quotable, more complex humor. Hollinghurst participates in this tradition of dark, often satiric comedy, but his employment of the figure of St. Sebastian illustrates an essential divergence from Waugh. Where the older author made use of the saint's dual role as a religious and homoerotic icon, Hollinghurst brings in Sebastian as nothing more than a modern reincarnation of *fin-de-siècle* camp. After *Brideshead Revisited* Waugh essentially dropped decadence, with some exceptions in his *Sword of Honour* trilogy, but held onto its religion. In *The Swimming-Pool Library*, Hollinghurst evacuates decadence of nearly all religious significance and reduces it to a secularized touchstone in the history of distinctly British queer identity. Stains's unmartyred Sebastian is wholly unrecognizable. He is the perfect symbol for the would-be artist's pornographic aesthetic. The young man in his photograph looks "ready for it," like any model on the cover of a dirty magazine. Staines takes a saint who was a symbol of self-torturing spiritual and sexual desire—not only for many of the decadents but also for writers such as Eliot and Waugh—and reduces him to a pretty, half-naked boy.

Hollinghurst's tendency to treat Catholicism as another garment in the dusty decadent wardrobe of camp fashion carries through into his later fiction. *The Line of Beauty*, winner of the 2004 Man Booker Award, is regularly compared to *Brideshead Revisited* and also makes explicit use of gay hagiography. An early review for *The New York Times* makes the connection to Waugh succinctly:

> Alan Hollinghurst's new novel, "The Line of Beauty," which won Britain's prestigious Man Booker Prize last month, reads like a contemporary retelling of Evelyn Waugh's classic "Brideshead Revisited": just change the setting from the period between the two World Wars to the Thatcher era of the 1980's, substitute Tory politics for Catholic doctrine, and make the homosexual relationships a lot more explicit.[5]

Set like the *Swimming-Pool Library* in 1980s London, the novel follows Nick Guest who has just moved in with the wealthy family of his Oxford classmate and unrequited love obsession, the beautiful aristocrat Toby Fedden. During Toby's alcohol, hash, and cocaine-fueled birthday party at an uncle's country estate, Nick describes another beautiful Oxford contemporary, the closeted Wani Ouradi, as "sweet-natured, very rich, and beautiful as a John the Baptist painted for a boy-loving pope."[6] As in his other work, Hollinghurst's characters readily identify the queerness of Catholic art without showing any interest in the religion itself. Hollinghurst's world is decadent in an explicit manner that would put the artists of the *fin de siècle* to shame, but this decadence has largely ceased to be dangerous. Spiritual angst no longer subverts orgies and intoxications. Modern Sebastian Flytes face the threat of public censure but experience none of the moral dilemmas that drove Waugh's character to the bottle and the cloister. As the queerness of decadence becomes mainstream, the decadence of Catholicism becomes quaint and tame by comparison. Hollinghurst makes allusive use of some decadent elements of Catholicism for their charm and muted shock value, but, unlike Firbank and Waugh, he shows no interest in the Catholic elements of decadence. Decadent Catholicism exists in the subconscious of Hollinghurst's world as the exquisite pose of an earlier generation whose last ghosts haunt the peripheries of the modern secular psyche.

DBC Pierre and the Decadence of the 1%

DBC Pierre's cosmopolitan background makes his work stubbornly resistant to national pigeonholing. Born Peter Finlay (1961) in Australia, he spent significant portions of his life in Mexico, the United States, and London before settling in the north of Ireland, where he lives today. He won the Man Booker Award one year before Hollinghurst for the novel *Vernon God Little* (2003), a disturbing comedy set in a cartoonish version of rural Texas in the wake of a school shooting. No one reading *Vernon God Little* would suspect its author of any knowledge of or inclination toward the literature of turn-of-the-century decadence, but Pierre's 2011 novel *Lights Out in Wonderland* stands out as the most self-consciously decadent text of the twenty-first century. By this, I mean that it not only makes explicit allusions to the long history of decadent literature from the *Satyricon* to *Dorian Gray*, but it also intentionally mimics, albeit with a modern inflection, the purple prose so foreign to most of the workmanlike style of contemporary literature. Unlike *The Swimming-Pool Library*, which primarily makes use of the queer camp of earlier decadent Catholic texts, *Lights Out in Wonderland* sets up the spiritually and artistically intoxicating legacy of literary decadence as a counterpoint to the soulless and utterly inartistic decadence of modern economic super elites.

The novel begins in an English sanitarium. There we meet a twenty-something radical socialist and activist named Gabriel Brockwell, who has just undergone a mental breakdown after conceding defeat at the hands of the shadowy forces behind globalized capitalism. Gabriel has given up the revolt against the 1% and decided to kill himself, but only after turning his final hours into "a perfect miniature of the age I leave behind, nothing less than a last wanton dive to oblivion."[7] This rejection of the will to live calls to mind the Schopenhauerian philosophy that plays such an important role in George Moore's *Mike Fletcher*, another novel about excess and suicide. In Gabriel's mind, the decision to end his life transforms him from an ineffectual socialist with daddy issues and a weasel-like appearance into "a sphinx with choir-boy eyes, as luminous and rude as a decadent portrait in oils."[8] This transformation contains a double allusion to Wilde. Gabriel's "decadent portrait in oils" is a probable reference to the enchanted portrait at the heart of *Dorian Gray*, and the "sphinx with choir-boy eyes" calls to mind the subject of Wilde's poem "The Sphinx" (1894), in which the speaker first marvels at and then passionately rejects the symbol of lust and pagan vice in favor of the crucifix:

You make my creed a barren sham, you wake foul dreams of sensual life,
And Atys with his blood-stained knife were better than the thing I am.

False Sphinx! False Sphinx! By reedy Styx old Charon, leaning on his oar,
Waits for my coin. Go thou before, and leave me to my crucifix,

Whose pallid burden, sick with pain, watches the world with wearied eyes,
And weeps for every soul that dies, and weeps for every soul in vain.[9]

Unlike Wilde's speaker, Gabriel has no interest in escaping the influence of the Sphinx or embracing the self-sacrifice of the cross. His death promises to save no one. Forfeiting his life is a purely personal act of defiance. It allows Gabriel to come as close as possible to freedom from the ubiquitous demands of credit, finance, and capital that characterize the shabby decadence of the twenty-first century.

In order to sustain this freedom, Gabriel must maintain a state of "nimbus" fueled by intoxication. But this intoxication is more than simple drunkenness. Nimbus becomes a semi-mystical ideal:

This glow around saints is the crucial clue to humanity's mission. Recall the moments when drink, music, and good company lit you full of fraternal love, forgiveness, and joy, then think: according to every doctrine those are the highest states we can reach as human beings. Whole faiths are dedicated solely to achieving them. They are qualities of Jesus and a countless majority of prophets and gods. Therefore never has a ritual been more above argument than intoxication for the purposes of raising a nimbus.[10]

Pierre indulges in a pastime familiar by now from the work of decadent and modernist artists, including Huysmans, Moore, Gray, Joyce, and Eliot, by paying homage to the work of Baudelaire. Gabriel's praise of intoxication as a "ritual" of almost religious significance that aids humanity in its war with existence bears the clear marks of Baudelaire's infamous prose poem "Enivrez-vous"

One must be forever drunken: that is the sole question of importance. If you would not feel the horrible burden of Time that bruises your shoulders and bends you to the earth, you must be drunken without cease. But how? With wine, with poetry, with virtue, with what you please. But be drunken. And if sometimes, on the steps of a palace, on the green grass by a moat, or in the dull loneliness of your chamber, you should waken up, your intoxication already lessened or gone, ask of the wind, of the wave, of the star, of the bird, of the timepiece; ask of all that flees, all that sighs, all that revolves, all that sings, all that speaks, ask of these the hour; and wind and wave and star and bird and timepiece will answer you: "It is the hour to be drunken! Lest you be the martyred slaves of Time, intoxicate yourselves, be drunken without cease! With wine, with poetry, with virtue, or with what you will."[11]

The protagonist of *Lights Out in Wonderland* does his best to fulfill Baudelaire's directive.

In search of a partner with whom to pursue the sensuous and spiritual intoxications of "nimbus" and express the decadence of the age in one last bender, Gabriel, supplied with ample cocaine and money stolen from his former revolutionary comrades, sets out for Tokyo, a mecca of postmodern decadence. There he meets his childhood friend, Smuts, a virtuoso chef who once rented a crematorium in order to roast a suckling pig whose internal organs had been replicated and replaced with black pudding, foie gras, and ravioli. Smuts now works in a restaurant specializing in poisonous fish ("It's the next big thing, poisons. Flavors aren't enough anymore"). In the establishment's exclusive, all-white tasting room, he introduces Gabriel to a miraculous wine called Marius: "Decadent times call for decadent wines."[12] Paradoxically, this particular decadent wine is the creation of a former billionaire playboy who "abandoned decadence to try and grow a grape with the answer to life inside it."[13] The near-sacramental language employed to describe this mysterious wine is in tension with the unorthodox methods used to produce it. Marius is made from grapes that feed on ancient, unspoiled soil and the hormones of copulating virgins: "Rumor says that virgins go to fornicate in the vines, that it's a pilgrimage for twisted convent girls and aristocrats.... These pressings are from a geological fluke dated to the first human ancestor. They're a correction of nature. They grow on prehistoric minerals, passion, and virgin's cum."[14] The name Marius alludes to Walter Pater's *Marius the Epicurean* (1885), the story of a second-century Roman youth who explores the competing philosophies of his day, including hedonism, and ends his life as an unbaptized Christian martyr. The name fits, as the wine itself inhabits the same liminal space between religious fervor and sensuous exploration occupied by so many decadent texts of more than a century ago.

But semi-sacramental wine fed on "virgin's cum" is about the only hint of anything like decadent Catholicism in Pierre's modern *homage* to the *fin de siècle*. Most of the novel is an exercise in excess for excess' sake. In Tokyo, a night fueled by Marius, liquor, cocaine, and poisonous fish leads to the death of a Yakuza mob boss, a ménage à trois with an octopus, and Smuts facing life in jail. Following this setback in Gabriel's plans for self-destruction, the remainder of the novel concerns itself with didactic reflections on the evil of unrestrained capitalism. As part of an absurd attempt to free his imprisoned friend, Gabriel finds himself in Berlin working as the doorman at a decadent banquet for a group of the world's richest men hosted in the tunnels beneath Hitler's behemoth Tempelhof Airport. Aside from a literal fountain of Marius, the feast includes "Caramelized Milk-Fed White Tiger Cub," "Giant Panda Paw with Borlotti Beans & Baby Root Vegetable," and, the pièce de résistance, a dish made from the hundred-year-old Galapagos tortoise, Lonesome George. Pierre makes the decadent roots of this feast and his novel almost painfully explicit: "And here, waiting for the greatest bacchanal since the fall of Rome, waiting for the feast of Trimalchio, Des Esseintes' last stand, Dorian Gray's big night out, waiting with the spirits of Salomé, Abbé Jules, Caragiale, Baudelaire, Hlaváček, Mirbeau, and Tonegaru, we smoke cigarettes at the curbside and bask in cool sun."[15] In the act of summoning the demon of literary decadence, Gabriel misses something. Trimalchio is a good imaginative cognate for Pierre's anonymous modern billionaires. They share a taste for excess and a general lack of taste. Des Esseintes and Dorian Gray would almost certainly deplore the philistine overindulgences of Pierre's 1%. Both characters sought, at least in theory, to make an art of pleasure. The nameless hedonists of *Lights Out in Wonderland* are, to put it lightly, unconcerned with art. Their grand banquet begins with a cocaine amuse-bouche and soon devolves into a mindless orgy:

> The banquet has collapsed to the floor, [*sic.*] Wonderland has become a writhing mass of cloth and flesh. All the room's cushions and rugs have been gathered, with guests squirming like maggots, grunting and rasping, skin glistening over Persian designs, sexual organs like weeping faces and veined worms forming unrepeatable artworks in the manner of Des Esseintes' jeweled turtle.
>
> A gazelle carcass lies on its side in the fountain. The nearest of its long, arched horns makes a breakwater against which a variety of flotsam bobs and whirls. Before I can list all the different things floating there, a guest lurches up and urinates long and hard into the wine. His frothy jet sends debris eddying over the horn.
>
> Another shadowy force crawls up and refills his goblet.[16]

There is a double allusion in the mention of "Des Esseintes' jeweled turtle." Just as Waugh calls attention to Rex Mottram's ridiculous imitation of Des Esseintes's bejeweled tortoise in *Brideshead Revisited*, Pierre casts aspersions on the nameless avatars of capital, who turn the *fin-de-siècle* art of decay into an unsophisticated bacchanalia of consumption. Rex and the "shadowy forces" represent a decadence shorn of art. Though Pierre does not share Waugh's religion, he shares his disdain for what both see as the soulless oligarchy of the modern era. Money has deadened the aristocrats of capital to all measures of value. The fountain of precious Marius, that last vestige of the sacramental in a secular world, becomes a urinal for the servants of mammon.

This image captures the didactic core of Pierre's novel, which rests on the simple moral that unrestrained capitalism can invert value to the point that the most sacred artistic fruits of this world become disposable trash in the hands of a soulless 1%. Compared to the parable of spiritual desolation at the heart of *Dorian Gray*, this message seems distinctly different. Its exigencies are social, material, and temporal. By contrast, the needs and obsessions of most of the decadents were personal, spiritual, and eternal. In this way, they share much more in common with their modernist inheritors than with the dominant literary voices of the last three or four decades.

Conversion to Catholicism helped define the literature of the British *fin de siècle*; apostasy has played a similar role in Anglophone literature of the last thirty years, especially in America. Three of the most influential writers of the late twentieth and early twenty-first centuries, Cormac McCarthy (1933), Don DeLillo (1936), Thomas Pynchon (1937), were all raised Catholic. The early influence of Catholicism on these writers makes itself felt in meaningful ways from time to time, but not as it did for the decadents. Catholicism in post-secular literature is almost never a legitimate source of salvation and inspiration as it was for Johnson, Dowson, Beardsley, Gray, and, perhaps, Wilde. At best, Catholic priests and nuns can provide an important glimpse of a world of abundant charity less dominated by capital, consumption, and degradation than the rest of the world. The nuns of DeLillo's *White Noise* (1985), who believe in neither God nor an afterlife, play a crucial role in preserving the humanity of the human race. After treating the protagonist for a gunshot wound, Sr. Hermann Marie explains the nuns' reason for persisting in an age of disbelief:

> It is our task in the world to believe things that no one else takes seriously. To abandon such beliefs completely, the human race would die.... There is no truth without fools. We are your fools, your madwomen, rising at dawn to pray, lighting candles, asking statues for good health, a long life.[17]

Such depictions of Catholicism suggest sympathy or nostalgia but not belief or inspiration. One never gets the impression that DeLillo considers Catholicism as a viable option for modern, educated people.

In rare but profound instances, Catholicism emerges in contemporary literature as a possible antidote to a tired postmodern nihilism. In the majority of cases, it functions as a haunting presence, an unidentified generator of shame, a last bastion for strange souls, or an impotent nemesis. It has, like decadence, found a place on the peripheries of postmodern literature. The two forces rarely emerge together. More and more, decadent Catholicism can only be found in the faintest dying echoes.

Notes

Anamnesis

1   W. B. Yeats, introduction to *The Oxford Book of Modern Verse 1892–1935* (Oxford: Clarendon Press, 1947), x.

2   Ibid., xi–xii.

3   I have attempted to maintain continuity in referring to the Catholic Church. Unless quoting directly or engaging with its use, I will avoid the term "Roman Catholicism." Though the title is comfortable for many Catholics today, it at times carries the suggestion of papist sectarianism in the context of British culture.

4   David Jones, *The Anathemata* (1952; repr., London: Faber and Faber, 2010), 205n1.

5   I have chosen to follow the general lead of my subjects in the capitalization of religious terms. There could hardly be two more different personalities than those of Wilde and Eliot, but both men thought of the Catholic institution as "the Church," never the church. Likewise, neither Aubrey Beardsley nor Evelyn Waugh would have considered referring to the many honorifics of the mother of Jesus Christ without capitalization (the Virgin, the Mother of God). These titles were natural and important to most of the authors with whom I deal in this book.

6   Kate Hext and Alex Murray, "Introduction," in *Decadence in the Age of Modernism*, ed. Kate Hext and Alex Murray, 1–26 (Baltimore, MD: Johns Hopkins University Press, 2019), 2.

7   Robert Volpicelli, "The New Decadence," review of *Modernism and the Reinvention of Decadence*, by Vincent Sherry; *Landscapes of Decadence*, by Alex Murray; and *Beginning at the End: Decadence, Modernism, and Postcolonial History*, by Robert Stilling, *Modernism/modernity* 26, no. 1 (2019): 214.

8   Ibid.

9   Ibid., 218.

10 Stanley Fish, "One University under God?" *Chronicle of Higher Education*, January 7, 2005, https://www.chronicle.com/article/One-University-Under-God-/45077.

11 Alex Murray's "Recusant Poetics: Rereading Catholicism at the Fin de Siècle" (*English Literature in Transition*, 2013) provides perhaps the only significant counterexample and makes the elision of Catholicism in his coedited *Decadence in the Age of Modernism* (2019) all the more glaring.

12 Joseph Bristow, "'A Poetess of No Mean Order': Margaret Sackville, Women's Poetry, and the Legacy of Aestheticism," in *Decadence in the Age of Modernism*, ed. Kate Hext and Alex Murray (Baltimore, MD: Johns Hopkins University Press, 2019), 112–13.

13 See Lewis, *Religious Experience and the Modernist Novel* (Cambridge: Cambridge University Press, 2010); Tonning, *Modernism and Christianity* (Basingstoke: Palgrave Macmillan, 2014); Pinkerton, *Blasphemous Modernism* (Oxford: Oxford University Press, 2017); Domestico, *Poetry and Theology in the Modernist Period* (Baltimore, MD: Johns Hopkins University Press, 2017).

14 James Joyce, *A Portrait of the Artist as a Young Man* (London: Signet Classics, 2006), 113; Oscar Wilde, *The Picture of Dorian Gray*, 1891, ed. Donald L. Lawler (New York: W. W. Norton, 1988), 103.

15 John Gray, *Silverpoints* (London: Elkin Matthews and John Lane, 1893), XXXIV; T. S. Eliot, *Inventions of the March Hare: Poems 1907–1917*, ed. Christopher Ricks (New York: Harcourt Brace, 1996), 78.

16 See George Cevasco, *The 1890s: An Encyclopedia of British Literature, Art, and Culture* (New York and London: Garland, 1993), 145. Cevasco defines decadence ambivalently:

> Critics differ as to whether or not the decadents wrote by formulas, had a point of view, or were moral, immoral, or amoral. To some readers, decadence refers to style, to others it describes behavior. Perversity of form, perversity of matter, or perversity of life are privileged in this book or that article, but something that is vaguely called decadence continues to describe qualities of the *fin de siècle*. Aesthetic values prevail over moral values, world-weariness is an affectation, new sensations are courted in desperation and in public. Decadence is self-conscious, and perhaps self-destroying, for the decadent impulse as we know it in Victorian literature ended with the century.

Cevasco self-consciously allows the attempt at definition to devolve into a catalog of radically different critical interpretations and unsatisfactory clichés (e.g., "perversity," "world-weariness," and self-destruction). Those looking for a good introductory history and taxonomy of the term "decadence" should review the introduction to Hext and Murray's *Decadence in the Age of Modernism* (2019). But they should not expect to find much, or anything, about Catholicism.

17 For details about the specific development of French decadence, see David Weir, *Decadence: A Very Short Introduction* (Oxford: Oxford University Press, 2018), 34–56.

18 See, for example, Edward Norman's *Anti Catholicism in Victorian England* (New York: Routledge, 2017) and Michael Wheeler's *The Old Enemies* (Cambridge: Cambridge University Press, 2006).

19 W. Somerset Maugham, *Of Human Bondage* (New York: Grosset & Dunlap, 1915), 26.

20 Claire Masurel-Murray, "Conversions to Catholicism among Fin de Siècle Writers: A Spiritual and Literary Genealogy," *Cahiers victoriens et édouardiens* 76 (2012): 105–6.

21 Ibid., 105.

22 *New American Bible*, Mt. 20: 1–16.

23   Vincent Sherry, *Modernism and the Reinvention of Decadence*, 4–5. Sherry cites
     Symons's shift in diction from "decadent" to "symbolist" as an intentional coding
     of the more provocative term, a coding that generations of critics subsequently
     repeated. I revisit this argument in my chapter on T. S. Eliot, who was profoundly
     influenced by Symons's work.

24   J. K. Huysmans, *Against Nature (À Rebours)*, trans. Robert Baldick (London:
     Penguin, 2003), 3–4.

25   Nordau, Max. *Degeneration*, trans. unknown (New York: D. Appleton and
     Company, 1895), 15.

26   Charles Baudelaire, *Flowers of Evil*, trans. James McGowan (Oxford: Oxford
     University Press, 1993), 97.

27   Respectively I allude to Dowson's "Carthusians," Beardsley's "Ballad of the Barber,"
     George Moore's *Mike Fletcher*, and Johnson's "Satanas," all of which receive
     attention in the following chapters.

28   William Carlos Williams, *The Autobiography of William Carlos Williams*, 1948
     (New York: New Directions, 1967), 189. Williams notes that all conversation ceased
     after Joyce's scolding of McAlmon.

29   Oscar Wilde, *De Profundis* (New York: G. P. Putnam's Sons, 1905), 90–1.

30   Ellis Hanson, *Decadence and Catholicism* (Cambridge, MA: Harvard University
     Press, 1997), 369.

31   This term, coined by sociologists Christian Smith and Melinda Lundquist Denton
     in their book *Soul Searching: The Religious and Spiritual Lives of American
     Teenagers* (2005), describes a set of commonly held beliefs among Americans,
     especially American youths, in the twenty-first century. The authors argue that
     for most Americans Moralistic Therapeutic Deism is essentially a watered-down
     Christianity, in which God serves more as a therapist-butler than lord and judge.
     Within this framework, the traditional notion of sin essentially disappears.

32   G. K. Chesterton, *Orthodoxy* (London: John Lane, 1909), 116.

33   Hanson, *Decadence and Catholicism*, 25.

34   Kahan openly disdains those celibacies traditionally tied to conservatism and
     orthodoxy. His study focuses explicitly on more radical and overtly subversive
     expressions of celibacy, which results in an inadequate appreciation for the diverse
     types of Catholic celibacy.

35   For a detailed discussion of Lee's interest in and horror at Marian devotions in
     Spain, see Leire Barrera-Medrano, "'Dolls in Agony': Vernon Lee in Southern
     Spain." *Cahiers victoriens et édouardiens* 83 (2016).

Chapter 1

1   G. K. Chesterton, *A Handful of Authors: Essays on Books and Writers* (New York:
     Sheed and Ward, 1953), 146.

2   Ibid., 144; T. S. Eliot, "A Preface to Modern Literature: Being a Conspectus, Chiefly of English Poetry, Addressed to an Intelligent and Inquiring Foreigner," *Vanity Fair* 21, no. 3 (1923): 44.

3   "A Truly Wilde Story: An interview with Joseph Pearce about the Life and Death of Oscar Wilde," Ignatiusinsight.com, 2000, http://www.ignatiusinsight.com/features/ jpearce_intervw_july04.asp. In an interview with the Ignatius Press, Pearce boldly asserted his opposition: "Ellmann gets all the facts and then mixes them up in such a way as to not clarify, but to muddy the waters. His is a postmodern biography. Wilde is presented as a relativist with no sense of good and evil. On the contrary, Wilde's art shows a consistency of objective morality, specifically Christian morality."

4   Lionel Johnson, "The Cultured Faun," in *Aesthetes and Decadents of the 1890s: An Anthology of British Poetry and Prose*, ed. Karl Beckson (Chicago: Academy Chicago Publishers, 1982), 111.

5   Ibid., 111–12.

6   Richard Griffiths, *The Pen and the Cross: Catholicism and English Literature, 1850–2000* (New York: Continuum, 2010), 47.

7   T. S. Eliot, *T. S. Eliot: Selected Essays 1917–1932* (New York: Harcourt, Brace, 1932), 349.

8   Richard Ellmann, *Oscar Wilde* (New York: Alfred A. Knopf, 1988), 57.

9   Lord Alfred Douglas, "Two Poems," *The Chameleon* 1, no. 1 (London: Gay and Bird 1894): 28.

10 Lord Alfred Douglas, *The Collected Poems of Lord Alfred Douglas* (London: Martin Secker, 1919), 113.

11 John Gray, *Silverpoints*, XXXIV.

12 R. K. R. Thornton, *The Decadent Dilemma* (London: Edward Arnold, 1983), 200.

13 Marion Thain, *"Michael Field": Poetry, Aestheticism, and the* Fin de Siècle (Cambridge: Cambridge University Press, 2007). Thain points out that most critics of Field's poetry are drawn to the reckless pagan sensuality of the early work and lose interest when the women convert to Catholicism (168). As evidence, she cites Angela Leighton's assertion that "faith did not re-energize their poetry, but turned it, paradoxically, towards the very flaccid and flowery decadence which they had largely avoided before" (ibid.). Leighton's assertion, made in 1992, demonstrates the surprisingly widespread ignorance of decadent Catholicism prior to Hanson's work. Her depiction of Field's simultaneous turn to Rome and attraction to "flowery decadence" as "paradoxical" overlooks the essential link between the two in most of the literature of the *fin de siècle*.

14 Michael Field, *Sight and Song* (London: Elkin Matthews and John Lane, 1892), 33.

15 For recent treatments, see Jill R. Ehnenn, *Women's Literary Collaboration, Queerness, and Late-Victorian Culture* (Ashgate: Burlington, VT, 2008), 92; Sarah

Parker, *The Lesbian Muse and Poetic Identity, 1889–1930* (New York: Routledge, 2015), 29.

16   G. K. Chesterton, "A Dead Poet," in *All Things Considered* (London: Methuen, 1915), 206.

17   See Ana Parejo Vadillo, "'Gay Strangers': Reflections on Decadence and the Decadent Poetics of A. Mary F. Robinson," *Cahiers victoriens et édouardiens* 78 (Autumn 2013). Vadillo links Meynell directly to larger discussions of decadent poetics: "Her [Meynell's] theories about the etymology of words in decadent writing embody a tempered vision of decadent poetics."

18   Murray Pittock, *Spectrum of Decadence: The Literature of the 1890s* (New York: Routledge, 2016), 130.

19   Francis Thompson, *Complete Poems of Francis Thompson* (New York: Modern Library, 1913), 88.

20   Ibid., 91.

21   Ibid., 93.

22   Those looking for such a discussion should see Murray Pittock, "Francis Thompson," in *Spectrum of Decadence: The Literature of the 1890s* (New York: Routledge, 2016), 149–55.

23   Matthew Sturgis, *Passionate Attitudes: English Decadents of the 1890s* (London: Macmillan, 1995), 86.

24   George Santayana, *Selected Critical Writings of George Santayana: Volume 1*, ed. Norman Henfrey (Cambridge: Cambridge University Press, 1968), 318.

25   Ramón Ruiz Amadó. "Diocese of Guadix," in *The Catholic Encyclopedia* 16 (New York: The Encyclopedia Press, 1914), http://www.newadvent.org/cathen/16043a.htm. Amadó employs the term in relation to the restoration of a Spanish diocese following the Reconquista: "The Almohades, in the twelfth century, destroyed this together with the other Andalusian sees; it was not restored until the time of the Catholic sovereigns. Cardinal Pedro González de Mendoza, Archbishop of Toledo, erected the new see on 21 May, 1492, in virtue of the Apostolic commission of Innocent VIII granted on August 4, 1486, restoring, by right of *postliminium*, the Apostolic rank possessed by the see previous to the Mohammedan invasion."

26   Augustine, *The City of God*, trans. Marcus Dods (New York: Modern Library, 2000), 412.

27   Richard Ellmann, *The Uses of Decadence: Wilde, Yeats, Joyce* (Bennington, VT: Bennington College, 1983), 308.

28   Translation mine.

29   Edward Caswall, *Lyra Catholica: Containing All the Hymns of the Roman Breviary and Missal* (New York: E. Dunigan, 1951), 156.

30   Ellmann, *Oscar Wilde*, 56.

31   Hanson, *Decadence and Catholicism*, 88.

32 Alex Murray, "Recusant Poetics: Rereading Catholicism at the *Fin de Siècle*," *English Literature in Transition, 1880–1920* 56, no. 3 (2013): 355–6.

33 Walter Pater, *The Renaissance: Studies in Art and Poetry*, 4th ed. (New York: Dover, 2013), 236–7 (italics mine).

34 Walter Pater, "Lacedaemon," in *Plato and Platonism* (London: Macmillan, 1907), 236–66. It was this notion of discipline in the service of perfection that led Pater to lengthy praise of ancient Sparta.

35 Lionel Johnson, *Post Liminium: Essays and Critical Papers by Lionel Johnson*, ed. Thomas Whittemore (New York: Mitchell Kennerley, 1912), 29.

36 Ibid.

37 Walter Pater, "A Novel by Mr. Oscar Wilde," *The Bookman* 1, no. 1 (November 1891): 59.

38 Hanson, *Decadence and Catholicism*, 27.

39 Johnson, *Post Liminium*, 3, 104, 155, 211, 219, 233, 239, 307. Johnson had an intimate knowledge of Augustine's work, and his essays repeatedly reference the saint as an authority on matters both spiritual and aesthetic.

40 Augustine, *City of God*, 466.

41 Jahan Ramazani, *Poetry and Its Others: News, Prayer, Song, and the Dialogue of Genres* (Chicago: University of Chicago Press, 2013), 131–3.

42 Ibid., 136.

43 Ibid., 139.

44 *The Catechism of the Council of Trent*, trans. Rev J. Donovan (Baltimore: Lucas Brothers, 1829), 183.

45 Ian Fletcher, "The Dark Angel," in *Interpretations: Essays on Twelve English Poems*, ed. John Wain (London and Boston: Routledge & Kegan Paul, 1972), 167.

46 Michel Foucault, *The History of Sexuality*, vol. 1, trans. Robert Hurley (New York: Pantheon Books, 1978), 20.

47 Ibid.

48 *The King James Bible*, Matt. 5.28.

49 Lionel Johnson, *Collected Poems*, 285 n1.

50 H. Montgomery Hyde, *The Love That Dare Not Speak Its Name: A Candid History of Homosexuality in Britain* (London: Harford, Brown & Co., 1970), 109.

51 Frederick Roden, *Same-Sex Desire in Victorian Religious Culture* (London: Palgrave Macmillan, 2002), 19.

52 In 2012, Richard Whittington-Egan self-published a biography of Johnson. Though certainly a work of merit, it has received little attention from scholars.

53 Jad Adams, *Madder Music, Stronger Wine: The Life of Ernest Dowson, Poet and Decadent* (London: I.B. Tauris, 2000), ix.

54 Quoted in *The Letters of Ernest Dowson* (Cranbury, NJ: Associated University Press, 1967), 421.

55 Arthur Symons, "Memoir," in *The Poems and Prose of Ernest Dowson*, 1900 (New York: Modern Library, 1919), 1.

56 Ibid., 4, 8.

57 Victor Plarr, *Ernest Dowson, 1888–1897: Reminiscences, Unpublished Letters, and Marginalia* (London: Elkin Mathews, 1914), 30.

58 Norman Alford, *The Rhymers' Club: Poets of the Tragic Generation* (New York: St. Martin's, 1994), 96.

59 John Gray, *Silverpoints*, XXIII.

60 Ibid.

61 Meredith Martin, "Did a Decadent Meter Exist at the *Fin de Siècle*?" in *Decadent Poetics: Literature and Form at the British* Fin de Siècle, ed. Jason David Hall and Alex Murray (New York: Palgrave Macmillan, 2013), 58. Martin rightly warns against oversimplifying Johnson's idealization of France and cites poems such as "In England" as evidence of Johnson's belief in English excellence.

62 The title, from Horace's *Odes*, translates as "I am not as I was in the reign of good Cynara." In the original, Horace implores Venus to wage no further erotic wars on him. He is old and argues that she should pester some younger man with desire.

63 Ellmann, *Oscar Wilde*, 565, 528.

64 Joseph S. Salemi, "The Religious Poetry of Ernest Dowson," *Victorian Newsletter* 72 (Fall 1987): 45.

65 Ernest Dowson, "Apple Blossom in Brittany," *The Yellow Book* 3 (October 1894): 102–3.

66 Ibid., 108–9.

Chapter 2

1 Ezra Pound, "Preface," in *The Poetical Works of Lionel Johnson* (London: Elkin Matthews, 1915), ix.

2 Ibid., viii–ix.

3 Ibid., iv.

4 T. S. Eliot, "Introduction: 1928," in *Ezra Pound: Selected Poems* (London: Faber and Faber, 1959), 9.

5 Quoted in T. S. Eliot, *Inventions*, 394–5.

6 I could draw on several examples but will limit myself to one. In a 1957 issue of the *Saltire Review*, Eliot professes that he read the "poets of the 'nineties" before going off to college. He claims that they were "the only poets ... who at that period in history seemed to have anything to offer me as a beginner." Quoted in T. S. Eliot, *Inventions*, 397.

7 Pound, "Preface," vii.

8   Ezra Pound, "Ferrex on Petulance," *The Egoist* 1, no. 1 (January 1914): 9.

9   Ezra Pound, *Personae* (London: Faber and Faber, 1934), 29.

10 Ezra Pound, *Collected Early Poems of Ezra Pound*, ed. Michael John King (New York: New Directions, 1976), 60.

11 J. J. Wilhelm, *Ezra Pound in London and Paris, 1908–1925* (University Park, PA: Penn State Press, 1990), 11.

12 Pound, "Preface," vx.

13 Oscar Wilde, *The Complete Letters of Oscar Wilde*, ed. Merlin Holland and Rupert Hart-Davis (London: Fourth Estate, 2000), 1173.

14 T. S. Eliot, "American Literature and the American Language," in *To Criticize the Critic and Other Writings* (New York: Farrar, Straus & Giroux, 1965), 58.

15 Quoted in Richard Ellmann, *Yeats: The Man and the Masks* (New York: Macmillan Co., 1948), 212.

16 James Longenbach, *Stone Cottage: Pound, Yeats and Modernism* (New York: Oxford University Press, 1988), 15.

17 Ibid., 26.

18 Quoted in ibid.

19 Ezra Pound, "The Later Yeats," *Poetry* 4, no. 2 (May 1914): 223.

20 Ibid.

21 W. B. Yeats, introduction to *The Oxford Book of Modern Verse*, xi.

22 For a more complete treatment of the orientalist trends in Yeats's early work, see Joseph Lennon, "W. B. Yeats's Celtic Orient," in *Irish Orientalism* (Syracuse: Syracuse University Press, 2004).

23 Richard Ellmann, *Yeats*, 36. Ellmann identifies the opposition between Mosada and the Church as "one that he [Yeats] was to employ continually for the next ten years to represent what he called the war of spiritual and natural order, all churches typifying to his mind the latter."

24 W. B. Yeats, *Mosada: A Dramatic Poem* (Dublin: Sealy, Bryers, and Walker, 1886), 1.

25 Several critics stress the importance of Johnson's collaboration with Yeats. For a recent and thorough example, see Gary H. Patterson's "Lionel Johnson's Celtic Twilight," in *At the Heart of the 1890s: Essays on Lionel Johnson* (New York: AMS Press, 2008).

26 Augustine, *Confessions*, trans. F. J. Sheed, ed. Michael Foley (Indianapolis, IN: Hackett, 2006), 210. 27.

27 R. K. R. Thornton, *The Decadent Dilemma*, 200.

28 Arthur Symons, "Editorial Note," *The Savoy* 1, no. 1 (January 1896): 5.

29 Warwick Gould, "'Lionel Johnson Comes First to Mind': Sources for Owen Aherne," in *Yeats and the Occult*, ed. George Mills Harper (New York: Maclean-Hunter Press, 1975), 255. As Gould points out, it is generally accepted that Aherne was modeled on Johnson.

30 W. B. Yeats, *The Tables of the Law & The Adoration of the Magi* (Stratford-upon-Avon: Shakespeare Head Press, 1914), 2.

31 Ibid., 3.

32 Ibid., 2.

33 W. B. Yeats, *The Collected Works of W. B. Yeats Vol. III: Autobiographies*, ed. William O'Donnell and Douglas N. Archibald (New York: Scribner, 1999), 241–2.

34 Ibid., 243.

35 W. B. Yeats, *Ideas of Good and Evil* (London: A. H. Bullen, 1903), 303.

36 Ibid., 300–1.

Chapter 3

1 W. H. Auden, *The Collected Poetry of W. H. Auden* (New York: Random House, 1945), 49.

2 Kate Hext and Alex Murray, "Introduction" to *Decadence in the Age of Modernism*, 5.

3 T. S. Eliot, "Tradition and the Practice of Poetry," in *T. S. Eliot: Essays from the Southern Review*, ed. James Olney (New York: Oxford University Press, 1988), 14.

4 For a survey of Untermeyer's campaign against Eliot, see Craig S. Abbott, "Untermeyer on Eliot," *Journal of Modern Literature* 15, no. 1 (Summer 1988): 105–99.

5 Louis Untermeyer, "New Poetry," *Yale Review* 26 (September 1936): 165.

6 See, for example, Ronald Schuchard, *Eliot's Dark Angel: Intersections of Life and Art* (New York: Oxford University Press, 1999); Vincent Sherry, *Modernism and the Reinvention of Decadence*; Ronald Bush, "In Pursuit of Wilde Possum: Reflections on Eliot, Modernism, and the Nineties," *Modernism/modernity* 11, no. 3 (September 2004): 469–85; and Cassandra Laity, "T. S. Eliot and A. C. Swinburne: Decadent Bodies, Modern Visualities, and Changing Modes of Perception," *Modernism/modernity* 11, no. 3 (September 2004): 425–48.

7 For a fuller account of what he calls Gray's "double conversion," see Jerusha Hull McCormack, *John Gray: Poet, Dandy, and Priest* (Hanover, NH: University Press of New England, 1991), 34.

8 This comment is taken from an 1894 review of Beardsley's *Salomé* and *Morte d'Arthur* illustrations in *The Studio: An Illustrated Magazine of Fine and Applied Art*. *The Studio* supported and praised Beardsley form its inception in 1893.

9 Ronald Schuchard, *Eliot's Dark Angel*, 43.

10 T. S. Eliot, *The Varieties of Metaphysical Poetry*, ed. Ronald Schuchard (London: Faber and Faber, 1993), 162.

11 Ibid.

12 T. S. Eliot, *The Letters of T. S. Eliot: Volume 2 (1923–1925)*, ed. Valerie Eliot and Hugh Haffenden (New Haven: Yale University Press, 2011), 739.

13 Lionel Johnson, "Some Letters of Lionel Johnson," *The Criterion* 3, no. 11 (April 1925): 361–3.

14 Quoted in Matthew Sturgis, *Aubrey Beardsley: A Biography* (New York: Overlook Press, 1999), 309.

15 Aubrey Beardsley, *The Letters of Aubrey Beardsley*, ed. Henry Mass, J. L. Duncan, and W. G. Good (Madison, NJ: Fairleigh Dickinson University Press, 1970), 459.

16 W. B. Yeats, *Collected Works*, 254.

17 Ibid.

18 Quoted in Jane Desmarais, *The Beardsley Industry: The Critical Reception in England and France, 1893–1914* (London: Ashgate Publishing, 1998), 21.

19 Ellis Hanson, *Decadence and Catholicism*, 29.

20 Ibid., 31.

21 T. S. Eliot, *Inventions*, 17.

22 Chris Snodgrass, *Aubrey Beardsley: Dandy of the Grotesque* (Oxford: Oxford University Press, 1995), 263.

23 Linda Zatlin, *Aubrey Beardsley and Victorian Sexual Politics* (Oxford: Oxford University Press, 1990), 87.

24 Emma Sutton, *Aubrey Beardsley and British Wagnerism of the 1890s* (Oxford: Oxford University Press, 2002), 100.

25 John Paul Riquelme, "T. S. Eliot's Ambivalences: Oscar Wilde as Masked Precursor," *The Hopkins Review* 5, no. 3 (Summer 2012): 376.

26 Aubrey Beardsley, "The Ballad of the Barber," *The Savoy* 3 (July 1896): 91.

27 Ibid., 93.

28 See Karl Beckson, *Aesthetes and Decadents of the 1890's: An Anthology of British Poetry and Prose* (Chicago: Academy, 1981), 6; and Carl R. Woodring and James S. Shapiro, eds. *The Columbia History of British Poetry* (New York: Columbia University Press, 1994), 524. Pope's *The Rape of the Lock* is yet another potential precursor of Beardsley's poem, especially since Beardsley completed illustrations for the narrative poem in 1896.

29 For comparative readings of "Saint Sebastian" and "Porphyria's Lover," see Ronald Schuchard, *Eliot's Dark Angel*, 11; and Donald Childs, *T. S. Eliot: Mystic, Son, and Lover* (London: Athlone Press, 1997), 88.

30 T. S. Eliot, *Inventions*, 78.

31 Edmund Gardner, "Joachim of Flora," in *The Catholic Encyclopedia*, vol. 8 (New York: Robert Appleton Company, 1910).

32 Leslie Toke, "Flagellants," in *The Catholic Encyclopedia*, vol. 6 (New York: Robert Appleton Company, 1909).

33 Frederick Rolfe, *In His Own Image* (London: John Lane, 1901), 255.

34 Ibid., 4.

35 John Davidson, *A Full and True Account of the Wonderful Mission of Earl Lavender, Which Lasted One Night and One Day; with a History of the Pursuit of Earl Lavender and Lord Brumm by Mrs. Scamler and Maud Emblem* (London: Ward & Downey, 1895), vii.

36 Ibid., ix.

37 Richard Le Gallienne, *Retrospective Reviews: 1893–1895 Vol. II* (London: John Lane, 1896), 224.

38 Quoted in T. S. Eliot, *Inventions*, 398.

39 Ibid.

40 Quoted in Stanley Weintraub, *Beardsley: A Biography* (New York: George Braziller, 1967), 59.

41 Elliot L. Gilbert, "Tumult of Images: Wilde, Beardsley, and 'Salome,'" *Victorian Studies* 26, no. 2 (Winter 1983): 133. Gilbert depicts Beardsley and Wilde as "collaborators."

42 Matthew Sturgis, *Passionate Attitudes*, 151.

43 Robert Ross, *Aubrey Beardsley*, 1909 (Folcroft, PA: Folcroft Library Editions, 1973), 33.

44 Quoted in Matthew Sturgis, *Passionate Attitudes*, 153.

45 Maureen T. Kravec, "Wilde's Salomé," *Explicator* 42, no. 1 (Fall 1893): 30.

46 Ibid.

47 T. S. Eliot "Preface to Modern Literature," 44. Eliot praises Wilde and his "circle" for exploding the propriety of their time. Not surprisingly, however, he also takes the opportunity to dismiss *Dorian Gray* as "perfect rubbish."

48 T. S. Eliot, *Selected Essays*, 349.

49 It is worth noting that scholars have long associated Eliot with a poetics of negation. For an early example, see *T. S. Eliot's Negative Way* (1982) by Eloise Knapp. For a more recent example, see Barry Spurr's "'Oh dark dark dark: They all go into the dark': The *Via Negativa* in the Poetry and Thought of T. S. Eliot" (2004). Though my use of the term *via negative* does not perfectly track with either of these works, they help to illustrate the importance of positive negation in Eliot's poetry.

50 T. S. Eliot, "The Lesson of Baudelaire," in *The Complete Prose of T. S. Eliot: The Critical Edition, Volume 2: The Perfect Critic, 1919–1926*, ed. Anthony Cuda and Ronald Schuchard (New York: Johns Hopkins University Press, 2014), 306.

51 Ibid.

52 J. K. Huysmans, *Against Nature*, 52–3.

53 Oscar Wilde, *Dorian Gray*, 98.

54 Peter Raby, *Aubrey Beardsley and the Nineties* (London: Collins and Brown, 1998), 44.

55 Oscar Wilde, *Salomé: A Tragedy in One Act*, trans. Lord Alfred Bruce Douglas (London: John Lane, 1907), 3.

56 Quoted in Stephen Calloway, *Aubrey Beardsley* (London: V&A Publications, 1998), 83.

57 Chris Snodgrass, *Aubrey Beardsley*, 145.

58 Quoted in ibid., 144.

59 Richard Ellmann, *Oscar Wilde*, 345.

60 B. C. Southam, *A Guide to the Selected Poems of T. S. Eliot*, 6th ed. (New York: Harvest, 1994), 52.

61 Lee Oser, *T. S. Eliot and American Poetry* (Columbia: University of Missouri Press, 1998), 36.

62 Petra Dierkes-Thrun, *Salome's Modernity: Oscar Wilde and the Aesthetics of Transgression* (Ann Arbor: University of Michigan Press, 2011), 44.

63 James H. Ledbetter, "Eliot's *The Love Song of J. Alfred Prufrock*," *The Explicator* 51, no. 1 (Fall 1992): 41.

64 See Stanley Sultan, *Eliot, Joyce, and Company* (Oxford: Oxford University Press, 1987), 258; Laurie MacDiarmid, *T. S. Eliot's Civilized Savage: Religious Eroticism and Poetics* (New York: Routledge, 2003), 27.

65 Oscar Wilde, *Salomé*, 54.

66 The use of "platter" could be inspired in part by Arthur Symons's "The Dance of the Daughters of Herodias" from *Images of Good and Evil* (1899).

67 Gabrielle McIntire, *Modernism, Memory, and Desire: T. S. Eliot and Virginia Woolf* (Cambridge: Cambridge University Press, 2007), 79.

68 Ibid.

69 Instances of this tendency appear in Rilquelme's "T. S. Eliot's Ambivalences: Oscar Wilde as Masked Precursor" and the article out of which this chapter emerged "'A Satirist of Vices and Follies:' Beardsley, Eliot, and Images of Decadent Catholicism." There are, of course, exceptions to this trend, such as Cassandra Laity's "T. S. Eliot and A. C. Swinburne: Decadent Bodies, Modern Visualities, and Changing Modes of Perception," which traces the influence of Swinburne from Eliot's early poetry to *Four Quartets*.

70 Schuchard, *Eliot's Dark Angel*, 19.

71 Ibid., 150.

72 George Orwell, "T. S. Eliot," *Poetry London* 2, no. 7 (October–November 1942): 56.

73 Ibid.

74 Ibid., 57.

75 Orwell could not have been reading a different version of "Whispers of Immortality" since Eliot's poem has remained unaltered since its publication in the *Little Review* in 1918.

76 Orwell, "T. S. Eliot," 57.

77 Ramazani, *Poetry and Its Others*, 144.

78 Ibid., Ramazani is not alone in arguing for Eliot's gradual but consistent development as a Christian poet. See Benjamin G. Lockerd, "Introduction," in *T. S. Eliot and the Christian Tradition* (Madison, NJ: Fairleigh Dickinson University Press, 2014), 1: "A consensus has begun to form on the subject, one of the primary tenets of which is that Eliot's conversion was not nearly as sudden as has been

assumed. Another is that his religious beliefs were of a piece with his ideas about literature, politics, and culture—but without being determined by them."

79 Allen Tate, "T. S. Eliot's *Ash Wednesday*," in *Essays of Four Decades* (Chicago: Swallow Press, 1968), 465.

80 Ibid., 467. Vincent Sherry argues that the word "symbolism" may be read as a coded stand-in for decadence. Were we to accept this theory of terminological coding, we might see in Tate's remarks an important commentary on the continuity of Eliot's partly decadent aesthetic.

81 Schuchard, *Eliot's Dark Angel*, 40.

82 T. S. Eliot, "A Preface to Modern Literature," 44. It is not altogether surprising that Eliot identifies Wilde as British rather than Irish, given Eliot's lack of sympathy for the growing agitation for Irish independence from the UK.

83 See Ian Fletcher, "The Dark Angel," for an in-depth analysis of the thematic connections between "The Dark Angel" and "Satanas."

84 Fletcher, "The Dark Angel," 178.

85 R. K. R. Thornton, *The Decadent Dilemma*, 200.

86 I address the confessional nature of Johnson's poem at length in Chapter 1, so I will not labor the point here.

87 Hanson, *Decadence and Catholicism*, 366.

Chapter 4

1 Simon Gikandi, "Race and Cosmopolitanism," *American Literary History* 14, no. 3 (2002): 599–600. Gikandi insists that even the positive elements of cosmopolitanism, such as internationalism, can mask an expansion of the very ills (racism, exclusion) that are commonly associated with the nation and nationalism. He suggests that such Euro-centric ambitions as "planetary humanism" are inherently limited and potentially insidious.

2 Tanya Agathocleous and Jason R. Rudy, "Victorian Cosmopolitanisms: Introduction," *Victorian Literature and Culture* 38, no. 2 (September 2010): 390. The editors of this special number identify themselves as part of a turn in literary studies away from the caricature of the nineteenth century as a period "predominantly associated with nationalism and imperialism."

3 Rebecca L. Walkowitz, *Cosmopolitan Style: Modernism Beyond the Nation* (New York: Columbia University Press, 2006), 10. Walkowitz argues that the modernist cosmopolitanism of writers such as Joyce and Woolf grew in part out of "the traditions of aestheticism and decadence," which taught them "to redefine the scope of international experience (by focusing on the personal, the intimate, and the artificial) and to resist the effects of heroic nationalism (by developing and analyzing marginal groups)."

4   Stanislaus Joyce, *My Brother's Keeper* (New York: Viking, 1958), 56–7. Stanislaus discusses *Silhouettes*, his sixteen-year-old brother's now-lost collection of juvenilia, as largely a collection of imitation-decadent prose poems.

5   See Geert Lernout, *Help My Unbelief: James Joyce and Religion* (London: Continuum, 2010), 84–7.

6   For thorough treatments of the influence of Moore on Joyce, see Karl Beckson, "Moore's *The Untilled Field* and Joyce's *Dubliners*: The Short Story's Intricate Maze," *English Literature in Transition 1880–1920* 15, no. 4 (January 1972): 291–304; and more recently, Richard Robinson, "'That Dubious Enterprise, the Irish Short Story': *The Untilled Field* and *Dubliners*," in *James Joyce in the Nineteenth Century* (Cambridge: Cambridge University Press, 2013), 46–60.

7   For more on Joyce as an inheritor of Moore's anti-Catholicism, see James H. Murphy, "Catholics and Fiction during the Union, 1801–1922," in *The Cambridge Companion to the Irish Novel* (Cambridge: Cambridge University Press), 109–10.

8   See David Weir, "Decadence and Modernism: Joyce and Gide," in *Decadence and the Making of Modernism* (Amherst: University of Massachusetts Press, 1995), 129.

9   See Adrien Frazier "Irish Modernisms, 1880–1930," in *The Cambridge Companion to the Irish Novel*, ed. John Wilson Foster (Cambridge: Cambridge University Press), 114; Adrian Frazier, *George Moore, 1852–1933* (New Haven: Yale University Press, 2000), 428.

10 T. S. Eliot, *The Letters of T. S. Eliot: Volume 1 (1898–1922), Revised Edition*, ed. Valerie Eliot and Hugh Haffenden (New Haven: Yale University Press, 2011), 641.

11 Patrick Kavanagh, "The Parish and the Universe," in *Poetry and Ireland since 1800: A Source Book*, ed. Mark Storey (London: Routledge, 1988), 205–6. I use the term "provincialism" as opposed to "parochialism" in light of Kavanagh's famous distinction:

> Parochialism and provincialism are [direct] opposites. The provincial has no mind of his own; he does not trust what his eyes see until he has heard what the metropolis—towards which his eyes are turned—has to say on any subject. This runs through all activities.
>
> The parochial mentality on the other hand is never in any doubt about the social and artistic validity of his parish. All great civilizations are based on parochialism—Greek, Israelite, English. In Ireland we are inclined to be provincial not parochial, for it requires a great deal of courage to be parochial. When we do attempt having the courage of our parish we are inclined to go false and to play up to the larger parish on the other side of the Irish Sea. In recent times we have had two great Irish parishioners James Joyce and George Moore.

12 Quoted in Richard Ellmann, *James Joyce*, 617.

13 Ibid.

14 Ibid., 618. Frazier takes Ellmann to task for factual inaccuracy in asserting, for example, that Joyce and Moore met only once when they actually met at least three times. Adrian Frazier acknowledges, however, that Ellmann's account of their meeting does not "misjudge the character of their relationship." See "Rapprochement with a Very Old Man: Joyce's London Meetings with George Moore," *Joyce Studies Annual* 3 (1992): 236.

15 George Moore, *Modern Painting* (New York: Charles Scribner's Sons, 1894), 31.

16 "George Moore (1852–1933) 1879 by Edouard Manet," Metmuseum.org, https://www.metmuseum.org/art/collection/search/436953.

17 "Minor Notices," *The Examiner* (January 26, 1878): 120.

18 Mark Llewellyn, "'Pagan Moore': Poetry, Painting, and Passive Masculinity in George Moore's *Flowers of Passion* (1877) and *Pagan Poems* (1881)," *Victorian Poetry* 45, no. 1 (Spring 2007): 78.

19 Frazier, *George Moore*, 49.

20 Llewellyn, "Pagan Moore," 91.

21 George Moore, *Flowers of Passion* (London: Provost & Co, 1878), 78.

22 Lord Alfred Tennyson, *The Complete Poems of Tennyson* (London: W. J. Black, 1925), 238.

23 Elizabeth Barrett Browning was familiar enough with this alternate meaning to use it in *Casa Guidi Windows* (London: Chapman & Hall, 1851), 14: "The chaplet's last beads fall / In naming the last saintship within ken, / And, after that, none prayeth in the land." A poet inclined to such painful archaisms as "meward" would surely be conversant with this secondary meaning.

24 Decades after writing this poem, Moore devoted substantial thought and effort to debunking the story of Christ's passion and resurrection. In his 1910 drama *The Apostle*, for example, Christ (un)miraculously survives his execution. Six years later, in his novel *The Brook Kerith*, Moore expanded on this theme, going so far as to have Jesus deny the existence of God and debate his own divinity with a zealous St. Paul.

25 George C. Schoolfield, *A Baedeker of Decadence* (New Haven: Yale University Press, 2003), 19.

26 Moore's *Confessions* is almost directly contemporaneous with Pater's autobiographical sketch, "The Child in the House" (1878), which plays in similar ways with the Lockean tabula rasa. See Kate Hext's *Walter Pater: Individualism and Aesthetic Philosophy* (Edinburgh: Edinburgh University Press, 2013), 34-7.

27 Munira H. Mutran, "'The Labyrinth of Selection' in *Confessions of a Young Man*," in *George Moore: Artistic Visions and Literary Worlds*, ed. Mary Pierse (Newcastle, UK: Cambridge Scholars Press, 2006), 78.

28 Hanson, *Decadence and Catholicism*, 10.

29 Moore first published "Nostalgia" under the equally uninspired title "Looking Back" in an 1881 issue of the *Spectator*, seven years before the first English edition

of *Confessions*. Yeats's "Happy Shepherd" appeared for the first time as a stand-alone poem under the title "Song of the Last Arcadian" in *The Wanderings of Oisin and Other Poems* (1889).

30 Frazier, *George Moore*, 242.

31 Oscar Wilde, *Poems with The Ballad of Reading Gaol* (London: Methuen, 1913), 243.

32 This now-famous phrase was coined by Arthur Symons in *The Symbolist Movement in Literature*.

33 Friedrich Nietzsche, *The Complete Works of Friedrich Nietzsche*, vol. 8, ed. Oscar Levy (New York: Macmillan, 1911), xxx.

34 David E. Cartwright, "Nietzsche on Schopenhauer's Moral Philosophy," in *Willing and Nothingness: Schopenhauer as Nietzsche's Educator*, ed. Christopher Janaway (Oxford: Clarendon, 1998), 133.

35 Peter Costello, "Pater, Moore, and Stevenson," in *Beauty and the Beast: Christina Rossetti, Walter Pater, R. L. Stevenson and Their Contemporaries*, ed. Peter Liebregts and Wim Tigges (Atlanta, GA: Rodopi, 1996), 131.

36 Fabienne Gaspari, "More Than Dramas of Sterility: Portraits of the Artist in Moore's Fiction," in *George Moore: Artistic Visions and Literary Worlds*, ed. Mary Pierse (Newcastle, UK: Cambridge Scholars Press, 2006), 20. Gaspari, who describes John Norton as "an aesthete who tries to turn his life both into a model of asceticism and a work of art, but constantly transgresses the limits between art and life," calls Norton's poem burning a form of suicide.

37 We can be reasonably certain the marginalia belong to Joyce. The red crayon is idiosyncratic. Because of his poor eyesight, Joyce used colored crayons in his manuscript work. Red crayon in particular appears throughout the manuscripts of *Stephen Hero* and *Ulysses*.

38 *Evelyn Innes*, 326.

39 Lily Young reemerges as a serious love interest later in the novel, but her death from a mysterious disease preserves both her virginity and Fletcher's freedom.

40 George Moore, *Ave* (London: William Heinemann, 1911), 2.

41 Ibid., 1.

42 Ibid., 3.

43 George Moore, *The Untilled Field* (Aeterna Press, 2010), 3.

44 Ibid., 13.

45 Ibid., 97.

46 I refer primarily to what William Empson so famously dubbed "the Kenner smear"—Hugh Kenner's attempt to reclaim Joyce as an essentially orthodox Catholic thinker.

47 George Moore, *Salve* (London: William Heinemann, 1912), 371–2.

48 Frazier, *George Moore*, 333.

49 Mary Lowe-Evans, *Catholic Nostalgia in Joyce and Company* (Gainesville: University Press of Florida, 2008). Recognition of this nostalgia is by no means an attempt to "baptize" Joyce, but it does acknowledge the importance of Catholicism as a partially positive force in Joyce's work.

50 William Empson, *Using Biography* (Cambridge, MA: Harvard University Press, 1984), 131–57.

51 Recent criticism has explored similarities between the two texts: Patrick Parrinder, "*A Portrait of the Artist*," in *A Portrait of the Artist as a Young Man: A Casebook*, ed. Mark A. Wollaeger, 85–128 (Oxford: Oxford University Press, 2003). Conor Montague, "A Class Apart: The Baptism of Stephen Dedalus," in *George Moore: Dublin, Paris, Hollywood*, ed. Conor Montague and Adrian Frazier, 123–36 (Dublin: Irish Academic Press, 2012).

52 Morse draws elaborate connections between Stephen and Baudelaire. J. Mitchell Morse, "Baudelaire, Stephen Dedalus, and Shem the Penman," *Bucknell Review* 7, no. 3 (1958): 183–98.

53 Hanson, *Decadence and Catholicism*, 46, 48.

54 The little office emerged in the eighth century at the famous abbey of Monte Cassino, founded by St. Benedict, the father of Western monasticism. It exemplifies the Marian devotion that, though by no means absent from Christianity of the late classical period, became central to the Western Church in the Middle Ages. By the eleventh century, the little office was common throughout Europe. See Toke, "Little Office of Our Lady," in *The Catholic Encyclopedia*, vol. 9 (New York: Robert Appleton Company, 1910).

55 James Joyce, *The Selected Letters of James Joyce*, ed. Richard Ellmann (New York: Viking, 1975), 165.

56 Ibid., 181.

57 Ellmann, *James Joyce*, 355.

58 The connection to Dowson has been made before. See Lothar Hönnighausen, *The Symbolist Tradition in English Literature: Pre-Raphaelitism and Fin de Siècle*, trans. Gisela Hönnighausen (Cambridge: Cambridge University Press, 1988), 90. Norbert Lennartz, "'The Ache of Modernism': James Joyce's *Pomes Penyeach* and Their Literary Context," *James Joyce Quarterly* 47, no. 2 (Winter 2010): 207.

59 Caroline Blyth, *Decadent Verse: An Anthology of Late-Victorian Poetry, 1872–1900* (London: Anthem, 2011), 16.

60 Ernest Dowson, "Of his Lady's Treasures," *Temple Bar* 98 (May–August 1893): 102. Here I quote the original version of the poem. "Of his Lady's Treasures; was later published with minor changes in its punctuation as "Villanelle of his Lady's Treasures." Originally the word "villanelle" appeared in parenthesis under the title "Of his Lady's Treasures," but apparently Dowson thought this was too subtle.

61 Wilde, *Poems with The Ballad of Reading Gaol*, 243.

62 I would deal with the subject of Joyce's blasphemous aesthetic at greater length had this not already been done masterfully in Steve Pinkerton's *Blasphemous Modernism*.

63 Emer Nolan, *Catholic Emancipations: Irish Fiction from Thomas Moore to James Joyce* (Syracuse: Syracuse University Press, 2007), 149.

Chapter 5

1 Edmund Wilson, "New Yorker," in *Evelyn Waugh: Collected Critical Heritage II*, ed. Martin Stannard (New York: Routledge, 1997), 245–6.

2 See Robert Murray Davis, *Brideshead Revisited: The Past Redeemed* (Boston: Twayne, 1990), 51; and Roberto A. Valderón García, "The Spoken and the Unspoken: The Homo-sexual Theme in E. M. Forster and Evelyn Waugh," in *Waugh without End: New Trends in Evelyn* Waugh *Studies*, ed. Carlos Villar Flor and Robert Murray Davis (Bern: Peter Lang, 2005), 175. In 1991, Davis denied any sexual activity between the two. Nearly a decade later, Garcia affirmed this position in an essay on homosexuality in the work of Waugh and E. M. Forster.

3 Two articles from *Logos: A Journal of Catholic Thought and Culture* epitomize this tendency: Douglas Lane Patey, "Evelyn Waugh's *Brideshead Revisited*," *Logos: A Journal of Catholic Thought and Culture* 3, no. 2 (2000): 9–30; and Dominic Manganiello, "The Beauty That Saves: *Brideshead Revisited* as a Counter-Portrait of the Artist," *Logos: A Journal of Catholic Thought and Culture* 9, no. 2 (Spring 2006): 154–70. Patey mentions homosexuality but only as a step in Charles Ryder's "progress from Sebastian Flyte, to Sebastian's sister Julia, to God" (20). Manganiello rightly identifies a "longing for eros" in Charles's relationship with Sebastian (160), but folds that longing into the same too-tidy pilgrim's progress from homosexual love to love for God.

4 Francesca Coppa, "'A Twitch upon the Thread': Revisiting *Brideshead Revisited*," in *Catholic Figures, Queer Narratives*, ed. Lowell Gallagher, Frederick S. Roden, and Patricia Juliana Smith, 149–62 (New York: Palgrave Macmillan, 2007), 160.

5 Ibid., 162.

6 Peter Christensen, "Homosexuality in *Brideshead Revisited*: 'Something Quite Remote from Anything the [Builder] Intended'," in *"A Handful of Mischief": New Essays on Evelyn Waugh*, ed. Donat Gallagher, Ann Pasternak Slater, and John Howard Wilson (Lanham, MD: Rowman & Littlefield, 2011), 137–8.

7 Benjamin Kahan, *Celibacies: American Modernism & Sexual Life* (Durham, NC: Duke University Press, 2013), 2.

8 Ibid.

9 Ibid., 5.

10 Ibid., 68.

11 Ibid., 142.

12   See Alex Murray, "Decadence Revisited: Evelyn Waugh and the Afterlife of the 1890s," *Modernism/modernity* 22, no. 3 (September 2015): 604. Near the end of his detailed and convincing survey of Waugh's shifting attitudes toward decadence over the course of his career, Murray characterizes *Brideshead* as a book "shot through with references to the literature of the fin de siècle."

13   John Ash, "A Conversation with Harry Mathews," *Review of Contemporary Fiction* 7, no. 3 (Fall 1987): 21.

14   Julian Jebb, "Interviews: Evelyn Waugh," *The Paris Review* 30 (Summer–Fall 1963): n.p.

15   Firbank originally called the book *Sorrow in Sunlight*, a title that Hollinghurst greatly prefers for obvious reasons.

16   Ronald Firbank, *Five Novels* (New York: New Directions, 1981), 116.

17   Evelyn Waugh, *Vile Bodies* (New York: Back Bay Books, 1999), 21.

18   Wilde's witty remark, which was first reported in Arthur Ransome's *Oscar Wilde: A Critical Study* (1912), was well known a decade later when Firbank composed his customs scene.

19   David Hilliard, "UnEnglish and Unmanly: Anglo-Catholicism and Homosexuality," *Victorian Studies* 25, no. 2 (Winter 1982), 199.

20   Osbert Sitwell, Introduction to *Five Novels*, by Ronald Firbank (New York: New Directions, 1981), viii.

21   Ibid., xxix.

22   Ibid., xxx.

23   See Allan Massie, "Is Baptizing a Puppy as Scandalous as Giving Holy Communion to a Grown Dog?" *The Telegraph*, September 29, 2013.

24   Firbank, *Five Novels*, 319–20.

25   Evelyn Waugh, *The Essays, Articles and Reviews of Evelyn Waugh*, ed. Donat Gallagher (London: Methuen, 1983), 56–7.

26   Wilde, *De Profundis*, 102.

27   Evelyn Waugh, *The Diaries of Evelyn Waugh*, ed. Michael Davie (London: Weidenfeld and Nicolson, 1976), 23.

28   Hanson, *Decadence and Catholicism*, 23.

29   Quoted in Roden, *Same-Sex Desire*, 63.

30   See, for example, Michael G. Brennan, *Evelyn Waugh: Fictions, Faith and Family* (New York: Bloomsbury Academic, 2013), 81.

31   Ibid., 8. The general paper for Waugh's Oxford entrance exam dealt with Rupert Brooke, the Pre-Raphaelites, and Arthur Symons's 1898 study of Beardsley. Unfortunately, Waugh's college, Hertford, no longer has the examination papers in its archive, so his earliest thoughts on the subject are lost. The earliest editions of Symons's text (1898) contain six drawings by Beardsley but do not include *Et in Arcadia Ego*. However, a 1948 edition published by the Unicorn Press and containing sixteen drawings, *Et in Arcadia Ego* among them, asserts on the inside

cover that it was first published in 1898. So, it is possible that Waugh was working with a text that included the illustration when he took the exam in 1921.

32 Evelyn Waugh, *Rossetti: His Life and Works* (London: Duckworth, 1928), 97.

33 Waugh viewed the painting at the Louvre in 1925. Poussin also produced an earlier version of *Les Bergers d'Arcadie* in 1627, which Waugh saw in 1932 (Brennan 81).

34 Virgil's *Eclogues* do not actually contain the phrase "et in arcadia ego," but, as M. Owen Lee points out, "'Et in Arcadia ego' is a phrase that may be thought to capture the essential spirit of Virgil's pastorals." See, M. Owen Lee, *Death and Rebirth in Virgil's Arcadia* (New York: SUNY Press, 1989), 89.

35 Pater, *The Renaissance*, 118.

36 Snodgrass, *Aubrey Beardsley*, 234.

37 The title also contains a subtle pun on Leonard Smithers's address at London's Royal *Arcade*. Beardsley seems to be commenting on the impending demise of *The Savoy*.

38 Brennan, *Evelyn Waugh*, 83.

39 Evelyn Waugh, *Put Out More Flags* (Boston: Little, Brown and Co, 1942), 46.

40 Ibid., 232.

41 Ibid.

42 Ibid., 237.

43 Christopher Hitchens makes the Flyte/flight observation in "'It's All on Account of the War,'" *The Guardian* (September 26, 2008), n.p.

44 Richard Kaye, "'A Splendid Readiness for Death': T. S. Eliot, the Homosexual Cult of Saint Sebastian, and World War I," *Modernism/modernity* 6, no. 2 (April 1999), 296.

45 Quoted in David Dooley, "Waugh's Road to Affirmation," in *Permanent Things*, ed. Andrew A. Tadie and Michael H. Macdonald (Grand Rapids, MI: Eerdmans, 1996), 63.

46 In a 1924 diary entry, for example, Waugh reports buying a book of Chesterton's letters. The timing seems significant for my discussion, since Alastair Graham, the model for Sebastian, converted to Catholicism and gave Waugh a Bible the very next day. Evelyn Waugh, *The Diaries*, 178.

47 Daniel Moran makes this element of the novel clear in his essay "*The Man Who Was Thursday*: Chesterton's Duel with the *Fin de Siècle*," *Logos: A Journal of Catholic Thought and Culture* 14, no. 4 (Fall 2011): 116–44.

48 G. K. Chesterton, *The Man Who Was Thursday: A Nightmare* (New York: Dodd, Mead, and Co., 1908), iii.

49 Ibid., italics mine.

50 Hanson, *Decadence and Catholicism*, 368.

51 Quoted in James A. Devereux, "Catholic Matters in the Correspondence of Evelyn Waugh and Graham Greene," *Journal of Modern Literature* 14, no. 1 (Summer 1987): 113. Waugh himself never shied away from conflict with those few Tartuffes among the US episcopacy. When Greene came under fire regarding a Cardinal's misreading and misunderstanding of *The Power and the Glory* (1940), Waugh quickly offered to issue a public statement on his friend's behalf.

52 Waugh, *The Diaries*, 297.

53 Paula Byrne, *Mad World: Evelyn Waugh and the Secrets of Brideshead* (New York: Harper, 2011), 326.

54 Ibid., 131.

55 Ibid.

56 Waugh, *The Essays*, 124.

57 Christensen, "Homosexuality in *Brideshead Revisited*," 156.

58 Grant Kaplan, "Celibacy as Political Resistance," *First Things* (January 2014), 53.

59 Ibid., 51–2.

60 David M. Halperin, "The Normalization of Queer Theory," *Journal of Homosexuality* 45, no. 2–4 (2003): 343.

61 Evelyn Waugh, *Men At Arms* (New York: Back Bay, 2012), 14.

62 *New American Bible*, 1 Cor. 7.1-7.

63 For a detailed discussion of the ways in which different readers have attempted to contest and affirm Plato's queerness by drawing on *The Symposium*, see H. Christian Blood, "The Trouble with Icons: Recent Ideological Appropriations of Plato's Symposium," *HELIOS* 35, no. 2 (2008): 197–222.

64 Plato. *Symposium*, in *Plato: Complete Works*, ed. John M. Cooper, 457–505 (Indianapolis, IN: Hackett, 1997), 211c–d.

Decadent Catholicism after Modernism

1 Alan Hollinghurst, *The Swimming-Pool Library* (New York: Vintage, 1989), 64.

2 Ibid., 179.

3 Ibid., 180.

4 Ibid., 43.

5 Michico Kakutani, "In Waugh's Territory, Shadowed by AIDS," *The New York Times* (November 23, 2004): E1.

6 Alan Hollinghurst, *The Line of Beauty* (New York: Bloomsbury, 2005), 59.

7 DBC Pierre, *Lights Out in Wonderland* (New York: W. W. Norton, 2011), 17.

8 Ibid., 15.

9 Oscar Wilde, *Poems with The Ballad of Reading Gaol*, 267–8.

10 Pierre, *Lights Out*, 70.

11 Charles Baudelaire, *The Poems and Prose of Charles Baudelaire*, trans. James Huneker (New York: Brentano's, 1919), 96.

12 Pierre, *Lights Out*, 73.

13 Ibid., 76.

14 Ibid., 77–8.

15 Ibid., 303.

16 Ibid., 333–4.

17 Don DeLillo, *White Noise* (New York: Penguin, 1999), 319.

Bibliography

Abbott, Craig S. "Untermeyer on Eliot." *Journal of Modern Literature* 15, no. 1 (Summer 1988): 105–99.

Adams, Jad. *Madder Music, Stronger Wine: The Life of Ernest Dowson, Poet and Decadent.* London: I.B. Tauris, 2000.

Agathocleous, Tanya and Jason R. Rudy. "Victorian Cosmopolitanisms: Introduction." *Victorian Literature and Culture* 38, no. 2 (September 2010): 389–97.

Alford, Norman. *The Rhymers' Club: Poets of the Tragic Generation.* New York: St. Martin's, 1994.

Amadó, Ramón Ruiz. "Diocese of Guadix." In *The Catholic Encyclopedia.* New York: The Encyclopedia Press, 1914. http://www.newadvent.org/cathen/16043a.htm.

Amis, Kingsley. *Everyday Drinking: The Distilled Kingsley Amis.* New York: Bloomsbury, 2008.

Ash, John. "A Conversation with Harry Mathews." *Review of Contemporary Fiction* 7, no. 3 (Fall 1987): 21–33.

Auden, W. H. *The Collected Poetry of W. H. Auden.* New York: Random House, 1945.

Augustine. *The City of God.* Translated by Marcus Dods. New York: Modern Library, 2000.

Augustine. *Confessions.* Translated by F. J. Sheed. Edited by Michael Foley. Indianapolis, IN: Hackett, 2006.

Baron, Scarlett. "'Will You Be as Gods?' (U 3.38): Joyce Translating Flaubert." *James Joyce Quarterly* 47, no. 4 (Summer 2010): 521–35.

Baudelaire, Charles. *Flowers of Evil.* Translated by James McGowan. Oxford: Oxford University Press, 1993.

Baudelaire, Charles. *The Poems and Prose of Charles Baudelaire.* Translated by James Huneker. New York: Brentano's, 1919.

Beardsley, Aubrey. "The Ballad of the Barber." *The Savoy.* Edited by Leonard Smithers 3 (July 1896): 90–3.

Beardsley, Aubrey. *The Letters of Aubrey Beardsley.* Edited by Henry Mass, J. L. Duncan, and W. G. Good. Madison, NJ: Fairleigh Dickinson University Press, 1970.

Beckson, Karl. Editor of *Aesthetes and Decadents of the 1890's: An Anthology of British Poetry and Prose.* Chicago: Academy, 1981.

Bittner, David. "Sebastian and Charles—More Than Friends?" *Evelyn Waugh Newsletter and Studies* 24, no. 2 (Autumn 1990): 1–3.

Blood, H. Christian. "The Trouble with Icons: Recent Ideological Appropriations of Plato's Symposium." *HELIOS* 35, no. 2 (2008): 197–222.

Bloom, Harold. "Introduction." In *Portrait of the Artist as a Young Man*. Edited by Harold Bloom, 8–9. Broomall, PA: Chelsea House, 1999.

Blyth, Caroline. *Decadent Verse: An Anthology of Late-Victorian Poetry, 1872-1900*. London: Anthem, 2011.

Brennan, Michael G. *Evelyn Waugh: Fictions, Faith and Family*. New York: Bloomsbury Academic, 2013.

Browning, Elizabeth Barrett. *Casa Guidi Windows*. London: Chapman & Hall, 1851.

Bush, Ronald. "In Pursuit of Wilde Possum: Reflections on Eliot, Modernism, and the Nineties." *Modernism/modernity* 11, no. 3 (September 2004): 469–85.

Byrne, Paula. *Mad World: Evelyn Waugh and the Secrets of Brideshead*. New York: Harper, 2011.

Calloway, Stephen. *Aubrey Beardsley*. London: V&A Publications, 1998.

Cartwright, David E. "Nietzsche on Schopenhauer's Moral Philosophy." In *Willing and Nothingness: Schopenhauer as Nietzsche's Educator*. Edited by Christopher Janaway, 116–50. Oxford: Clarendon, 1998.

Caswall, Edward. *Lyra Catholica: Containing All the Hymns of the Roman Breviary and Missal*. New York: E. Dunigan, 1951.

The Catechism of the Council of Trent. 1566. Translated by Rev J. Donovan. Baltimore: Lucas Brothers, 1829.

Cevasco, G. A. *The 1890s: An Encyclopedia of British Literature, Art, and Culture*. New York and London: Garland, 1993.

Chesterton, G. K. *All Things Considered*. London: Methuen, 1915.

Chesterton, G. K. *A Handful of Authors: Essays on Books and Writers*. New York: Sheed and Ward, 1953.

Chesterton, G. K. *The Man Who Was Thursday: A Nightmare*. New York: Dodd, Mead, and Co., 1908.

Chesterton, G. K. *Orthodoxy*. London: John Lane, 1909.

Childs, Donald. *T. S. Eliot: Mystic, Son, and Lover*. London: Athlone Press, 1997.

Christensen, Peter. "Homosexuality in *Brideshead Revisited*: 'Something Quite Remote from Anything the [Builder] Intended'." In *"A Handful of Mischief." New Essays on Evelyn Waugh*. Edited by Donat Gallagher, Ann Pasternak Slater, and John Howard Wilson, 137–59. Lanham, MD: Rowman & Littlefield, 2011.

Coppa, Francesca. "'A Twitch upon the Thread': Revisiting *Brideshead Revisited*." In *Catholic Figures, Queer Narratives*. Edited by Lowell Gallagher, Frederick S. Roden, and Patricia Juliana Smith, 149–62. New York: Palgrave Macmillan, 2007.

Costello, Peter. "Pater, Moore, and Stevenson." In *Beauty and the Beast: Christina Rossetti, Walter Pater, R. L. Stevenson and Their Contemporaries*. Edited by Peter Liebregts and Wim Tigges, 127–39. Atlanta, GA: Rodopi, 1996.

D'Arcy, Margaretta. "The Metamorphosis of George Moore." In *George Moore: Dublin, Paris, Hollywood*. Edited by Conor Montague and Adrian Frazier, 39–52. Dublin: Irish Academic Press, 2012.

Davidson, John. *A Full and True Account of the Wonderful Mission of Earl Lavender, Which Lasted One Night and One Day; with a History of the Pursuit of Earl Lavender and Lord Brumm by Mrs. Scamler and Maud Emblem.* London: Ward & Downey, 1895.

Davis, Robert Murray. *Brideshead Revisited: The Past Redeemed.* Boston: Twayne, 1990.

DeLillo, Don. *White Noise.* New York: Penguin, 1999.

Desmarais, Jane Haville. *The Beardsley Industry: The Critical Reception in England and France, 1893–1914.* London: Ashgate, 1998.

Devereux, James A. "Catholic Matters in the Correspondence of Evelyn Waugh and Graham Greene." *Journal of Modern Literature* 14, no. 1 (Summer 1987): 111–26.

Dierkes-Thrun, Petra. *Salome's Modernity: Oscar Wilde and the Aesthetics of Transgression.* Ann Arbor: University of Michigan Press, 2011.

Dooley, David. "Waugh's Road to Affirmation." In *Permanent Things.* Edited by Andrew A. Tadie and Michael H. Macdonald, 48–65. Grand Rapids, MI: Eerdmans, 1996.

Douglas, Lord Alfred. *The Collected Poems of Lord Alfred Douglas.* London: Martin Secker, 1919.

Douglas, Lord Alfred. "Two Poems." *The Chameleon* 1, no. 1. London: Gay and Bird (1894): 25–8.

Dowson, Ernest. "Apple Blossom in Brittany." *The Yellow Book* 3 (October 1894): 93–109.

Dowson, Ernest. "Of His Lady's Treasures." *Temple Bar* 98 (May–August 1893): 102. London: Richard Bentley & Son, 1893.

Dowson, Ernest. *The Letters of Ernest Dowson.* Cranbury, NJ: Associated University Press, 1967.

Dowson, Ernest. *The Poems of Ernest Dowson.* Edited by Mark Longaker. Philadelphia: University of Pennsylvania Press, 1962.

Ehnenn, Jill R. *Women's Literary Collaboration, Queerness, and Late-Victorian Culture.* Burlington, VT: Ashgate, 2008.

Eliot, T. S. "American Literature and the American Language." In *To Criticize the Critic and Other Writings,* 43–60. New York: Farrar, Straus & Giroux, 1965.

Eliot, T. S. *The Complete Poems and Plays: 1909–1950.* New York: Harcourt Brace, 1980.

Eliot, T. S. "Introduction: 1928." In *Ezra Pound: Selected Poems,* 7–21. London: Faber and Faber, 1959.

Eliot, T. S. *Inventions of the March Hare: Poems 1907–1917.* Edited by Christopher Ricks, 7–21. New York: Harcourt Brace, 1996.

Eliot, T. S. "The Lesson of Baudelaire." In *The Complete Prose of T. S. Eliot: The Critical Edition, Volume 2: The Perfect Critic, 1919–1926.* Edited by Anthony Cuda and Ronald Schuchard, 306–8. New York: Johns Hopkins University Press, 2014.

Eliot, T. S. *The Letters of T. S. Eliot: Volume 1 (1898–1922), Revised Edition.* Edited by Valerie Eliot and Hugh Haffenden. New Haven: Yale University Press, 2011.

Eliot, T. S. *The Letters of T. S. Eliot: Volume 2 (1923–1925)*. Edited by Valerie Eliot and Hugh Haffenden. New Haven: Yale University Press, 2011.

Eliot, T. S. *The Letters of T. S. Eliot: Volume 4 (1928–1929)*. Edited by Valerie Eliot and Hugh Haffenden. New Haven: Yale University Press, 2011.

Eliot, T. S. "A Preface to Modern Literature: Being a Conspectus, Chiefly of English Poetry, Addressed to an Intelligent and Inquiring Foreigner." In *Vanity Fair* 21, no. 3 (1923): 44, 118.

Eliot, T. S. *Selected Prose of T. S. Eliot*. Edited by Frank Kermode. New York: Farrar, Straus and Giroux, 1975.

Eliot, T. S. "Tradition and the Practice of Poetry." In *T. S. Eliot: Essays from the Southern Review*. Edited by James Olney, 11–23. New York: Oxford University Press, 1988.

Eliot, T. S. *T. S. Eliot: Selected Essays 1917–1932*. New York: Harcourt, Brace, 1932.

Eliot, T. S. *The Varieties of Metaphysical Poetry*. Edited by Ronald Schuchard. London: Faber and Faber, 1993.

Eliot, T. S. "Whispers of Immortality." *The Little Review* 5, no. 5 (1918): 11–12.

Ellmann, Richard. "James Joyce, Irish European." Speech. 1966. James Joyce Collection, The Harry Ransom Center.

Ellmann, Richard. *James Joyce: New and Revised Edition*. New York: Oxford University Press, 1982.

Ellmann, Richard. *Oscar Wilde*. New York: Alfred A. Knopf, 1988.

Ellmann, Richard. *The Uses of Decadence: Wilde, Yeats, Joyce*. Bennington, VT: Bennington College, 1983.

Ellmann, Richard. *Yeats: The Man and the Masks*. New York: Macmillan Co, 1948.

Empson, William. *Using Biography*. Cambridge, MA: Harvard University Press, 1984.

Field, Michael. *Sight and Song*. London: Elkin Matthews and John Lane, 1892.

Firbank, Ronald. *Five Novels*. New York: New Directions, 1981.

Fish, Stanley. "One University under God?" *Chronicle of Higher Education*. January 7, 2005. https://www.chronicle.com/article/One-University-Under-God-/45077.

Fletcher, Ian. "The Dark Angel." In *Interpretations: Essays on Twelve English Poems*. Edited by John Wain, 153–78. London and Boston: Routledge & Kegan Paul, 1972.

Foucault, Michel. *The History of Sexuality*, vol. 1. Translated by Robert Hurley. New York: Pantheon Books, 1978.

Frazier, Adrian. *George Moore, 1852–1933*. New Haven: Yale University Press, 2000.

Frazier, Adrian. "Irish Modernisms, 1880–1930." In *The Cambridge Companion to the Irish Novel*. Edited by John Wilson Foster, 97–112. Cambridge: Cambridge University Press, 2006.

Frazier, Adrian. "Rapprochement with a Very Old Man: Joyce's London Meetings with George Moore." *Joyce Studies Annual* 3 (1992): 228–36.

García, Roberto A. Valderón. "The Spoken and the Unspoken: The Homo-sexual Theme in E. M. Forster and Evelyn Waugh." In *Waugh without End: New Trends in Evelyn Waugh Studies*. Edited by Carlos Villar Flor and Robert Murray Davis, 155–79. Bern: Peter Lang, 2005.

Gardner, Edmund. "Joachim of Flora." In *The Catholic Encyclopedia*, 8, 406–07. New York: Robert Appleton Company, 1910.

Gaspari, Fabienne. "More Than Dramas of Sterility: Portraits of the Artist in Moore's Fiction." In *George Moore: Artistic Visions and Literary Worlds*. Edited by Mary Pierse, 12–23. Newcastle, UK: Cambridge Scholars Press, 2006.

"George Moore (1852–1933) 1879 by Edouard Manet." Metmuseum.org. https://www.metmuseum.org/art/collection/search/436953

Gikandi, Simon. "Race and Cosmopolitanism." *American Literary History* 14, no. 3 (2002): 593–615.

Gilbert, Elliot L. "Tumult of Images: Wilde, Beardsley, and Salome." *Victorian Studies* 26, no. 2 (Winter 1983): 133–59.

Gould, Warwick. "'Lionel Johnson Comes First to Mind': Sources for Owen Aherne." In *Yeats and the Occult*. Edited by George Mills Harper, 255–84. New York: Maclean-Hunter Press, 1975.

Gray, John. *Silverpoints*. London: Elkin Matthews and John Lane, 1893.

Greene, Graham. *Collected Essays*. London: Bodley Head, 1969.

Griffiths, Richard. *The Pen and the Cross: Catholicism and English Literature, 1850–2000*. New York: Continuum, 2010.

Halperin, David M. "The Normalization of Queer Theory." *Journal of Homosexuality* 45, no. 2–4 (2003), 339–43.

Hanson, Ellis. *Decadence and Catholicism*. Cambridge, MA: Harvard University Press, 1997.

Hargrove, Nancy D. "T. S. Eliot's Year Abroad, 1910–1911: The Visual Arts." *South Atlantic Review* 71, no. 1 (Winter 2006): 89–131.

Hext, Kate. *Walter Pater: Individualism and Aesthetic Philosophy*. Edinburgh: Edinburgh University Press, 2013.

Hext, Kate and Alex Murray. "Introduction." In *Decadence in the Age of Modernism*. Edited by Kate Hext and Alex Murray, 1–26. Baltimore, MD: Johns Hopkins University Press, 2019.

Hilliard, David. "UnEnglish and Unmanly: Anglo-Catholicism and Homosexuality." *Victorian Studies* 25, no. 2 (Winter 1982): 181–210.

Hitchens, Christopher. "'It's All on Account of the War.'" *The Guardian*. September 26, 2008. Theguardian.com. https://www.theguardian.com/books/2008/sep/27/evelynwaugh.fiction

Hollinghurst, Alan. *The Line of Beauty*. New York: Bloomsbury, 2005.

Hollinghurst, Alan. *The Swimming-Pool Library*. New York: Vintage, 1989.

Hönnighausen, Lothar. *The Symbolist Tradition in English Literature: Pre-Raphaelitism and Fin de Siècle*. Translated by Gisela Hönnighausen. Cambridge: Cambridge University Press, 1988.

Huysmans, J. K. *Against Nature (À Rebours)*. Translated by Robert Baldick. London: Penguin, 2003.

Hyde, Harford Montgomery. *The Love That Dare Not Speak Its Name: A Candid History of Homosexuality in Britain*. London: Harford, Brown & Co., 1970.

Jebb, Julian. "Interviews: Evelyn Waugh." *The Paris Review* 30 (Summer–Fall 1963): n.p. Theparisreview.org. https://www.theparisreview.org/interviews/4537/evelyn-waugh-the-art-of-fiction-no-30-evelyn-waugh

Johnson, Lionel. *The Collected Poems of Lionel Johnson.* Edited by Ian Fletcher. New York and London: Garland Publishing, 1982.

Johnson, Lionel. "The Cultured Faun." In *Aesthetes and Decadents of the 1890s: An Anthology of British Poetry and Prose.* Edited by Karl Beckson, 110–13. Chicago: Academy Chicago Publishers, 1982.

Johnson, Lionel. *Post Liminium: Essays and Critical Papers by Lionel Johnson.* Edited by Thomas Whittemore. New York: Mitchell Kennerley, 1912.

Johnson, Lionel. "Some Letters of Lionel Johnson." *The Criterion* 3, no. 11 (April 1925): 356–63.

Jones, David. *The Anathemata.* London: Faber and Faber, 2010.

Joyce, James. "Gas from a Burner." Harry Ransom Center. The University of Texas at Austin, 1912.

Joyce, James. *A Portrait of the Artist as a Young Man.* London: Signet Classics, 2006.

Joyce, James. *The Selected Letters of James Joyce.* Edited by Richard Ellmann. New York: Viking, 1975.

Joyce, James. *Ulysses.* Edited by Hans Walter Gabler. New York: Vintage Books, 1986.

Joyce, Stanislaus. *My Brother's Keeper.* New York: Viking, 1958.

Kahan, Benjamin. *Celibacies: American Modernism & Sexual Life.* Durham, NC: Duke University Press, 2013.

Kakutani, Michico. "In Waugh's Territory, Shadowed by AIDS." *The New York Times* (November 23, 2004): E1.

Kaplan, Grant. "Celibacy as Political Resistance." *First Things* (January 2014): 49–53.

Kavanagh, Patrick. "The Parish and the Universe." In *Poetry and Ireland since 1800: A Source Book.* Edited by Mark Storey, 204–6. London: Routledge, 1988.

Kaye, Richard. "'A Splendid Readiness for Death': T. S. Eliot, the Homosexual Cult of Saint Sebastian, and World War I." *Modernism/modernity* 6, no. 2 (April 1999): 107–34.

The King James Bible. Camden, NJ: Thomas Nelson, 1972.

Kravec, Maureen T. "Wilde's Salomé." *Explicator* 42, no. 1 (Fall 1893): 30–3.

Laity, Cassandra. "T. S. Eliot and A. C. Swinburne: Decadent Bodies, Modern Visualities, and Changing Modes of Perception." *Modernism/modernity* 11, no. 3 (September 2004): 425–48.

Ledbetter, James H. "Eliot's *The Love Song of J. Alfred Prufrock.*" *The Explicator* 51, no. 1 (Fall 1992): 41–45.

Le Gallienne, Richard. *Retrospective Reviews: 1893–1895 Vol. II.* London: John Lane, 1896.

Lee, M. Owen. *Death and Rebirth in Virgil's Arcadia.* New York: SUNY Press, 1989.

Lennartz, Norbert. "'The Ache of Modernism': James Joyce's *Pomes Penyeach* and Their Literary Context." *James Joyce Quarterly* 47, no. 2 (Winter 2010): 197–211.

Lernout, Geert. *Help My Unbelief: James Joyce and Religion*. London: Continuum, 2010.

Lewis, Pericles. *Religious Experience in the Modernist Novel*. New York: Cambridge University Press, 2010.

Llewellyn, Mark. "'Pagan Moore': Poetry, Painting, and Passive Masculinity in George Moore's Flowers of Passion (1877) and Pagan Poems (1881)." *Victorian Poetry* 45, no. 1 (Spring 2007): 77–92.

Lockerd, Benjamin G. "Introduction." In *T. S. Eliot and the Christian Tradition*. Edited by Benjamin G. Lockerd, 1–32. Madison, NJ: Fairleigh Dickinson University Press, 2014.

Longenbach, James. *Stone Cottage: Pound, Yeats and Modernism*. New York: Oxford University Press, 1988.

Lowe-Evans, Mary. *Catholic Nostalgia in Joyce and Company*. Gainesville: University Press of Florida, 2008.

MacDiarmid, Laurie. *T. S. Eliot's Civilized Savage: Religious Eroticism and Poetics*. New York: Routledge, 2003.

Mahoney, Kristin. *Literature and the Politics of Post-Victorian Decadence*. Cambridge: Cambridge University Press, 2015.

Manganiello, Dominic. "The Beauty That Saves: Brideshead Revisited as a Counter-Portrait of the Artist." *Logos: A Journal of Catholic Thought and Culture* 9, no. 2 (Spring 2006): 154–70.

Martin, Meredith. "Did a Decadent Meter Exist at the *Fin de Siècle*?" In *Decadent Poetics: Literature and Form at the British* Fin de Siècle. Edited by Jason David Hall and Alex Murray, 46–64. New York: Palgrave Macmillan, 2013.

Mason, Stuart. *Bibliography of Oscar Wilde*. London: T. W. Laurie, 1914.

Massie, Allan. "Is Baptizing a Puppy as Scandalous as Giving Holy Communion to a Grown Dog?" *The Telegraph*. September 29, 2013.

Masurel-Murray, Claire. "Conversions to Catholicism among Fin de Siècle Writers: A Spiritual and Literary Genealogy." *Cahiers Victoriens et Édouardiens* 76 (2012): 105–25.

Maugham, W. Somerset. *Of Human Bondage*. New York: Grosset & Dunlap, 1915.

McCartney, George. *Confused Roaring: Evelyn Waugh and the Modernist Tradition*. Bloomington and Indianapolis: Indiana University Press, 1987.

McCormack, Jerusha Hull. *John Gray: Poet, Dandy, and Priest*. New York: AMS Press, 2008. Brandeis University Press, 1991.

McIntire, Gabrielle. *Modernism. Memory, and Desire: T. S. Eliot and Virginia Woolf*. Cambridge: Cambridge University Press, 2007.

"Minor Notices." *The Examiner* (January 26, 1878): 120.

Montague, Conor. "A Class Apart: The Baptism of Stephen Dedalus." In *George Moore: Dublin, Paris, Hollywood*. Edited by Conor Montague and Adrian Frazier, 123–36. Dublin: Irish Academic Press, 2012.

Moore, George. *Ave*. London: William Heinemann, 1911.

Moore, George. *Confessions of a Young Man*. Edited by Susan Dick. Montreal and London: McGill-Queen's University Press, 1972.

Moore, George. *Flowers of Passion*. London: Provost & Co, 1878.

Moore, George. *Mike Fletcher: A Novel*. London: Ward and Downey, 1889.

Moore, George. *Modern Painting*. New York: Charles Scribner's Sons, 1894.

Moore, George. *Salve*. London: William Heinemann, 1912.

Moore, George. *The Untilled Field*. Aeterna Publishing, 2010.

Moran, Daniel. "*The Man Who Was Thursday*: Chesterton's Duel with the *Fin de Siècle*." *Logos: A Journal of Catholic Thought and Culture* 14, no. 4 (Fall 2011): 116–44.

Morse, J. Mitchell. "Baudelaire, Stephen Dedalus, and Shem the Penman." *Bucknell Review* 7, no. 3 (1958): 183–98.

Murphy, James H. "Catholics and Fiction during the Union, 1801–1922." In *The Cambridge Companion to the Irish Novel*. Edited by John Wilson Foster, 97–112. Cambridge: Cambridge University Press, 2006.

Murray, Alex. "Decadence Revisited: Evelyn Waugh and the Afterlife of the 1890s." *Modernism/modernity* 22, no. 3 (September 2015): 593–607.

Murray, Alex. "Recusant Poetics: Rereading Catholicism at the *Fin de Siècle*." *English Literature in Transition, 1880–1920* 56, no. 3 (2013): 355–73.

Mutran, Munira H. "'The Labyrinth of Selection' in *Confessions of a Young Man*." In *George Moore: Artistic Visions and Literary Worlds*. Edited by Mary Pierse, 75–84. Newcastle, UK: Cambridge Scholars Press, 2006.

Nietzsche, Friedrich. *The Complete Works of Friedrich Nietzsche*. Edited by Oscar Levy, vol. 8. New York: Macmillan, 1911.

Nolan, Emer. *Catholic Emancipations: Irish Fiction from Thomas Moore to James Joyce*. Syracuse: Syracuse University Press, 2007.

Nordau, Max. *Degeneration*. Translator unknown. New York: D. Appleton and Company, 1895.

Norman, Edward. *Anti-Catholicism in Victorian England*. New York: Routledge, 2017.

Orwell, George. "T. S. Eliot." *Poetry London* 2, no. 7 (October–November 1942): 56–9.

Oser, Lee. *T. S. Eliot and American Poetry*. Columbia: University of Missouri Press, 1998.

Parker, Sarah. *The Lesbian Muse and Poetic Identity, 1889–1930*. New York: Routledge, 2015.

Parrinder, Patrick. "A Portrait of the Artist." In *A Portrait of the Artist as a Young Man: A Casebook*. Edited by Mark A. Wollaeger, 85–128. Oxford: Oxford University Press, 2003.

Pater, Walter. "A Novel by Mr. Oscar Wilde." *The Bookman* (November 1891): 59–60.

Pater, Walter. *Plato and Platonism*. London: Macmillan, 1907.

Pater, Walter. *The Renaissance: Studies in Art and Poetry*, 4th ed. New York: Dover, 2013.

Paterson, Gary H. *At the Heart of the 1890s: Essays on Lionel Johnson*. New York: AMS Press, 2008.

Patey, Douglas Lane. "Evelyn Waugh's *Brideshead Revisited*." *Logos: A Journal of Catholic Thought and Culture* 3, no. 2 (2000): 9–30.

Pearce, Joseph. "A Truly Wilde Story: An Interview with Joseph Pearce about the Life and Death of Oscar Wilde." *IgnatiusInshight.com* (2000). http://www.ignatiusinsight.com/features/jpearce_intervw_july04.asp.

Pearce, Joseph. *The Unmasking of Oscar Wilde*. London: HarperCollins, 2000.

Pinkerton, Steve. *Blasphemous Modernism*. Oxford: Oxford University Press, 2017.

Pierre, DBC. *Lights Out in Wonderland*. New York: W. W. Norton, 2011.

Pittock, Murray. *Spectrum of Decadence: The Literature of the 1890s*. New York: Routledge, 2016.

Plarr, Victor. *Ernest Dowson, 1888–1897: Reminiscences, Unpublished Letters, and Marginalia*. London: Elkin Mathews, 1914.

Plato. "Symposium." In *Plato: Complete Works*. Edited by John M. Cooper, 457–505. Indianapolis, IN: Hackett, 1997.

Poe, Edgar Allan. *The Complete Tales and Poems*. Edited by Wilbur S. Scott. New York: Castle Books, 2011.

Pound, Ezra. *Collected Early Poems of Ezra Pound*. Edited by Michael John King. New York: New Directions, 1976.

Pound, Ezra. "Ferrex on Petulance." *The Egoist* 1, no. 1 (January 1914): 9–10.

Pound, Ezra. "The Later Yeats." *Poetry* 4, no. 2 (May 1914): 223.

Pound, Ezra. *Personae*. London: Faber and Faber, 1934.

Pound, Ezra. "Preface." In *The Poetical Works of Lionel Johnson*. Edited by Ezra Pound, v–xix. London: Elkin Matthews, 1915.

Pound, Ezra. *Selected Poems*. Edited by T. S. Eliot. London: Faber and Faber, 1959.

Raby, Peter. *Aubrey Beardsley and the Nineties*. London: Collins and Brown, 1998.

Ramazani, Jahan. *Poetry and Its Others: News, Prayer, Song, and the Dialogue of Genres*. Chicago: University of Chicago Press, 2013.

Riquelme, John Paul. "T. S. Eliot's Ambivalences: Oscar Wilde as Masked Precursor." *The Hopkins Review* 5, no. 3 (Summer 2012): 353–79.

Roden, Frederick S. *Same-Sex Desire in Victorian Religious Culture*. London: Palgrave Macmillan, 2002.

Rolfe, Frederick. *In His Own Image*. London: John Lane, 1901.

Ross, Robert. *Aubrey Beardsley*. Folcroft, PA: Folcroft Library Editions, 1973.

Salemi, Joseph S. "The Religious Poetry of Ernest Dowson." *Victorian Newsletter* 72 (Fall 1987): 44–7.

Santayana, George. *Selected Critical Writings of George Santayana: Volume 1*. Edited by Norman Henfrey. Cambridge: Cambridge University Press, 1968.

Schoolfield, George C. *A Baedeker of Decadence*. New Haven: Yale University Press, 2003.

Schuchard, Ronald. *Eliot's Dark Angel: Intersections of Life and Art*. New York: Oxford University Press, 1999.

Schuchard, Ronald. "Wilde's Dark Angel and the Spell of Decadent Catholicism." In *Rediscovering Oscar Wilde*. Edited by C. George Sandulescu, 371–96. Gerrards Cross, Buckinghamshire: Colin Smythe, 1994.

Sherry, Vincent. *Modernism and the Reinvention of Decadence*. New York: Cambridge University Press, 2015.

Sitwell, Osbert. "Introduction." *Five Novels* by Ronald Firbank. New York: New Directions, 1981.

Snodgrass, Chris. *Aubrey Beardsley: Dandy of the Grotesque*. Oxford: Oxford University Press, 1995.

Southam, B. C. *A Guide to the Selected Poems of T. S. Eliot*. 6th ed. New York: Harvest, 1994.

Spurr, Barry. '*Anglo-Catholic in Religion:' T. S. Eliot and Christianity*. Cambridge: Lutterworth, 2010.

Sturgis, Matthew. *Aubrey Beardsley: A Biography*. New York: Overlook Press, 1999.

Sturgis, Matthew. *Passionate Attitudes: English Decadents of the 1890s*. London: Macmillan, 1995.

Sultan, Stanley. *Eliot, Joyce, and Company*. Oxford: Oxford University Press, 1987.

Sutton, Emma. *Aubrey Beardsley and British Wagnerism of the 1890s*. Oxford: Oxford University Press, 2002.

Symons, Arthur. "Editorial Note." *The Savoy* 1, no. 1 (January 1896): 5.

Symons, Arthur. "Memoir." In *The Poems and Prose of Ernest Dowson*. 1900. New York: Modern Library, 1919.

Tate, Allen. "T. S. Eliot's *Ash Wednesday*." In *Essays of Four Decades*, 462–70. Chicago: Swallow Press, 1968.

Tennyson, Alfred. *The Complete Poems of Tennyson*. London: W. J. Black, 1925.

Thain, Marion. "*Michael Field*": *Poetry, Aestheticism, and the Fin de Siècle*. Cambridge: Cambridge University Press, 2007.

Thompson, Francis. *Complete Poems of Francis Thompson*. New York: Modern Library, 1913.

Thornton, R. K. R. *The Decadent Dilemma*. London: Edward Arnold, 1983.

Toke, Leslie. "Flagellants." In *The Catholic Encyclopedia*, vol. 6, 89–93. New York: Robert Appleton Company, 1909.

Toke, Leslie. "Little Office of Our Lady." In *The Catholic Encyclopedia*, vol. 9, 294–95. New York: Robert Appleton Company, 1910.

Tonning, Erik. *Modernism and Christianity*. New York: Palgrave Macmillan, 2014.

Untermeyer, Louis. "New Poetry." *Yale Review* 26 (September 1936): 165–6.

Vadillo, Ana Parejo. "'Gay Strangers': Reflections on Decadence and the Decadent Poetics of A. Mary F. Robinson." *Cahiers victoriens et édouardiens* 78 (Autumn 2013): n.p. http://journals.openedition.org/cve/856.

Volpicelli, Robert. "The New Decadence." Review of *Modernism and the Reinvention of Decadence*, by Vincent Sherry; *Landscapes of Decadence*, by Alex Murray; and *Beginning at the End: Decadence, Modernism, and Postcolonial History*, by Robert Stilling. *Modernism/modernity* 26, no. 1 (2019): 213–18.

Walkowitz, Rebecca L. *Cosmopolitan Style: Modernism beyond the Nation*. New York: Columbia University Press, 2006.

Waugh, Evelyn. *Brideshead Revisited: The Sacred and Profane Memoirs of Captain Charles Ryder*. New York: Back Bay, 2012.

Waugh, Evelyn. *The Diaries of Evelyn Waugh*. Edited by Michael Davie. London: Weidenfeld and Nicolson, 1976.

Waugh, Evelyn. *The Essays, Articles and Reviews of Evelyn Waugh*. Edited by Donat Gallagher. London: Methuen, 1983.

Waugh, Evelyn. *Men at Arms*. New York: Back Bay, 2012.

Waugh, Evelyn. *Put Out More Flags*. Boston: Little, Brown and Co, 1942.

Waugh, Evelyn. *Rossetti: His Life and Works*. London: Duckworth, 1928.

Waugh, Evelyn. *Vile Bodies*. New York: Back Bay Books, 1999.

Weintraub, Stanley. *Beardsley: A Biography*. New York: George Braziller, 1967.

Weir, David. *Decadence: A Very Short Introduction*. Oxford: Oxford University Press, 2018.

Weir, David. *Decadence and the Making of Modernism*. Amherst, MA: University of Massachusetts Press, 1995.

Wheeler, Michael. *The Old Enemies: Catholic and Protestant in Nineteenth-Century English Culture*. Cambridge: Cambridge University Press, 2006.

Wilde, Oscar. *The Complete Letters of Oscar Wilde*. Edited by Merlin Holland and Rupert Hart-Davis. London: Fourth Estate, 2000.

Wilde, Oscar. *De Profundis*. New York: G. P. Putnam's Sons, 1905.

Wilde, Oscar. *The Picture of Dorian Gray*. Edited by Donald L. Lawler. New York: W. W. Norton, 1988.

Wilde, Oscar. *Poems*. Boston: Roberts Brothers, 1881.

Wilde, Oscar. *Poems with The Ballad of Reading Gaol*. London: Methuen, 1913.

Wilde, Oscar. *Salomé: A Tragedy in One Act*. Translated by Lord Alfred Bruce Douglas. London: John Lane, 1907.

Wilhelm, J. J. *Ezra Pound in London and Paris, 1908–1925*. University Park, PA: Penn State Press, 1990.

Williams, William Carlos. *The Autobiography of William Carlos Williams*. 1948. New York: New Directions, 1967.

Wilson, Edmund. "New Yorker." In *Evelyn Waugh: Collected Critical Heritage II*. Edited by Martin Stannard, 245–8. New York: Routledge, 1997.

Woodring, Carl R. and James S. Shapiro, eds. *The Columbia History of British Poetry*. New York: Columbia University Press, 1994.

Yeats, W. B. *The Collected Poems of W. B. Yeats*. New York: Macmillan Company, 1951.

Yeats, W. B. *The Collected Works of W. B. Yeats Vol. III: Autobiographies*. Edited by William O'Donnell and Douglas N. Archibald. New York: Scribner, 1999.

Yeats, W. B. *Ideas of Good and Evil*. London: A. H. Bullen, 1903.

Yeats, W. B. "Introduction." In *The Oxford Book of Modern Verse 1892–1935*. Edited by W. B. Yeats, v–xlii. Oxford: Clarendon Press, 1947.

Yeats, W. B. *Mosada: A Dramatic Poem*. Dublin: Sealy, Bryers, and Walker, 1886.

Yeats, W. B. *The Tables of the Law & The Adoration of the Magi*. Stratford-upon-Avon: Shakespeare Head Press, 1914.

Yeats, W. B. *The Trembling of the Veil*. London: T. Werner Laurie, 1922.

Yeats, W. B. *The Wanderings of Oisin and Other Poems*. London: Kegan Paul, Trench & Co, 1889.

Zatlin, Linda. *Aubrey Beardsley and Victorian Sexual Politics*. Oxford: Oxford University Press, 1990.

Index